Readers of the Lost Ark

Readers of the Lost Ark

Imagining the Ark of the Covenant from Ancient Times to the Present

KEVIN M. MCGEOUGH

OXFORD
UNIVERSITY PRESS

Oxford University Press is a department of the University of Oxford.
It furthers the University's objective of excellence in research, scholarship,
and education by publishing worldwide. Oxford is a registered trade mark of
Oxford University Press in the UK and in certain other countries.

Published in the United States of America by Oxford University Press
198 Madison Avenue, New York, NY 10016, United States of America.

© Oxford University Press 2025

All rights reserved. No part of this publication may be reproduced, stored in a retrieval system, transmitted, used for text and data mining, or used for training artificial intelligence, in any form or by any means, without the prior permission in writing of Oxford University Press, or as expressly permitted by law, by license or under terms agreed with the appropriate reprographics rights organization. Inquiries concerning reproduction outside the scope of the above should be sent to the Rights Department, Oxford University Press, at the address above.

You must not circulate this work in any other form and you must
impose this same condition on any acquirer

CIP data is on file at the Library of Congress

ISBN 9780197653883

DOI: 10.1093/9780197653913.001.0001

Printed by Marquis Book Printing, Canada

For Shawn

Contents

Acknowledgments	ix
Map of Israel and Environs	xiii
Map of Ethiopia and Environs	xiv
Introduction	1
1. What Was the Ark and What Did It Do?	11
2. The Archaeology of the Ark and Iron Age Religion	31
3. Rethinking the Ark without the Temple: The Ark in Early Synagogues and Churches	53
4. Medieval Theology: The Ark as Metaphor	76
5. The "Real" Raiders of the Lost Ark: From Jerusalem to Japan	95
6. The Ark of Indiana Jones and Other Cinematic Arks	119
7. Toys and Teaching Tools: Models of the Ark in Communities of Faith and Fandom	140
8. The Romance of Solomon and Sheba: Ethiopian Ark Traditions	161
9. Aliens, Radios, and Conspiracies: The Many Arks of Pseudoarchaeology	175
Conclusion	200
Bibliographic Essay	213
Bibliography	227
Scriptural References	239
Subject Index	241

Acknowledgments

There are many people to whom I owe thanks for their support and assistance over the course of my study of the Ark of the Covenant. First, I would not have written this book without the encouragement of James Linville, who emailed me, out of the blue, asking me if I felt like writing a book on the Ark of the Covenant. Jim put me in touch with Steve Wiggins at Oxford University Press, who had been searching for someone to write such a monograph. Steve's vision for the book matched my own idea that a reception history of the Ark would be an interesting way to explore different aspects of biblical interpretation over the past two thousand years, and the two of us agreed on a preliminary outline relatively quickly.

I especially want to thank the anonymous reviewers of this book, who offered thoughtful and constructive suggestions. Sadly, due to space constraints, I was unable to follow through with all of these suggestions. To make this volume even remotely affordable, I have had to remove or shorten a number of detailed discussions on Rabbinic thought, medieval art, Early Modern and later Masonic treatments of Solomon's Temple, Islamic understandings of the Ark, toys, video games, and wax museums. Despite this, I think the volume still manages to capture the different varieties of receptions of the Ark, from ancient times to the present.

The University of Lethbridge has been a supportive place for the research and writing of this book. I have been privileged to hold a Tier I Board of Governor's Research Chair in Archaeological Theory and Reception, bringing with it teaching relief, which has allowed me to write a book like this on top of my more typical research duties. A University of Lethbridge Research Fund grant supported my travel to Israel for this project. Both the research chair and the grant are overseen by our Office of Research and Innovation Services. From that office, I want to thank Dena McMartin, Emma Dering, and Natasha Chaykowski for their assistance. Claudia Malacrida and Erasmus Okine, both formerly of this office, also offered research supports that laid the groundwork for my study of the Ark.

The University of Lethbridge has a wonderful library and library staff. I want to acknowledge Rhys Stevens, the archaeology subject librarian, for

X   ACKNOWLEDGMENTS

his efforts to make sure that we have access to the resources that our program needs, despite their often seemingly idiosyncratic nature. The staff in charge of interlibrary loans made research in such a remote location as Lethbridge possible, and I am often shocked at how quickly they manage to find materials with the most cryptic of bibliographic clues.

My own department, Geography & Environment, nurtures the kind of research reflected by this book. As a department where physical scientists, social scientists, and humanists work together, our interesting conversations and diverse research outputs are a testament to the value of interdisciplinarity. Much of my theoretical orientation has been influenced by thinking about "space" in conversation with these colleagues. I am also affiliated with the Department of History & Religious Studies, and the members of that department are just as supportive of my research. Both departments are in the Faculty of Arts & Science, led by an encouraging and empathetic dean's office.

A number of friends and colleagues have helped me with specific elements of this book. Steve Harvey helped me track down Egyptological- related images, and Aidan Dodson has allowed me to use one of his images from KV 62. Shlomo Izre'el from Tel Aviv University discussed with me different approaches to popular writing, as well as various aspects of the Ark and Israel (ancient and modern). Also from Tel Aviv University, Zvi Lederman offered numerous assistances and ideas. John Harding and Shayne Dahl answered various questions about Japanese religion, questions that they were surprised would come from someone studying the Ark of the Covenant. Marcus Dostie has prepared the maps for this book, and his expertise in geography and cartography makes life easier for everyone in my department. Jason Laurendeau and Carly Adams discussed many elements of autoethnography, colonialism, and play, sharing with me their own works at various stages. Their son, Quinn Adams Laurendeau, helped me find some Ark of the Covenant video game Easter Egg Arks (although that discussion was cut for space constraints, so you will have to find the "walk throughs" for them on the Internet yourself).

Over the past two years, I had conversations with many colleagues and friends who helped me in the articulation of my ideas. Jerimy Cunningham, a specialist in the American Southwest with whom I share a lab (which much to his horror is partially filled with Bible commentaries), has had to endure many conversations about the Ark of the Covenant. C. James MacKenzie consistently offers unique perspectives on popular religious practice. I want to thank James Linville again, but here for his various comments to me on contemporary American religious beliefs. Other colleagues (outside of the University of Lethbridge) with whom I discussed this project and are deserving of thanks include William Caraher (University of North Dakota), Steven Garfinkle (Western Washington University), Jacob Lauinger (The Johns Hopkins University), Jana Mynářová (The Charles University), Benjamin Porter (University of California, Berkeley), and Bruce Routledge (University of Liverpool).

Of course, I have to thank my parents, who facilitated my earliest engagement with the Ark. My wife, Elizabeth Galway, with whom I am collaborating on research relating to the intersection of archaeology and children's literature, has been relatively understanding about the influence that the Ark of the Covenant has had over our lives for the past few years. My daughter, Lucy, has assisted me in many elements of this book, especially concerned with toy and video game versions of the Ark. She undoubtedly knows more about the Ark than most preteens, and I fear that I have infected her with my love for both what is ancient and what is unusual.

Finally, I would like to thank my long-time friend and colleague, Shawn Bubel, who features in this book (much to what will likely be to her dismay when she reads this). We have been traveling to the Middle East together since our days as undergraduate students at the University of Lethbridge, and we have been running the archaeology program together at that same school for over twenty years. I can't imagine a better archaeological partner or friend. This book is dedicated to her.

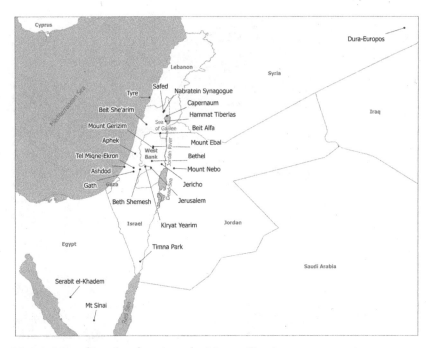

Map 1 Map of Israel and environs by Marcus Dostie

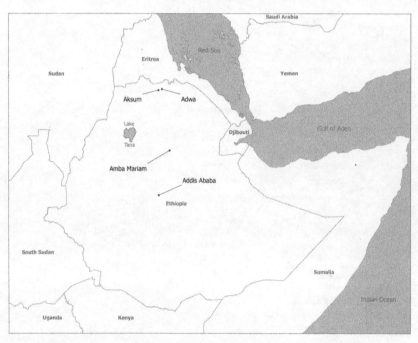

Map 2 Map of Ethiopia and environs by Marcus Dostie

Introduction

I remember my excitement so vividly. I was five. My father was *finally* taking me to see the movie I had been endlessly harassing him about. This was the movie where Han Solo was an archaeologist and he was doing something related to ancient Egypt. There is no way that I knew exactly what he was doing in ancient Egypt, but I had seen a clip from the film where Han Solo was dressed all in white robes, holding up a staff where the sunlight shone through a crystal and lit up a model of an ancient city. This seemed amazing to my five-year-old mind (and it is still pretty great in my forties). By five, I was already very interested in Egypt, which is not atypical of those of us in the field. Many scholars who work in the region recall similar feelings, an almost primordial sense of interest in an ancient culture, with this being especially true for Egyptologists. Thus, my two main interests in life up to that time (ancient Egypt and *Star Wars*), or at least the two main interests that I can still remember and have continued to hold my attention, were combined in this one film with its provocative, but relatively incomprehensible title for a five-year-old, *Raiders of the Lost Ark*.

So my father and mother put my younger sister and me in our 1975 burgundy Pontiac Parisienne and took us to the Green Acres drive-in theater in Lethbridge, Alberta. It was summer and in southern Alberta, it takes a long time for the sun to go down in July. The wait, for my sister and me, was interminable. Finally, the film began and I started watching *Raiders of the Lost Ark*, crowded with my sister between my parents, in the front seat of the Pontiac, trying to see over the dash. It was amazing. I couldn't believe it. There was actually something better than *Star Wars*, and Indiana Jones was even cooler than Han Solo. I've seen *Raiders* so many times since then that it is impossible for me to remember what particular elements of this film stood out to me. But I do remember that over the next year or so, my friends and I desperately tried to swing across different kinds of playground equipment using ropes found in construction sites as make-shift whips. I certainly wouldn't let my daughter scavenge materials from a construction site, but the 1980s were a different time for children. I'm sure that cramped into the front

Readers of the Lost Ark. Kevin M. McGeough, Oxford University Press. © Oxford University Press 2025.
DOI: 10.1093/9780197653913.003.0001

seat of our Pontiac, the physicality and kinetic energy of *Raiders* was at least partially what captured my imagination, likely more than the actual treasure Indy was seeking, the Ark of the Covenant.

This drive-in had a doubleheader, and my dad, a lover of World War II films, had chosen a showing that well-suited him. The film that started after *Raiders* was *Das Boot*, and my first memory of that was my sister and I rolling around in agony in the back seat wondering why we had to stay to watch this; my dad told us just to go to sleep. He can't remember if he made it through all three hours then, or whether his kids or his wife forced him to leave early. I actually imagine that, despite a relatively large German-speaking population in southern Alberta, many cars didn't stay for that second showing; *Das Boot*, while an amazing film, certainly doesn't have the same widespread appeal that *Raiders* does. The two films do have a connection. The submarine used at the end of *Raiders* was loaned to Spielberg by the *Das Boot* filmmakers and appears in both movies.

I asked my parents recently, but they don't really remember what they thought of a three-year-old and five-year-old watching that film. In the 1980s, there was a looser concept of what constituted a family film. There were often only a few cinemas in a city and so the films that played on the screen had to appeal to parents with young kids, adults, and especially the teenagers who would keep going to the same film over and over again. I imagine that my parents had the same sense of trepidation that I had when I showed *Raiders* to my daughter when she was six. My wife thought it was a bad idea because of the violence and adult themes, but she relented as the options to keep our daughter entertained during one of the COVID-19 lockdown periods were becoming stale. And I couldn't take any more random Netflix kids cartoons. I just didn't have it in me.

There was one scene in *Raiders* that I was worried about though (and worried about my wife's rage if it led to nightmares later), but at least I knew it was coming. My parents didn't. This is the final scene, when Belloq, the lead villain, opens the Ark of the Covenant. Ghosts fly out, swirl around the Nazis, and then, as the mysterious music becomes quite shrill, an energy force from the Ark melts the faces and explodes the heads of the bad guys, while Indy implores Marion, his romantic interest, to keep her eyes shut. As a five-year-old, I didn't keep my eyes shut, and I loved it. My mother was probably thinking murderous thoughts toward my father, and plotting that he would be the one to stay up with us through the night, shepherding us through our nightmares (which, for the record, neither I nor my sister

INTRODUCTION   3

had). Forty years later, I was nervously watching my daughter, worried that perhaps I was traumatizing her by making her watch something age-inappropriate that I loved. But she was fine, not bothered in any way by the scene. Afterward, I asked my daughter what she thought, and her response was both devastating and relieving: "That film was pretty boring. Except for when the faces melted. That was interesting."

My first thinking about the Ark of the Covenant, and most of my thinking about the Ark for about fifteen years after, was mediated by this experience and the repeated (and by repeated, I really mean repeated) viewings of *Raiders of the Lost Ark*. As someone who wasn't raised in a religious household, all I knew about the Ark was that it was some kind of biblical artifact. It, according to the film, had been stolen by a pharaoh named Shishak and taken to Egypt. I assumed that the Bible actually described it as a very powerful weapon and it had the Ten Commandments in it, because of what the audience is told in the movie's exposition. The Ark's power as a weapon and its general importance as an artifact were why it was significant, according to the logic of the film. While I didn't think it had any magical powers, I had no reason to disbelieve any of the movie's historical description of the Ark. It was plausible to me that the Bible did contain stories of the Ark's magical powers. I didn't really know, or care, what "the covenant" was, and I didn't question why Shishak would steal this object and take it to Egypt.

Yet I don't think that my friends who came from Christian households had much more knowledge of the Ark than this either. I grew up with a great many religious friends. Lethbridge is a very religiously conservative town, not diverse in the way that we normally think of diversity today, but diverse in its own way with its large population of Mormons, Hutterites, Mennonites, Dutch Reform Calvinists, and Evangelical Christians, along with the varieties of liberal Protestants and Catholics typical of smaller communities in Canada. In any case, I don't remember the Ark coming up very frequently in the many discussions of religion I had with childhood friends who came from faith communities who prioritized conversion. The Jewish community in Lethbridge is very small, and perhaps my Jewish friends had encountered the Ark through synagogue, but I don't remember us ever talking about it. I feel that it is safe to say that the general impressions I had of the Ark as a child in the 1980s were fairly in line with the impressions that many North Americans had of the Ark at that time, and that they were mostly mediated through the vision of it offered by Steven Spielberg and George Lucas, the filmmakers responsible for *Raiders*.

4   READERS OF THE LOST ARK

My lack of knowledge about the Ark didn't necessarily stop me from being interested in it. And, in fact, I think that my vague sense of the Ark was that it was one of the most important objects in Judaism, if not *the* most important object. I felt that it must have an important role in the Bible. I felt that it was something that would be worth searching for, archaeologically, and that it might be something discoverable even if my own feelings about the historicity of any biblical story were fairly agnostic leaning toward extreme skepticism. Eventually I dove into some of the popular writing about the Ark, which was probably supported by catching the occasional television program that featured the Ark, shows like *In Search Of* that explored mysteries like aliens, Atlantis, and Bigfoot. This was before the rise of infotainment channels like History and Discover, and before the Internet, so there wasn't the same volume of weird information about the Ark available as there is now.

By the time I got to university, I did have a pretty good sense of what the Ark was. One of my friends whose father was a leader in a Mormon community which had separated itself from the main church in Salt Lake City had a biblical concordance. We worked through every mention of the Ark in the Bible, confirming for ourselves that the physical depiction of the Ark in *Raiders* seemed to reflect the biblical description. It was a golden box, with cherubim on top (whatever those were), that was carried on poles by two people. It was where Moses put the broken tablets of the Ten Commandments. It did seem to have supernatural powers and be particularly dangerous, but that danger didn't seem to be related to opening it up and looking inside.

Yet what also struck me at university was how the Ark of the Covenant seemed to be of zero interest to the professors teaching me archaeology and religious studies. It did not come up in class. Ever. And this didn't seem to be out of step with professional archaeology in general. As I started using an actual academic library and gaining access to scholarly sources on the Ark, I realized that there were not all that many studies on the subject. There were a few at the time, and there are many more now (I discuss those in the bibliographic essay at the end of this book). But really, academics don't have all that much to say on the topic. Compared to the vast amount of public interest in the Ark of the Covenant, and how captivating it seems in the context of Indiana Jones, academic research on it is fairly limited. As I became a "professional" scholar of the ancient Near East, initiated through the various guild requirements of graduate school, concentrating on gaining foundational knowledge needed for the work, like historical chronologies,

INTRODUCTION 5

changes in pottery forms over time, biblical criticism, and ancient languages, I stopped caring about the Ark.

My own experiences mirror larger trends in who engages with ideas about the Ark. Sure, there are occasional scholarly articles about the Ark, and every once in a while a really good extended study (again, these are discussed in the essay at the end of this book). But the more interesting thinking about the Ark has been by the nonspecialist public. The Ark has captivated people's imaginations since ancient times and, while most of this thinking has been in tandem with readings of the Bible, much has expanded far beyond the limited references in the Old Testament. Ancient Jewish writers recorded beliefs that the Ark had been hidden in a secret location that would only be revealed when the Messiah came. These old traditions of the Ark having been stored in a clandestine locale seem to continue into the twenty-first century, with modern authors making similar claims, sometimes linking the Ark to apocalyptic ideas, but more often tying its hiddenness to the larger themes of what we call pseudoarchaeology, unwarranted and bad arguments lacking evidence but masquerading as real science. Many of the themes of pseudoarchaeology are based on conspiracy thinking, connecting the Ark to secret societies or alien visitations, and often both.

In other words, the Ark has been and still is very meaningful to some communities outside of the academic realms of archaeology and biblical studies. For those who do not do this work professionally, the Ark evokes all sorts of ideas of mystery, power, religion, and antiquity. For some, the Ark is one of many symbols of how powerful elites are secretly controlling the globe. It doesn't matter how or why they are doing this, but the fact that they are is simultaneously comforting and destabilizing, a curious mix of emotions that gives traction to such ideas, now spread easily and cheaply through the Internet, reaching far larger audiences in more accessible ways. For others, the Ark provides a locus for community, a kind of fan culture, where Indiana Jones fans can obsess over making their own models of the Ark and argue over whose replica best reflects that from the original film. Indiana Jones fandom isn't manifest at the same scale as fandom for other franchises, like *Star Trek* or *Star Wars*, but the intensity of those fans reflects this kind of new community that has been emerging since the 1960s. As someone who gleefully bought a set of Indiana Jones promotional watches manufactured only in Japan, from a distant seller over EBay, I can't say that my commentary on this group is entirely neutral. For observant Jews, the Ark is remembered when they visit synagogue, and the Torah scrolls are removed from the

6 READERS OF THE LOST ARK

cabinet that it stands in to represent the original Ark of the Covenant, connecting modern Judaism with its origins in antiquity. These are just some of the ways that the Ark is meaningful today, but there are many more.

So why does the Ark mean so many different things to such disparate groups of people? Is it just that these are people seeking communities for themselves? Perhaps. This is likely part of the story. But a key part of it also has to be some intrinsic qualities of the Ark itself. Something about it makes it very susceptible to interpretation and imagination. Something has to captivate people, enough so that I want to write this book and that you are now reading it. I think that much of what makes the Ark so evocative is that there is just the right balance of certainty and ambiguity surrounding it. Its "thinginess" is tangible. The Bible tells us exactly what it looks like so we can fully visualize it, both as individuals and in unanimity with others who are visualizing it. As we will see, there aren't too many variations in its physical depictions. Yet, at the same time, it is surrounded by ambiguity. What was it and why did it matter? It carries with it notions of religious power, and it has a charismatic ancient pedigree. And on top of that, the Bible is pretty mute on what happened to it. So, despite the lack of physical ambiguity, there is lots of room for imaginative interpretation surrounding the Ark.

Here, the work of a scholar named Malcolm Quinn is very valuable. He studied the swastika, trying to understand why this obscure design could come to have so much power today. Quinn calls it a "metasymbol," a symbol that points to many meanings and has certain qualities but is also ambiguous enough for the new users of the symbol to manipulate it however they want. The swastika references ancient times, but without really any particular meaning. And in the early years of the twentieth century, it didn't really mean much to the general public, who mostly wouldn't have been able to recognize it, let alone name it. The Nazis were able to adopt this symbol quite easily because it was so ambiguous in meaning, but they could present it as a symbol of a supposed ancient Aryan heritage. Because it was ancient but also not bearing much in terms of overt meaning, the Nazis could use it to evoke whatever meanings they wanted it to have, without needing to be very specific. It could immediately stand for National Socialism without other symbolic meanings overshadowing those intended by Hitler. Now, of course, the swastika cannot be separated from Nazi ideology and the horrors of World War II, and so it is no longer an empty symbol in the way that it used to be.

I am not, in any way, saying here that the Ark should be correlated with the Nazis, despite the entirely coincidental fact that the villains in *Raider of the*

INTRODUCTION   7

Lost Ark were the Nazis. But I am suggesting that like the swastika, the Ark of the Covenant works as a metasymbol just as Malcolm Quinn describes. The Ark points to ancient biblical history and ancient religion very broadly. It has an almost concrete physicality in that we all imagine it looking the same way. What it *exactly* means, however, is pretty vague. It is just vague enough for interpreters to understand it how they want to, with some constraints. It is an ancient religious artifact associated with the Old Testament. It looks like it is described in the Bible. And it was seemingly lost, or at least hidden from society, in ancient times. This makes the Ark a really provocative artifact to imagine with, and, not surprisingly, there have been many creative interpretations.

Creative interpretations are the subject of this book. Well, the main subject anyways. The first two chapters will discuss what we actually know about the "real" ancient Ark, first what is known from the Bible, and second what is known from archaeology. After that though, this book will trace how the Ark has been interpreted in different times and places. It will provide a history of "readers of the Lost Ark" rather than raiders, although there is a chapter on the Ark in film, and especially *Raiders of the Lost Ark* (how could there not be?).

In scholarly circles, this is what we call "reception history." This book offers not a history of the Ark itself, but how the Ark has been received over time. The study of reception is a fairly common type of research, which emerged especially from the study of the Bible and Greco-Roman literature. Rather than studying the Bible, or Plato, or the writings of Marcus Aurelius directly, scholars who "do" reception history, study how people have understood these texts in different historical contexts. Partially this has to do with people reading the same works of literature over the course of two thousand years and needing to find something else to say about these writings. But more, it is because there has been two thousand years of thinking about those works and that thinking is interesting in its own right. Reading literature is not just about the author; the reader of that literature is part of how that literature becomes meaningful. And while literary scholars will disagree about the relative scale of importance between author and reader/reading community in this relationship, most will agree that that relationship is key. Certainly, those of us who practice reception history are just as, if not more interested, in readers than authors.

Some types of receptions are more obvious subjects of academic interest. It would be difficult to study European painting from the medieval and Early

8 READERS OF THE LOST ARK

Modern periods without, to some extent, considering how they treat biblical and classical literature, since these were the predominant subjects of that art. Popular culture offers another obvious subject for reception studies scholars. I, for example, have done a lot of work on how the ancient world is presented in movies (and if you keep reading this book, you'll encounter that in Chapter 6). Popular culture is usually distinguished from elite or high culture as the culture of the masses or general public. The term is kind of nebulous and who counts as elite and who counts as the masses, and what differentiates these groups is quite murky and changes over time. In any case, art created in response to ancient literature, whether it be a Shakespearean play or a Frank Miller comic book, is fairly typically the subject of reception studies.

Yet reception studies is really more than just the study of art and literature. It can be about how people are inspired to make meaning more broadly. In this book we will see how the Ark functions, not so much to generate new communities, but how the Ark is rethought as new communities are generated. When the Second Temple in Jerusalem was destroyed by the Romans in 70 CE, Judaism stopped being centered in that city and that building. The practice of Judaism shifted to the synagogue, and the Ark, once a symbol of the Temple (although the First Temple, the one built by Solomon), was integrated figuratively into synagogue architecture and liturgical practices. Studying how the Ark has been reimagined sheds light on how Judaism itself was and continues to be reimagined. Early Christian communities likewise thought about the Ark within the context of their new community, partially as a means of drawing connections with older Israelite traditions and forging new ideas for the future. The Letter to the Hebrews in the New Testament discusses the contents of the Ark, whereas the book of Revelation describes John's vision of the Ark in Heaven as the seventh trumpet sounds ushering in the final judgment upon the earth. Hebrews ruminates on the received traditions, and Revelation creates a new one.

The forging of new traditions in relation to older ones about the Ark continues to this day. Perhaps the most famous of these involves the Church of St. Mary of Zion in Aksum Ethiopia. Ethiopians claim that that church is the current resting place of the Ark of the Covenant. This was popularized by Graham Hancock in his *The Sign and the Seal* (1992), a book that is consistently one of the best-selling "archaeology" books, much to the chagrin of professionals in the field. It has now become accepted among many that this is a *possible* location of the Ark, if not a likely one. In any case, the idea that

INTRODUCTION 9

this church in a contested location in Ethiopia may hold the Ark tells an interesting story of the adoption of Judaism and Christianity in Africa. Without a doubt, the idea of the Ark plays an absolutely central role in Ethiopian religious life.

This concern for the location of the "lost" Ark reflects a kind of Victorian-era sensibility in regard to the Bible and in regard to any mystery of the world. There are many older legends of the lost Ark that will be discussed in this book, and these concerns resurfaced in Victorian times. With the triumph of scientific reasoning and industrial technology in nineteenth-century England, there developed a stream of thinking called positivism in which it was believed that science would eventually reveal the solutions to anything that was once mysterious. Biblical scholars embraced archaeology, believing that they could find material confirmation of biblical history (beyond the stories of Genesis), not really believing that the historical portions of the Bible would show themselves to be ahistorical. Merged with the new globalization that came with Victorian imperialism, adventurers sought out discoveries like the Ark of the Covenant that could be brought to England, continental Europe, or the United States, and celebrated as a kind of intellectual bounty.

Real Victorian explorers and fictional accounts of them from the nineteenth century are the obvious inspiration for Indiana Jones and the various pseudoarchaeological accounts of late twentieth and early twenty-first explorers looking for the Ark. Victorian veritas in art has also meant that the paintings of the nineteenth century have had an outsized impact on how we view the Ark of the Covenant, as the style of these paintings was such that they were meant to be realistic and seemingly based on historical research. And while the actual academic credentials of much Victorian painting should be questioned, their physical "real-ness" means that they make for easy visual reference tools for filmmakers and other artists looking to replicate the Ark in present-day materials. As we shall explore, contemporary visions of the Ark are difficult to separate from nineteenth-century imaginings.

Yet what has come to dominate twenty-first-century imaginings of the Ark are the works of pseudoscholars. The motivations of these people vary. Some are interested amateurs exploring a hobby that, for whatever reason, never became a profession. Some are conspiracy thinkers looking to subvert what they perceive to be the false realities perpetuated by governments, churches, and other groups for various reasons. Others are more mercenary in their motivations. Some of these mercenary motivations are financial.

10 READERS OF THE LOST ARK

Digital content creators find it easier to sell documentaries about ancient alien power sources than ancient social history. And authors, like Graham Hancock, sell far more books than I ever will, by peddling conspiracy stories written like mystery novels. Other mercenary motivations are perhaps more disturbing. After the events of January 6, 2021, and the US capital uprising involving the so-called QAnon shaman, and the earlier QAnon attacks on the antiquities of the Pergamon Museum in Berlin, it has become apparent that pseudoarchaeological views of the ancient world are playing a destabilizing role in contemporary geopolitics. While the Ark is not a major focus of these groups, the logics (or illogics) used to imagine the Ark in pseudoarchaeological works are similar and something that should be of grave concern to all of us.

The rest of this book shall explore these and other issues related to the lost Ark. The first few chapters will try to get a handle on what the Ark actually was and what contemporary ancient sources had to say about the Ark and similar kinds of religious equipment. The rest of the book, however, will examine different "readers of the lost Ark" and the ways that different communities have come to imagine and reimagine the Ark and the Bible. Where this book may differ from most other books about the Ark is that I am not trying to discover the lost Ark. I have no idea if there even was an Ark, let alone where it would be now.

1

What Was the Ark and What Did It Do?

According to the book of Exodus, on the first day of the third month after having left Egypt, Moses and the Israelites entered the Sinai Desert. There they encamped at the foot of Mount Sinai, where God addressed the people through Moses. God instructed Moses to make sure that the people stayed away from the mountain, not to get too close to Him, but that they would see the smoke and fire of His descending from above and hear the blasting of a trumpet proclaiming His presence. After God appeared, Moses ascended the mountain where God spoke the words that have come to be known as the Ten Commandments or the Decalogue, beginning with the statement: "I am Yahweh your God, who brought you out of Egypt, out of the house of bondage. You shall have no other gods before me." With those words, a new turning point in the history of Israel begins, for this is when God gives the Israelites the laws that they will be expected to live by. Before this, the Israelites were bound to God by the covenant made with Abraham. This was the promise that Abraham's descendants would one day inherit the land of Canaan, "the promised land." When Moses ascended Sinai, the promise was about to be fulfilled, finally after many generations and many years of hardship for the Israelites. They were about to inherit the land of Canaan.

Before they were to take possession of the territory, however, God would give the Israelites the laws that they would be expected to live by in that promised land. The first laws, the Ten Commandments, were foundational and unconditional, applicable to any situation. The Israelites were not to murder, were to honor their parents, and were not to covet their neighbor's ox or donkey. These and the other Ten Commandments were not the only laws offered on Sinai; other laws are more situationally specific, with distinct penalties for particular acts, and a level of detail that seems less fitting to a theophany on a mountain than the declarative statements of the Decalogue like "You shall not commit adultery." Rather, they detail what to do if someone's bull injures another person's bull, or what to do if someone digs a pit and someone else's donkey falls in it. Sorceresses and committers of

Readers of the Lost Ark. Kevin M. McGeough, Oxford University Press. © Oxford University Press 2025.
DOI: 10.1093/9780197653913.003.0002

12 READERS OF THE LOST ARK

bestiality are to be put to death, but foreigners and widows are to be treated charitably.

After detailing these various laws that scholars have come to call the Covenant Code, God goes on to explain that he will send a messenger to Canaan before the Israelites. He describes how these nations will be thrown into confusion but that the Israelites were not to make covenants with these peoples, or let them live in the area, seemingly contradicting His previous statement that foreigners were to be treated well (but presumably that isn't to be the case until the Israelites have fully inherited the land).

Moses reports all of this to the people, and their answer is described using the Hebrew idiom "with one voice," meaning all in agreement. They declare: "All of the words which Yahweh spoke, we shall do." In other words, they have agreed to the terms of the new agreement, an agreement they will break almost immediately after this by fashioning a golden calf. Moses got to work right away, writing down all of God's words. He then builds an altar and sanctifies the new agreement with an offering, and then reads the words he had just written out to the people, the terms of which they agree to once again. Once this is finished, Moses is called up to the top of the mountain, to receive the tablets of the Ten Commandments, where he enters into the cloud of God's presence, and stays for forty days and forty nights. To the Israelites looking up from below, the presence of God on Sinai looked like what is written in Hebrew as a "consuming fire."

While the Israelites nervously viewed this consuming fire, Moses is given instructions on the tabernacle that he is to have built. This first requires an offering of the materials needed to construct it, and the building materials demanded are very specific. Then God gives instructions for what to build, and the first thing that is to be built is the Ark. This is the first time that such an object is mentioned in the Bible, and its description is very specific. The New International Version (NIV) translation of this passage, Exodus 25:10–22, reads:

> Have them make an ark of acacia wood—two and a half cubits long, a cubit and a half wide, and a cubit and a half high. Overlay it with pure gold, both inside and out, and make a gold molding around it. Cast four gold rings for it and fasten them to its four feet, with two rings on one side and two rings on the other. Then make poles of acacia wood and overlay them with gold. Insert the poles into the rings on the sides of the ark to carry it. The poles are to remain in the rings of this ark; they are not to be removed.

WHAT WAS THE ARK AND WHAT DID IT DO? 13

Then put in the ark the tablets of the covenant law, which I will give you. Make an atonement cover of pure gold—two and a half cubits long and a cubit and a half wide. And make two cherubim out of hammered gold at the ends of the cover. Make one cherub on one end and the second cherub on the other; make the cherubim of one piece with the cover, at the two ends. The cherubim are to have their wings spread upward, overshadowing the cover with them. The cherubim are to face each other, looking toward the cover. Place the cover on top of the ark and put in the ark the tablets of the covenant law that I will give you. There, above the cover between the two cherubim that are over the ark of the covenant law, I will meet with you and give you all my commands for the Israelites.

The description is very vivid. Some of the technical terms are a bit unclear today. We are not sure what an "atonement cover" (*kapōret* כַּפֹּרֶת) is, for example, other than that it is some type of cover and that the word is related to the Hebrew word usually translated as "atonement," the price paid as a ransom. The common translation for *kapōret* in English is "mercy seat." This is thanks to Martin Luther's German translation of the word as *Gnadenstuhl*, and William Tyndale, who translated that word into English. English readers may also be confused by the word *cherubim*, which has come to mean chubby, angelic-looking babies resting on clouds, but in ancient Hebrew more likely refers to a sphinxlike figure or a winged adult (we will discuss this more in Chapter 2). Beyond these issues of contemporary translation, the visual description of the Ark seems to be clear.

However, biblical scholars like to complicate things. If they didn't, there wouldn't be much to do reading the same text over and over again for the past two thousand years. One of the scholarly approaches to the Bible is what is called hermeneutics, which just means interpretation. By reading and rereading, new readers offer new interpretations that build off of older ones. With the description of the Ark, which again seems to be straightforward on first impression, the issue of the relationship among these different components of the Ark is debated. Menaham Haran, for example, sees three elements: the mercy seat, the cherubim, and the Ark as all fundamentally separate parts. The cherubim represent God's physical presence, the mercy seat functions as a throne, and the Ark itself is the chest to hold God's laws. Whether the biblical writers thought of these components as distinct is unclear, but Hanan's argument is certainly something for us to consider.

14 READERS OF THE LOST ARK

Not only does the book of Exodus give us God's description of the Ark, it repeats that description when we read about the construction of the Ark by Bezalel, son of Uri of the tribe of Judah. Exodus 35:30–31 tells us that the Lord had made Bezalel particularly skilled at this kind of craftsmanship. As the Israelites bring offerings to Bezalel and his team, the offerings being the necessary construction materials, Bezalel builds the Tabernacle and the Ark. In Exodus 37:1–9, we read of the construction of the Ark, and the description there matches that provided in Exodus 25. We then read in Exodus 40 that after the Tabernacle and the Ark have been constructed, Moses places the tablets of the Ten Commandments within the Ark, attaches the poles, and puts the mercy seat upon it. He brings it into the Tabernacle and hides it behind the curtain (*pārōchet*), just as Yahweh instructed.

That screen is important for the safety of the priests, it would seem. The Ark becomes a piece of equipment that only the priestly tribe, the Levites, is allowed to work with. The first chief priest is Moses's older brother Aaron, and his descendants are referred to as the Levites. Yet even with this elite pedigree, the Levites' work can still be dangerous. Aaron's two sons, Nadab and Abihu, die because they don't give a proper offering to the Lord. So, after their deaths, Moses explains to Aaron all of the rules that need to be followed to avoid such a tragedy again. In Leviticus 16, after discussing medical issues like skin blemishes, bodily discharges, and menstruation, Moses discusses the rules surrounding the Ark. He warns that Aaron should never go behind the screen that hides the Ark, because the Lord will appear in a cloud above the mercy seat. Aaron needs to be ritually clean and make the proper sacrifices before approaching the Ark. Burning the right incense will create smoke that will hide God's presence from Aaron, preventing Aaron's death. Menahem Haran calls this power of the Ark a "contagious holiness," and the idea that holy items and spaces presented a danger to those who were not ritually prepared seems to have been widespread in the ancient Near East.

Narratively here, the purpose of the Ark is clear. It is where God will meet with the Israelites and give them their commandments, to invigilate the laws that He has demanded be followed. But as we shall see, the Ark becomes a part of the equipping of the Temple, and so just as much as it is assumed to have been a container for holding God's laws, it is also described in ways that suggest it functioned as a kind of furniture, a throne for God. The mercy seat comes to be taken as the seat, while the Ark is a footrest or throne base. This is somewhat consistent with Near Eastern art, where kings are often depicted seated on a throne with an inscription on the base of the statue beneath their feet. Here then, the equivalent of the inscription would be the laws of God within the Ark. Furthermore, its placement in the Tabernacle and later the Temple reflects other Near Eastern temple practices where the statue of a god is kept in a temple, and priests offer that statue the things a living being would need (food, drink, music, prayers of adoration). For an aniconic religion like the worship of Yahweh, a religion where images of the divine were prohibited, no statue would be allowed, so an empty throne seems like it would be an appropriate substitute.

The Israelites are said to have wandered in the wilderness for forty years. As they wandered, they needed to carry the Ark and the Tabernacle in which it resided. Some scholars have suggested that the portability of both the Ark and the Tabernacle is meaningful, that the Ark makes sense as a portable throne of the deity. As we shall discuss in Chapter 2, such devices for transporting deities are well known from Egypt. According to Numbers 4:4–8, one particular branch of the Levites, the Kohathites, were in charge of covering and transporting the Ark properly. These verses offer a bit of an interpretive problem, however. The Kohathites are assigned the task of putting the poles into the Ark to prepare it for transport. Yet in Exodus 25:15, God commands that the poles are never to be removed. It is not really possible to harmonize the two verses, other than perhaps to acknowledge that the Israelites frequently disobeyed the Lord and may have done so here. That does not help us understand, however, if the poles were really meant to be removable.

When the Israelites depart from Sinai, the Ark leads the way and is credited with finding them a place to stay. The book of Numbers also records what needs to be said whenever the Ark moved in those first few days of traveling after leaving Sinai, what scholars call "the Song of the Ark." Numbers 10:35–36 reads, in the NIV translation:

> Whenever the ark set out, Moses said,
> "Rise up, Lord! May your enemies be scattered;
> may your foes flee before you."
> Whenever it came to rest, he said,
> "Return, Lord, to the countless thousands of Israel."

Saying this every time the Ark moved may have grown tiresome, but given the dangers the Ark posed, it makes sense to have warned the camp. Yet the song probably reflects a much older tradition about the Ark, one that is not

16   READERS OF THE LOST ARK

preserved in the biblical text. At least that is what we often presume when we read these songs which occasionally interrupt the narrative of the first five books of the Bible.

The Name(s) of the Ark

Despite the clarity of Exodus 25 and the repeated description of the Ark in Exodus 35, these passages leave some ambiguities. Here it is not described as the Ark of the Covenant, but just as an "ark of acacia-wood." Acacia wood is clear. But what, exactly, is an ark? The Hebrew word is ʾārōn אֲרוֹן and that is important. This word also appears in Genesis 50:26, there referring to the coffin in which Joseph is interred in Egypt. Most English versions of the Bible translate the word in Genesis as coffin, and that is likely the best choice given the context of the verse. There it may refer to a very particular kind of Egyptian funerary equipment, and perhaps the Egyptian connection is more important than it seems. In the next chapter, we shall explore some of the possible Egyptian analogues for the Ark of the Covenant, so the fact that another appearance of the word ʾārōn אֲרוֹן in the Hebrew Bible is in an Egyptian context, referring to what is essentially a wooden box, may not be coincidental. That God describes this equipment to Moses, who lived all of his life in Egypt, seems wholly consistent with the story.

The connection to Genesis 50 is not likely apparent to most English-language readers of the Old Testament. They are more likely to connect the Ark of the Covenant to Noah's Ark, the ship that the patriarch was commanded to build in Genesis 6:14. Like Exodus 25, Genesis 6 presents the words of God, demanding that a wooden box be built. For English-language readers, both of these wooden boxes that God commands be built are "arks." This is because of the Latin word, arca, meaning chest. For readers of the ancient Greek translation of the Bible, called the Septuagint or LXX, both of these wooden boxes that God demands be built are called kibōtós, which is a Greek word for box. Now the third century BCE translator(s) of Genesis and Exodus had many options in Greek to choose from, but kibōtós was selected for both passages. The most likely motivation was that a kibōtós usually seems to refer to a wooden chest for storing valuables, but there are other possible explanations for this translation choice. The collection box in the Temple mentioned in 2 Kings 12:10 is also anʾ ārōn אֲרוֹן and is a really clear instance of a wooden box for storing valuables. Whatever the reason,

WHAT WAS THE ARK AND WHAT DID IT DO?   17

the ancient Greek translation of the Hebrew Bible uses *kibōtós* for Noah's Ark as well. Yet in Hebrew, the words used in Genesis 6 and Exodus 25 are not the same. Noah's Ark is not an `*ārōn* אָרוֹן but a *tēbâh* תֵּבָה (spelled תֵּבַת in Genesis 6 because of certain features of Hebrew grammar that need not be brought up here). So, while the ancient Hebrew writers also thought both Noah's Ark and the Ark of the Covenant were boxes, they used different words. The Greek translation, the Septuagint, was very influential, however, and so translators who worked from that source usually translated *kibōtós* the same way in both Genesis and Exodus. So it became convention to think of Noah's Ark and the Ark of the Covenant with the same word "ark." In fact, as we shall see in later chapters, early Rabbinical and Christian interpreters became confused by how these words were used and presumed that there was some connection between the two Arks, even a connection as simple as physical appearance, that perhaps they both looked kind of the same. However, there is no ancient Hebrew linguistic connection between these two wooden boxes that God commanded to be built.

So far, what I've described about the Ark isn't very confusing. In its first reference in the Old Testament, it is a wooden box that God demands to have built, and God uses a different word to describe it that He then used for another wooden box He demanded be built, Noah's Ark. It's when we dive into other references to the Ark in the Bible that things become more confusing. C. L. Seow counts 195 references to the Ark in the Bible, and only 53 of those instances do not also involve some descriptive element like "of the Covenant." Despite the fact that most English-language readers think of the Ark as the Ark of the Covenant, this is not its most common descriptor. That honor goes to Ark of God, Ark of the Lord, Ark of the God of Israel, or Ark of the Lord of all of the Earth, basically the word *Ark* followed by a name used for God. These names for the Ark in the Bible are somewhat interchangeable, more related to the preferred term for God rather than a preferred name for the Ark. The longest of these names is found in 1 Samuel 4:4, and it is a little bit different: "the Ark of the Covenant of the Lord of Hosts, who is enthroned (or sits) upon the cherubim." Some suggest that this is the original designation of the Ark, that this is the earliest form of its name, and other references to it in the Bible just use a shortened form. That makes sense, given the nature and length of the name, but it is not an assertion that can be proven because of the nature of the evidence.

Yet these references to the Ark in relation to the name of God are more interesting than they may seem at first. The complexities of ancient Hebrew

18 READERS OF THE LOST ARK

translation become really apparent when one tries to understand references to the Ark in Joshua 3:11. In that passage, Joshua says to the people: "Behold, the Ark of the Covenant, the Lord of all of the Earth is passing in front of you over the Jordan River." Most English translations treat this passage as meaning the Ark of the Covenant that belongs to the Lord of all the Earth—in other words, the Ark of the Covenant that belongs to God. That isn't what the Hebrew says, although it is possible that the Hebrew writer meant this. What is more likely grammatically, but maybe not seemingly as logical, is that the writer is calling the Ark itself the Lord of all of the Earth. Grammatically this makes the most sense. In the Hebrew version, there is a certain level of poetry that cannot be captured in the translation as the words translated as "Ark" and "Lord" are very similar, `ārōn אֲרוֹן and `ādōn אֲדוֹן, respectively. There is only one letter different in each word, the resh (r) in Ark and the dalet (d) in Lord. This is far less difference than it may seem like to English readers because the Hebrew letters resh and dalet are so similar in appearance that they were often confused for one another.

Gods and religious things in the ancient Near East were often given brief descriptive titles following their names, what scholars call epithets. This is the most likely explanation for this passage, based on the Hebrew. "The Lord of all of the Earth" is the epithet used to describe the Ark of the Covenant. In that case, it suggests that the Ark is actually standing in for God. That all makes sense in the context of the passage, where Joshua is saying to the Israelites that when they see the Ark passing in front of them, they will be seeing God Himself actually passing in front of them. As we shall see in the next chapter, this would be expected of similar kinds of religious equipment used in ancient Egypt. All that being said, there are three possibilities for translating this passage. The translation I think is most likely is "the Ark of the Covenant, the Lord of all of the Earth." It could also be "the Ark of the Covenant of the Lord of all of the Earth." The third possibility, and the type of possibility that fills Hebraists with dread, is that this is a mistake and an ancient scribe mistook a resh for a dalet. In that case, the translation should be: "the Ark of the Covenant, the Ark of all of the Earth." While I think that that is very unlikely and that the first option is the most likely, the ancient Hebrew is ambiguous. There is no way to know with certainty which translation is to be preferred. It is this kind of ambiguity, however, that has meant that the Old Testament can be translated over and over again and each translation offers the possibility for new readings and new interpretations. In other words, two thousand years of previous effort hasn't meant that the translation work is finished!

The role that the Ark plays in the book of Joshua does not make it easy to determine if the Ark is a powerful item in and of itself or if it is powerful because God is present with it. That the Ark played a role in warfare was hinted at already in Numbers 14:44. In that passage, the Israelites have defied Moses and gone off to fight the Canaanites and Amalekites before God has commanded them to do so. The passage reads, in the NIV translation: "neither Moses nor the ark of the Lord's covenant moved from the camp." Numbers continues, explaining that the Israelites were beaten, and the implication here is that the Ark was required for military success. It seems likely that it was needed as a means of making the Lord present, but the passage is ambiguous. Joshua brings the Ark into battle, according to the book named after him, and its presence seemed to be important, if not essential, for the conquest of Canaan.

Perhaps the first sign of the Ark's power under Joshua's leadership is when it heaps up the waters of the Jordan River to allow the Israelites to cross into the Promised Land, just as Moses parted the Sea of Reeds to leave Egypt. In Joshua 3, Joshua tells the people that when they see the Ark move, it is time for them to move. They need to follow behind it (keeping a distance of 2000 cubits because of the danger it poses), but keep it in view so that they will know where to go. The priests move ahead with the Ark, and Joshua tells them to go stand in the middle of the Jordan. Those who visit the Jordan River in the twenty-first century may not be so impressed with this feat, as it if often just a trickle today. But the Old Testament tells us that the Israelites crossed in the flood season, and yet despite this, according to Numbers 3:16 (NIV), the "water from upstream stopped flowing. It piled up in a heap a great distance away, at a town called Adam in the vicinity of Zarethan, while the water flowing down to the Sea of the Arabah (that is, the Dead Sea) was completely cut off." The priests waited in the middle of the river and all of the Israelites were able to pass on dry ground. The same event is described in Psalm 114, but that Psalm doesn't mention the Ark.

The heaping up of the waters of the Jordan inspired the construction of a sanctuary at Gilgal, according to Joshua 4. Before the priests moved and the waters settled again, Joshua ordered one man from each tribe, twelve in total, to take a stone (they would have been large stones) from right where the priests were standing. They then set these stones up at Gilgal, which became a monument to this event. Likely this story was told in the book of Joshua to

20 READERS OF THE LOST ARK

explain the origins of a shrine at Gilgal. An obscure reference in the book of Judges suggests that Gilgal was where the Ark was kept initially. Judges 2:1 reads: "The messenger of the Lord went up from Gilgal to Bochim." While it is speculative to presume that the messenger of the Lord was the Ark, since "messenger" is not used elsewhere in relation to the Ark, the passage does suggest that the religious center of the Israelites was thought to have changed at this time, similarly implying that Gilgal was the first religious center in the Promised Land. We do not know where Bochim was located, but it was likely near Bethel, as in Judges 20:27, that is where the Ark is located and where the Israelites go to ask questions of the Lord.

Returning to Gilgal, that site is located on the eastern side of the site of Jericho, one of the oldest continuously inhabited cities in the world, ironically except for the period when we think the conquest would have occurred. At that time, Jericho seems to have been mostly abandoned. The story of the battle of Jericho, as told in Joshua 6, is well known through songs and artistic depictions. This is the first Canaanite city taken by the Israelites. And their strategy is given to them by Yahweh, who tells them, in Joshua 6:3–5 (NIV):

> March around the city once with all the armed men. Do this for six days. Have seven priests carry trumpets of rams' horns in front of the ark. On the seventh day, march around the city seven times, with the priests blowing the trumpets. When you hear them sound a long blast on the trumpets, have the whole army give a loud shout; then the wall of the city will collapse and the army will go up, everyone straight in.

They do so and it works. The combination of the Ark and the trumpets is enough to make the walls of Jericho "come tumbling down," as the folk song goes.

After these events, the Bible tells of how the Ark came to be associated with another important site. The covenant between God and the Israelites is renewed in the presence of the Ark in a ceremony at Mount Ebal, recorded in Joshua 8:30–34. There Joshua built an altar and made an offering. Then, in the presence of all of Israel, who were explicitly "standing on both sides of the ark of the covenant of the Lord" (NIV translation of Joshua 8: 33), he wrote on stones a copy of the Law of Moses and then read it out to the assembled people.

Most English-language speakers familiar with the Bible are likely already conditioned to think of the Ark as the Ark of the Covenant. The Hebrew word for "covenant" is *berît*, and this name makes sense, given how the Ark is introduced in the Bible. It is a piece of equipment that God demands be built as He is making His covenant with Israel, and it is where He wants the tablets of the Ten Commandments to be stored. This is the name used by one particular source from which the first five books of the Bible (also known as the Pentateuch) was compiled—the so-called Deuteronomist (or D for short).

A similar name as the Ark of the Covenant is the Ark of the Testimony, or at least that is how it is commonly translated. The Hebrew word that "Testimony" is a translation for is `*ēdût*, which is basically a synonym for covenant. Semantically, the Ark of the Covenant and the Ark of the Testimony are essentially the same, even if they do not seem so similar in English. Yet just because the words *covenant* and *testimony* refer to similar ideas, it does not mean that this distinction is not important. Bible scholars presume that writers chose words for a reason. The Ark of the Testimony seems to be used very purposefully and consistently in the Hebrew Bible, reflecting another source from which the Pentateuch was composed— the so- called Priestly source (or P for short).

Perhaps a word or two about these biblical sources is important for those who may be new to biblical studies. In the nineteenth century, German scholars came up with a means of understanding why there seems to be so much repetition and disagreement in the first five books of the Bible. For example, it is very unclear how many animals Noah was said to have taken on to the Ark with him (the boat, not the Ark of the Covenant). If you read Genesis 6:19–20, it is clear that two of each animal (a male and female) were to be brought on board. Yet if you continue to read, on to Genesis 7:1–3, it is clear that seven pairs (fourteen of each animal in total) were to be brought aboard. Similar repetitions and inconsistencies are found in other parts of Genesis, such as the story of the creation of the world or in the two similar stories of Abraham and Sarah going to Egypt (Genesis 12 and 20), with Abraham pretending to be Sarah's brother in each. Then in Genesis 26, their son Isaac does the same thing, pretending his wife, Rebekah, is his sister. The stories are not the same, but they are so similar it would be very strange to posit that this happened three times! The explanation for this was not bad editing or scribal error, *per se*, but rather that when the Bible was written down in the form it appears today, there were different versions of these stories available to the editor. Rather than choosing which version should be authoritative enough to make it into the Bible, the different versions were all included, leaving it for the reader to decide.

22   READERS OF THE LOST ARK

Scholars who study these kinds of problems in the Bible are doing something called source criticism, trying to identify the original versions of parts of the Bible and reconstruct what those original sources may have been like. One of the major clues that these scholars use is vocabulary; writers often use the same vocabulary over and over again, and ancient authors are no exception. The clearest evidence for this in the first five books of the Bible is the names used for God. That and other evidence was used, in the nineteenth century, to identify four main sources for the Pentateuch. The J source uses the name Yahweh to refer to God, which is translated as "The Lord" in English. J here means Jahwist, which is German for Yahwist. The E source uses the word *elohim* to refer to God, which is translated as "God" in English. The D source stands for the Deuteronomist, who, while not being the sole author of Deuteronomy, tended to make arguments that reflected values that one would associate with that book. The already mentioned P source was mostly interested in priestly issues, issues related to the practical functioning of religious activities related to the Temple in Jerusalem. So, getting back to the Ark of the Covenant, when it is called the Ark of the Testimony, most scholars take that as a sign that they are reading something originally derived from the P source. So, to return to the topic that this tangent started on, while the name Ark of the Testimony basically means the same things as the Ark of the Covenant, the use of this different term is likely indicative of the original source from which that section of the Bible was taken.

When these sources describe similar moments in biblical history, differences in the accounts create biblical inconsistencies, which troubled early commenters and scholars of the Bible. One of the most readily apparent contradictions related to the Ark can be found when the accounts of its construction in Exodus and Deuteronomy are compared. In Exodus 37:1–9, as already discussed, Bezalel builds the Ark at the same time that he builds the Tabernacle. However, in Deuteronomy, the situation is different. According to Deuteronomy 10:3, the Ark is built in the immediate aftermath of the Golden Calf incident, before Bezalel constructs the Tabernacle. God commands Moses to build an Ark of acacia wood and to carve two tablets of stone to reinscribe the Ten Commandments, after Moses had smashed the original ones. This is not long before it was supposed to have been built according to Exodus, but it is different enough to be jarring. What has been made of this discrepancy? Modern scholars take this as evidence of different sources, and rather than trying to figure out which version is "correct," they try to understand how the different versions reflect different source contexts.

Ancient scholars, however, were not comfortable with this kind of discrepancy and tried to harmonize the different versions, an approach that will be discussed in Chapter 3. Some early commentators argued that there were two Arks, a temporary one built by Moses and then a permanent one built by Bezalel. Others took Moses's proclamation in Deuteronomy 10:3 less literally. That is to say, when Moses states: "I made an ark," he simply means that he eventually had one made, and he is referring to the work later done by Bezalel.

Rost's Ark Narrative and Source Criticism as Reception History

Source criticism is not limited to the Pentateuch. Scholars have conducted such studies on the appearance of the Ark of the Covenant in other parts of the Bible. Most influential has been the work of Leonhard Rost, who went so far as to name one of these original sources for the Bible as "The Ark Narrative." Rost (1896–1979) was a German theologian who, in 1926, published what has come to be a classic work in the study of the origins of the kingdom of Israel, *The Succession to the Throne of David*. Rost was particularly interested in historical theology, in thinking about how God came to be involved in human history and how different people made different theological arguments in specific historical contexts. In his influential book, he argued that 1 Samuel 4:1b–7:1 and 2 Samuel 6:1–23 were originally one continuous narrative that was divided when the Bible was put into its current form. It was originally a collection of stories that had been written or at least compiled by Jerusalem priests who would have told them to visitors to Jerusalem highlighting the miraculous nature of the Ark of the Covenant in order to impress them. Rost notes that while the Ark seems to play a role in historical events, the details of those events are somewhat vague in Samuel. Furthermore, the story centers on the loss of the Ark and a major military defeat for the Israelites. However, Rost argued that by concentrating on the miracles of the Ark, these accounts shift focus from military losses to the power of God.

The Ark narrative begins with the Israelites losing a major battle to the Philistines, a battle referred to variously as the Battle of Aphek (where the Philistines camped) or the Battle of Eben-Ezer (where the Israelites camped). Regardless, the battle took place somewhere between those two

24 READERS OF THE LOST ARK

sites, so neither name really works. Four thousand Israelites were killed in the first engagement so the elders of Israel recommend that they bring the Ark to the battleground, in order that (according to the NIV translation of 1 Samuel 4:3): "He may go with us and save us from the hand of our enemies." However, despite terrifying the Philistines, who are aware of the reputation of the Ark, it does not help the Israelites. They lose thirty thousand men when their camp at Eben-Ezer is attacked, including the prophet Eli's two sons, Hophni and Phineas. They also lose the Ark of the Covenant itself. When news of the death of his sons reaches Eli, the prophet falls off his chair, breaks his neck, and dies. His daughter-in-law who is pregnant also dies upon hearing the news, but she survives just long enough to give birth to a son and name him Ichabod, which means "no glory," because "the Glory has departed from Israel" (1 Samuel 4: 21 [NIV]).

After the birth of Ichabod, the story shifts to the perspective of the Philistines. They first take the Ark that they have captured in battle to Ashdod, where they install it in the Temple of Dagon. The next morning, the Philistines find that the cult statue of the god Dagon has fallen on its face beside the Ark. They put it back up, but the next morning, it has fallen again, this time breaking across the threshold of the temple. The Bible explains that this is why no priest of Dagon will step directly on the threshold of the Temple of Dagon. However, what finally convinces the community of Ashdod that the Ark is trouble is that they all become afflicted with tumors. The Septuagint and Vulgate add that the city is overrun with rats as well, but that does not appear to be part of the original Hebrew story. The people demand to the Philistine rulers that the Ark be removed from Ashdod, so it is sent to another Philistine city, Gath. Similar problems befall the people of Gath so it is sent to a third Philistine city, Ekron. But as it is entering the city, the Ekronites are well aware of its reputation and demand that it be sent away.

The Philistines decide to return the Ark to Israel, but given the problems that it has caused, they send it back with a gift as an offering. The priests and the diviners recommend that the offering consist of five gold model tumors and five gold model rats. The models of rats and tumors, while seeming like unusual gifts, were chosen because these had been the nature of the plagues. The number five was chosen because there were five main cities of Philistia and so one rat and one tumor offering were sent on behalf of each ruler. These are intended as an offering to the God of Israel, but the diviners and priests of Philistia devise a test to see if it is indeed He who has brought these troubles upon them. They hitch two ritually pure cows to a cart, but they

WHAT WAS THE ARK AND WHAT DID IT DO? 25

take the calves of those cows away, thinking that the cows will be drawn to these calves. They send the cart away believing that if the cart goes toward Beth Shemesh, back to Israelite territory, and the cows do not follow after their calves, this will be a sign that it was the Israelite god who brought this punishment upon them. The cows walked straight to Beth Shemesh, and the five rulers of the Philistine cities followed the cart to the border and watched from there.

While the people were outside harvesting wheat in the valley, they were first quite happy to see the Ark returning (1 Samuel 6:13). The cart comes to a stop in the field of Joshua of Beth Shemesh, beside a large rock. The people immediately chop up the wood of the cart so that they can offer the cows as burnt offerings to the Lord. The Levites, the only ones allowed to touch the Ark, pull it off the cart and set it and the gifts of gold on the large rock, which we are told in 1 Samuel 6:18 (NIV): "is a witness to this day in the field of Joshua of Beth Shemesh." However, the story does not end happily here for the people of Beth Shemesh. Seventy of them are killed by God because they looked at the Ark. Some scholars suggest that the mention of the Levites was added later and that the Beth Shemeshites who were smote were the ones who had taken the Ark off the cart, as there were no Levites among them. Whatever was the case in the original story, to prevent further catastrophe, the people of Beth Shemesh call for someone to take the Ark away. This falls to the men of Kiryat Yearim, who take the Ark to their community, where it remains for twenty years, under the care of Eleazar, the son of Abinadab.

Here the Ark narrative breaks in the book of Samuel, picking up again in 2 Samuel 6. The story shifts to David, now king, who takes all of the able-bodied men to Kiryat Yearim, now called Baalah in the Bible, to get the Ark and bring it to Jerusalem. In the received version of the biblical story, David is now in a strong position, having defeated the Philistines, his enemies, and cemented his kingship. Proponents of the theory that the Ark narrative was one long story suggest that this was a direct continuation, and would have originally been told immediately after the installation of the Ark at Kiryat Yearim. This is the crux of the debate regarding the Ark narrative thesis— whether the story now involving David seems like part of the same literary piece. Regardless, the events that transpire show that the installation of the Ark in Jerusalem was part of the installation of David as king and cemented Jerusalem as a capital city.

The procession of the Ark to Jerusalem is an elaborate one, but as is typical of events involving the Ark, it is beset with tragedy. In this case, poor Uzzah,

26 READERS OF THE LOST ARK

the son of Abinadab who had cared for the Ark for the past twenty years, reaches out to steady the Ark as it comes in danger of falling. This enrages Yahweh, as Uzzah should not have touched the Ark. So Yahweh strikes down the poor man. David becomes angry and refuses to bring the Ark into the citadel of Jerusalem and sends it instead to the house of Obed-edom, the Gittite. It stays there for three months and brings great blessings on the house, and so seeing that, David changes his mind, wanting such blessings for himself. The king reconvenes the procession, this time giving an offering every six paces. David dresses in a linen ephod, plays music, and dances through the streets. His wife, Michal, daughter of Saul, the king he has deposed, watches this display, and we are told that she came to "despise him in her heart." There the story transitions from the Ark narrative to one regarding the dynasty of David.

Other parts of the Bible emphasize the special connection between David and the Ark, and may offer competing visions of David's transfer of the Ark to Jerusalem. The books of Chronicles, written much later than the books of Samuel, emphasize David's relationship to the Ark. In 1 Chronicles 13:3–4, it is hinted that Saul had not treated the Ark properly and offers a praiseworthy evaluation of David in this regard. This reflects the Chronicler's apologetic treatment of David, wanting to depict him in a favorable light. The Chronicler emphasizes this good relationship rather than concentrating on the many negative relationships of David's described in Samuel.

Perhaps the original Ark narrative was much longer than that which is received in Samuel. Psalm 132 is perhaps the most important potentially alternative view of the Ark's journey to Jerusalem and David's relationship to it. In the Psalm we read that David vowed that he would not rest until he brought the Ark back to Jerusalem (or, as written in the Psalm, "a resting place for Yahweh." The Psalm also writes about the Ark being in "Ephrathah," in "the field of Jaar." The Ark narrative as we know it certainly does not mention a camping place for the Ark. It is supposed to be at Abinadab's house. Jaar is likely Kiryat-Yearim, but scholars are not in agreement about where Ephrathah is. So is this a different, but similar tradition as recounted in the Ark narrative? Or does it suggest that parts of the version of the Ark narrative that we read now have been lost or were removed as part of the editorial process?

Scholars continue Rost's legacy by discussing and debating which biblical verses were original to the Ark narrative and which were added by later editors. They debate the original intention of the Ark narrative and how that

WHAT WAS THE ARK AND WHAT DID IT DO? 27

narrative is transformed by the addition of new lines or by interspersing the story with new material. They debate whether the story of David and the Ark really fits with the story of the Ark being captured by the Philistines. Does the Davidic story of the Ark provide a happy conclusion to the questions about Israelite chosen-ness that would have emerged after such significant losses to the Philistines? Or does the emphasis on David's installation in Jerusalem seem too different from stories involving the miracles of the Ark in foreign lands? There will not be any resolution to debates about the Ark narrative. This is the nature of source criticism in the Bible. New readers study the text, trying to gain new insights into the book by reconstructing different original sources or thinking about different genres of writing that may have been transformed into the Bible as we know it. As frustrating as it may be to not be able to find *the* answer, this is part of what makes biblical studies so interesting. This literature is so complex that, even though people have been reading the same words for at least two thousand years, new interpretations still remain possible.

The Ark in Jerusalem

The Davidic stories of the Ark suggest that not only was it thought to be the location through which God manifested Himself on earth, it was also a significant symbol of royal authority. That it may have earlier been a sign of tribal authority is perhaps suggested in the books of Judges and Samuel. The first locations it was held in were Gilgal, Bethel, and Shiloh, all sites within the territory of Ephraim. This seems too coincidental merely to be explained by the geography of the conquest of the land. David taking the Ark for himself and transferring it to Jerusalem may have been a means of asserting his authority over a powerful tribe that had maintained loyalty to Saul. However, this involves much reading between the biblical lines. Regardless, the transfer of the Ark to Jerusalem signifies the centralization of power there and under the house of David.

The story of the Ark does not end with its transfer to Jerusalem by David, however. Its final resting place in Jerusalem is in the Temple, built by David's son Solomon. It is transferred to the Temple in 1 Kings 8. The account there tells of a massive procession ceremony involving all of the elites of Israel and considerable sacrificial offerings. A description of the Ark in the Temple is given in 1 Kings 8:6–9 (NIV):

28   READERS OF THE LOST ARK

The priests then brought the ark of the Lord's covenant to its place in the inner sanctuary of the temple, the Most Holy Place, and put it beneath the wings of the cherubim. The cherubim spread their wings over the place of the ark and overshadowed the ark and its carrying poles. These poles were so long that their ends could be seen from the Holy Place in front of the inner sanctuary, but not from outside the Holy Place; and they are still there today. There was nothing in the ark except the two stone tablets that Moses had placed in it at Horeb, where the Lord made a covenant with the Israelites after they came out of Egypt.

Solomon makes a statement to those gathered there, announcing, among other things, that he has built a Temple for the Lord and that he has (1 Kings 8:21, NIV) "provided a place there for the ark, in which is the covenant of the Lord that he made with our ancestors when he brought them out of Egypt." Solomon then gives a prayer of dedication, and the Temple is consecrated. It is filled with a cloud, like that which had filled the Tabernacle when God was present.

Once the Ark is installed in the Temple in Jerusalem, it becomes less prominent in the biblical story. Perhaps there were ritual processions in which it was removed from the Temple and people could see it. Some scholars have argued that Psalms 24, 47, and 68 may reflect such processions, since they talk about the Lord's presence in relation to what seems to be the Temple or, in the case of 68, a procession. The Ark is not mentioned in any of these Psalms, and so scholars must make these arguments by reading between the lines.

The last king that the Bible mentions having seen the Ark of the Covenant may be Hezekiah. In 2 Kings 19:14–19, King Hezekiah enters the Temple and prays "before the Lord" for assistance against the threat of King Sennacherib, the Assyrian king set to destroy Jerusalem. The prophet Isaiah informs Hezekiah that the Lord has heard his prayers and Sennacherib's army is vanquished by God. The Assyrians are forced to retreat. The same events are recounted in the book of Isaiah (37:14–17). However, neither book mentions the Ark directly, so this is merely speculative. Yet the Bible may also suggest that Josiah was the last king to see the Ark. There is a cryptic reference in the book of Chronicles, written well after the Iron Age, and so usually taken as less trustworthy for Ark scholars. In 2 Chronicles 35:3, King Josiah tells the Levites to bring the Ark back to the Temple and stop carrying

WHAT WAS THE ARK AND WHAT DID IT DO? 29

it on their shoulders. Why they would have been doing so is unclear, and the whole verse is somewhat mysterious.

The Bible does not make it clear what happened to the Ark of the Covenant. It just disappears from the story. Since it was so closely associated with God, it seems, from a biblical perspective, that it should not be able to have been destroyed or just discarded. It must be somewhere and must be there on purpose. Indiana Jones fans tend to like the theory that it went missing very early on, during the sacking of Jerusalem in the reign of Rehoboam, Solomon's son, by the Egyptian pharaoh Sheshonq (Shishak in most biblical translations), described in 1 Kings 14:25–28. 1 Kings 14:26 mentions that he carries off the "treasures of the House of the Lord אֹצְרוֹת בֵּית יְהוָֹה," but the Ark isn't specifically mentioned. It could have been destroyed by one of the later kings of Judah that are said to have engaged in apostasies, such as Jehoash or Manasseh, both of whom plundered the Temple according to the books of Kings. Menachem Haran, for example, argues that the Ark was removed from the Temple while Manasseh ruled. That king, according to the Bible (2 Kings 21), reversed the religious reforms of Hezekiah, and installed elements of polytheism in the Temple, such as an image of the goddess of Asherah. There would have been no room in the Holy of Holies for both the Ark and an image of Asherah.

Perhaps the Ark was carried off or destroyed when the Babylonian King Nebuchadnezzar destroyed the Temple. The apocryphal book 1 Esdras 1:54 mentions that the Babylonians took away the vessels of the Ark of God but does not directly say that they took away the Ark itself. However, none of the contemporary or near contemporary accounts of the Babylonian destruction of Jerusalem mention anything of the Ark. This is not surprising in regard to the Babylonians; the Ark would have just been one of many treasures plundered. It seems harder to understand why the literature surrounding the exile of the Judahites would not mention this. Yet the prophet Jeremiah predicts this set of circumstances, that the Ark would be forgotten. Jeremiah 3:16–17 reads (NIV):

> "In those days, when your numbers have increased greatly in the land," declares the Lord, "people will no longer say, 'The ark of the covenant of the Lord.' It will never enter their minds or be remembered; it will not be missed, nor will another one be made. At that time they will call Jerusalem the Throne of the Lord, and all nations will gather in Jerusalem to honor

30 READERS OF THE LOST ARK

the name of the Lord. No longer will they follow the stubbornness of their evil hearts."

According to the prophet, Jerusalem will become the new Ark, a theme I will pick up Chapter 3.

Despite how concerned modern readers are with the fate of the Ark, the Hebrew Bible seems not to have been interested in this topic at all. Since the Bible was compiled later, perhaps the Ark was of no interest to the writers. Perhaps it had fallen out of religious usage by the end of the Iron Age. Perhaps it never existed at all and was just an invention of writers who also crafted stories about Moses and King David. As we shall see in the next chapter, historians and archaeologists hold varying stances toward the historicity of the Bible. We will return to the question of the fate of the Ark throughout this book. Now though, having surveyed what the Old Testament tells us about the Ark, let's turn to what archaeology can tell us. And spoiler alert, despite movies and bad History channel documentaries to the contrary, archaeology does not tell us what happened to the Ark. Archaeology might, however, help us better understand what the Ark was.

2

The Archaeology of the Ark and Iron Age Religion

For twenty years I have been sending off undergraduates from my department at the University of Lethbridge with my colleague Dr. Shawn Bubel to excavate at the archaeological site of Tell Beth Shemesh in Israel. Shawn and I have been best friends for years, and she is the partner with whom I run our archaeology program. So it is strange that, despite this, I can count on one hand the number of times that I have actually visited Beth Shemesh. Writing this book offered a good excuse for us to take a trip to the site during a season when excavations had been paused for a variety of reasons, the least of which being the COVID-19 pandemic that had made the prospect of shepherding twenty undergraduates on their first visit to the Holy Land unappealing to us, let alone for the university administrators and insurance agents who would have to agree to this. The two of us had found ourselves in Israel for different reasons, but both wanted to go to the site, so we rented a Nissan Micra from a Ben Gurion Airport car rental agency. A very tiny car with a manual transmission, it was the only car that was available in Israel where tourism was starting to rebound as the pandemic seemed to abate.

Beth Shemesh is located between Tel Aviv and Jerusalem, in a very busy section of the country. The site is divided by a highway; a new highway extension will cut further through the archaeological remains on the east side of the site. Some of those remains are being recorded through salvage excavations by the Israel Antiquities Authority, hurried excavations that are conducted to allow infrastructure to develop. The future highway extension will be on the east side of the site. Shawn's team has been digging on the west side of the highway, so we parked the very small car in a turnoff on that side. We got out of the car and stepped over the barbed wire that limits access to the site. I cursed myself for wearing flip-flops as thorns and barbs cut into my feet. I never let our undergraduate students wear flip-flops on an archaeological site, but I wasn't smart enough to take my own advice.

Readers of the Lost Ark. Kevin M. McGeough, Oxford University Press. © Oxford University Press 2025.
DOI: 10.1093/9780197653913.003.0003

32   READERS OF THE LOST ARK

We walked to the section of the site where Shawn has been spending her summers for the past twenty years. There she worked with a team led by Shlomo Bunimovitz and Zvi Lederman of the Institute of Archaeology of Tel Aviv University in collaboration with Dale Manor of Harding University. There, this team has been training undergraduate students in the basics of field archaeology while concentrating on uncovering the remains of the city from the Middle Bronze Age (c. 2000–1550 BCE) to its destruction by the Assyrians in 701 BCE. They have been able to trace the city's transformation from a massive Canaanite city to a city that straddled the border between Israel and Philistia.

Of the many remarkable finds Shawn's team has made over the years, the one that interests me the most is the Iron Age temple uncovered in the last few seasons of excavations. Their team is still analyzing those discoveries, but it is clear that this building is from the period in which biblical tradition suggests that the Ark of the Covenant would have been at the site. Their excavations made international news with the discovery of this temple. For within it they found a massive stone table, consisting of a huge stone slab atop two smaller stones. That a table would have been found in a temple may not seem so surprising. But the size of this table is unusual. And when considered in relation to the story of the Ark at Beth Shemesh from Samuel, it becomes even more captivating. In 1 Samuel 6:13–15, when the Ark arrives at Beth Shemesh on the wagon, sent by the Philistines from Ashdod, the Israelites who were out reaping in the field take the Ark off of the wagon and put it on a "large stone." Verse 18 clarifies that this stone is still in the field today.

Could this stone, part of the stone table of the temple, be *the* stone upon which the Israelites put the Ark? Shawn's team does not go so far as to say "yes." The table is not really where the Bible says the stone was located. The fields in which the Israelites would have been working when the Ark arrived are down the hill from the site. Nonetheless, her collaborator Shlomo Bunimovitz suggested that the author of the biblical story might have known about the gigantic stone table at Beth Shemesh, that perhaps this large table at Beth Shemesh was well known in the Iron Age and possibly later. At some point in the Iron Age, this temple was destroyed, with its pottery smashed and covered in animal dung, perhaps reflecting changing views of proper religious practice and antagonism toward earlier activities. The writers of the biblical story would not actually have been able to see the stone, the table, or the temple. They might, however, have been aware of traditions about it.

THE ARCHAEOLOGY OF THE ARK AND IRON AGE RELIGION   33

The stone table at Beth Shemesh, and its possible connection to the biblical story of the Ark, reflects one of the major problems scholars have in using archaeology to understand the Bible. In the nineteenth century, when biblical archaeology began, archaeologists would travel to the Holy Land expecting to find material confirmation of biblical evidence. They didn't really expect to find proof that the Bible was inaccurate, and they didn't really know what kind of evidence would confirm biblical stories. As the archaeology of the region matured as a discipline, and as biblical studies moved more toward literary criticism than to historical analysis, it became apparent that archaeology did not really work as a means of verifying the Bible. Archaeology provides different kinds of historical evidence than the Bible does. Biblical archaeology is not as simple as digging with the Bible in one hand and a trowel in the other.

Further complicating the matter is that the Bible, in the form that we have it now, was written down hundreds of years after many of the events it purports to describe. Sometimes the anachronisms are obvious, such as in the book of Genesis when camels are mentioned well before they were present in the region or in Exodus when Egyptian cities are called by names from much later periods. These anachronisms don't matter much. It's similar to when one notices a car from a later time in a period movie. It doesn't mean that the story isn't accurate. It just means that the person telling the story has, for whatever, reason, used materials from the wrong era to tell the story. Maybe they had no idea that camels were not present in the Bronze Age Levant. Or maybe they used the city name Pi-Rameses because they felt that their audience may be more familiar with that than an older name for a city that no longer existed.

Historians face other, more significant problems with the fact that the Bible was written much later than many of the events described in it. For literature and historical writing take on different meanings in different contexts. The same story can mean different things in different situations, even when the words are the same. Think of the difference between the 1944 Laurence Olivier version of Shakespeare's *Henry V*, which worked as a nationalist rally cry for England and the Allied powers during World War II, versus Kenneth Branagh's 1989 version, which explores the horrors of violence. The two films use the same text but could not be further from one another in tone. The same kind of historical sensitivity needs to be allowed for in biblical interpretation. That is not to say that there are no universal truths explored in the Bible. Just as Shakespeare's St. Crispin's Day speech, spoken by Henry V

34 READERS OF THE LOST ARK

on the eve of the Battle of Agincourt, resonates with audiences four hundred years later, so, too, is the Bible filled with writings that are deeply meaningful no matter the context of the reader.

For historians and archaeologists, however, context is everything. And so, depending on the context from which one thinks the biblical stories were written down, the meaning changes dramatically. This becomes part of much of the debate among biblicists and archaeologists: what is the context in which the Bible was written down, and how does that context relate to the earlier periods discussed in the Bible? The stories of the Ark of the Covenant stand right at the center of current debates in the field, about the historicity of the United Monarchy, the origins of the Iron Age Kingdom centered in Jerusalem, and the emergence of the people that would come to be known as Israelites. About these issues, evidence from the Bible and archaeological investigations are in ironic agreement as both sets of evidence are absolutely ambiguous! In other words, archaeologists and biblicists are equally able to marshal evidence that supports or denies the historicity of the political circumstances described in the Bible in relation to stories about the Ark.

The United and Divided Monarchies: Historical Debates and Archaeological Ambiguities

The Iron Age political history of Israel, according to the Bible, is one in which a new state forms, breaks apart due to civil war, and then both states are destroyed by larger Mesopotamian empires. According to the Bible, the Israelites ask the prophet Samuel for a king, so that they can be like other nations. Samuel warns them that this is a bad idea but anoints Saul as king anyways. After some turmoil, David takes over after Saul, establishes Jerusalem as the capital, and the Davidic dynasty as the lineage to rule over Israel. However, his son Solomon is his only descendent to rule a United Monarchy, and upon Solomon's death, civil war divides the country in two: a kingdom in the north that retains the name Israel and a kingdom in the south named Judah, where Jerusalem remains the capital. Israel is destroyed in 722 or 721 BCE by a Mesopotamian empire that scholars call Neo-Assyrian. Judah is destroyed in 586 or 587 BCE by the Neo-Babylonians, another Mesopotamian empire. The Neo-Babylonians destroy the Temple (in which the Ark was stored) and carry many Judahites off to exile in the city of Babylon, located in what is today known as Iraq. The Judahites did not remain in exile for long, however.

THE ARCHAEOLOGY OF THE ARK AND IRON AGE RELIGION   35

When the Persians destroyed the Neo-Babylonian Empire in 539 BCE, they allowed exiled peoples to return to their homeland. The Judahites returned to their land, which became known as Yehud, and it became a province under the control of the Persians. The same region comes to be called Judea when it falls under the sway of the Hellenistic kingdoms of Alexander the Great and his successors, and then the Romans. At some point during this time, the Bible was written down in the form we know today.

So why does this matter for thinking about the Ark of the Covenant? Depending on when the Bible was written down, there would have been different political meanings that lie beneath those stories. Now, we imagine that literature and historical accounts continue to have different meanings for any new readers, and so it is not surprising that these meanings would change over time. The crux of the issue is that scholars have different opinions on whether the first part of that political story really happened, whether there ever was a United Monarchy and an historical King David. There are multiple variations on the scholarly arguments, but they can be simplified into three general categories of thinking about the veracity of the Ark's era of biblical history: a maximalist perspective, a minimalist perspective, and variations of a moderate perspective that falls in between these. One's stance on those issues makes a big difference for how one understands the role of the Ark. Still, no matter which of these perspectives one operates from, the reasons for telling stories about the Ark tend to center on Jerusalem, the Temple there, and the argument that this is the location where God wants to be worshipped and that it is the location from which the people should be ruled.

A maximalist perspective treats the historicity of the books of Samuel and the stories surrounding the Ark as generally reliable. Usually, a maximalist scholar will still presume that the version of the stories we have received was written down much later than the events of the early Iron Age. But they also presume that the writers used sources from the period that were generally trustworthy and that they attempted to write a history the way that modern historians do. The ancient author's theological editorials about those events will not be presumed to be akin to the analysis of modern historians, but those editorials are easy to identify and ignore. Maximalist scholars may or may not take the miraculous stories of the Ark at face value, but they will, in most cases, presume that the ancient Israelites used the Ark in their religious activities. They will assume that the installation of the Ark in Jerusalem was an important moment in David's kingship.

36 READERS OF THE LOST ARK

Minimalist scholars, in extreme cases, would take all of the stories about the period of the Ark as much later tales used to justify the present-day needs of the biblical author. These stories may have been written down in the context of the Roman province of Judea, literally centuries after the Iron Age. Miraculous stories of the Ark were just propaganda used by the elites of Greco-Roman Judea to justify the authority of the Second Jerusalem Temple and to glorify a mythical King David and a golden age that never was. Why would they do this? It would have been part of an effort to create a Judean national identity that was distinct from Greco-Roman culture, and these stories would have justified the power of the priests in Jerusalem. For minimalist scholars, stories of the Ark would be just that—stories. Perhaps there would have been some kind of analogous religious equipment in the Second Temple, but mostly the miraculous stories of the Ark would be intended to justify, through historical antecedent, the power of the Jerusalem Temple in the Roman era and the primacy of the religious practices of that institution over other means of worshipping Yahweh. Judea, at the time, was a location of contested political and religious power with a diversity of Jewish groups, including Samaritans and Christians. Stories about the Ark and the Temple would have been powerful propaganda for encouraging fidelity to the Temple and supporting the authority of the Sanhedrin (the group of Elders who acted as a religious authority and met in the Temple).

The perspectives that fall between the poles of maximalist and minimalist are a bit more varied, and to capture them all here would require a book devoted entirely to this topic. Generally though, these scholars tend to believe that there never was a United Monarchy— that there was no King Saul, King David, or King Solomon. Rather, the stories of the United Monarchy are stories told about two hundred years later in the kingdom of Judah as a means of glorifying Jerusalem as the capital and to argue for the religious authority of the Iron Age Jerusalem Temple. The rhetorical function of the Ark may seem similar to the role it would play in more extreme minimalist views, but the context would be slightly different. Rather than arguing for the primacy of the Jerusalem Temple and its religious practices within the context of a Hellenized Judea under the control of the Romans, these scholars take the Ark stories as arguments for the primacy of religious practices associated with the southern kingdom. These literary arguments would have been enacted in tandem with the Judahite kings who had come to power in Jerusalem and claimed descent from King David. They also may have provided an argument that the land of the now-destroyed northern

THE ARCHAEOLOGY OF THE ARK AND IRON AGE RELIGION   37

kingdom more legitimately belonged to Judah. While scholars debate exactly what arguments were made through biblical literature, most working from this perspective would suggest that stories about the Ark would have functioned as propaganda for the religious (and perhaps political) leaders of the southern kingdom.

So why do many archaeologists feel that there was no United Monarchy? The reasons are complex. Most archaeologists are confident that during what they call the Iron IIb period (925–701 BCE), the region we now think of as Israel was divided into two kingdoms, a more powerful northern kingdom named Israel and a southern kingdom named Judah with its capital in Jerusalem, much as is described in the book of Kings. Generally, most archaeologists see much of the book of Kings as a relatively trustworthy historical source, but one with its own political and religious agenda, as one would expect of the history writing of the time. There are enough extra-biblical references, especially in Mesopotamian sources, to the events and figures mentioned in Kings that it would be hard to imagine that these kingdoms did not exist. Likewise, the archaeological evidence shows clear evidence of small states such as those described in the Bible, again meaning that there is no reason to presume a different historical situation.

It is really the period of the United Monarchy that is the problem, for archaeologists disagree on whether we have material evidence for this period and for the United Kingdom led by Saul, David, and Solomon. Archaeologists call this period the Iron IIa (1000–925 BCE), and its brevity is part of the issue. External dating techniques are profoundly useful, but seventy-five years used to go missing within the margin of error for such techniques, and the established chronology is based on this older evidence. Archaeologists also use changes in pottery styles to date levels at sites, since pottery changes over time and is preserved very well. Imagine how Coke bottles have changed over the past one hundred years. The same is true for ancient pottery and for periods we have good radiocarbon dates for: we can correlate those radiocarbon dates with ceramics. However, scholars currently disagree vehemently on how radiocarbon dates and pottery correlate for the early Iron II, and these dates and often these fights get nasty.

It is also a problem that many of the structures that would have been built in the Iron IIa period were used in later periods. The best archaeological evidence for these buildings is from their final use, although we can often identify earlier phases of uses for buildings. However, since we do not have agreement on which pottery dates to the Iron IIa (if any could be said

38   READERS OF THE LOST ARK

to at all), archaeologists do not agree on whether we have any archaeological evidence that could be associated with David's kingdom. While some archaeologists think that many buildings from this period have been preserved, others would date these buildings to a later time. In theory, the location where there would be the best evidence for the United Monarchy, for a palace built by David and a Temple built by Solomon, would be in Jerusalem. There is, however, a significant complication to this. The palace and temple complex would have been located in a part of Jerusalem called the Temple Mount. This is the same site as where the Second Temple was built, of which the Western Wall (what people used to call the Wailing Wall) still remains. It is also the location of the Dome of the Rock, the third most holy site in Islam, and any kind of archaeological investigation there is illegal and inappropriate. There are many more reasons why the existence of the United Monarchy is debated. Exploring all of these problems here would mean that we would run out of room to talk about the Ark!

Luckily for me, the dispute about the historicity of the United Monarchy is not a debate that I have to settle here. I can't say that I fall strongly in any camp, meaning that I don't have a consistent take on the historicity of the United Monarchy. I think that we can use archaeology to better understand these stories about the Ark and that that is not dependent on these biblical events having actually happened or there having been a United Monarchy. As you shall see, I think that there likely was an historical Ark, but I remain agnostic about when this Ark was built and by whom. In any case, I believe that archaeology can still tell us more about the Ark and the stories about the Ark, either because it informs us about the material realities surrounding those events or the material realities that inspired the authors of these stories. We have already discussed how the big stone table in the temple at Beth Shemesh may have been the stone the Ark was put atop, or how memories of there being a large stone table there inspired later writers to describe it in their story of the Ark. The same kinds of logic can likewise inform us about stories of the Ark in other situations.

I want now to return to Beth Shemesh, or at least very near to the site, and think about how archaeological investigations can help expand our understanding of biblical literature, without treating archaeology as a tool to verify or reject biblical history. When we dismiss this kind of question, we see that archaeology actually provides different but, to my mind, even more interesting information, by helping us better understand the context in which biblical literature was written. Looking to the north of Beth Shemesh, to Kiryat

Yearim, we can see how geographical considerations help us better understand those elements of the Ark story. This is where the Ark was sent after the Beth Shemeshites wanted it out of their town because of the hardships it was causing.

Ancient Kiryat Yearim has been identified with the mound of Deir el-'Azar, in the center of the town of Abu Ghosh. Identifying archaeological sites with places mentioned in the Bible was one of the central concerns of biblical archaeology in the nineteenth century, a field called historical geography. This is a very multidisciplinary type of work. Scholars use the geographical descriptions of places mentioned in the Bible to get a general sense of where to expect these biblical places. They compare contemporary place names (usually names given to the site in Arabic) with the ancient Hebrew names to see if they are linguistically related. They consider local traditions, especially traditions that have been passed down in ecclesiastical contexts (since churches were often established in locations where ancient peoples believed biblical things happened). Sometimes archaeologists are really lucky and will find an inscription with the site's ancient name.

Kiryat Yearim is one site whose identity has been confirmed based on many of these types of lines of evidence. In the nineteenth century, a number of explorers visited the site of Abu Ghosh, attempting to decide whether it should be connected with ancient Kiryat Yearim. Located here was Our Lady Ark of the Covenant Church, a church that had been founded based on the assumption that this was where the Ark stayed after leaving Beth Shemesh. The first of these explorers was the American biblical geographer, Edward Robinson. Robinson normally treated local church traditions with suspicion, because most of these beliefs reflected what people thought in the Byzantine era. This was an era of great church building in the Holy Land but also an era that was over a thousand years later than the events of the Bible. The people who established the churches thought that these were the locations of biblical events, but Robinson thought that since those events happened so long before the churches were founded, these traditions were untrustworthy. Yet Robinson was convinced of the identification in this case because the location of the site made sense. The British explorers who visited after Robinson were not convinced. Both Claude Conder and Lord Kitchener rejected Abu Ghosh as Kiryat Yearim for a number of reasons. Since this site is also called Baalah in the Bible, they believed that they should have been able to find a place where the god Baal was worshipped on the site, which they could not do. They also thought that the local name for the site, el-Kiiryah, was not

40 READERS OF THE LOST ARK

similar enough to Kiryat Yearim to justify the identification. Other geographical factors related to tribal boundaries likewise convinced them that this was not the site. Despite their concerns, most modern Bible scholars agree with Robinson and reject Conder and Kitchener's rejection of the identification. The location matches well with biblical accounts, the name is similar in a meaningful way, and the local tradition shows a long belief that this was the site. As we shall see, the archaeology does not necessarily confirm the identification in the way that archaeologists would hope, but what has been discovered there well fits the Ark stories.

Recently Kiryat Yearim was excavated for two seasons by another archaeological team involving scholars from Tel Aviv University, this one led by Israel Finkelstein from that institution and Thomas Römer from the University of Lausanne and the Collège de France. In its present context it does not seem like it, but it was one of the largest mounds in the Iron Age and it holds a commanding presence in the region near Jerusalem. The top of the mound seems to have been artificially flattened, and the excavations of Finkelstein and Römer have shown that the site was surrounded by massive fortifications. The fortifications were used for many years, well into the Islamic period, but the excavators date the initial construction of these fortification walls to the Iron IIb (the period of the Divided Monarchy, after the Ark would have been present at the site). That being said, the ceramic evidence recovered by them would allow that these could have been first constructed as early as the end of the Late Bronze Age. Finkelstein, however, is one of the most prominent proponents of the moderate stance toward the historicity of the Bible, arguing that there was no Davidic kingdom but there was a later kingdom of Judah. This stance compels him to assume that major construction events in this region took place no earlier than the Iron IIb period.

Whatever the precise date of the fortifications of Kiryat Yearim, these excavations have shown that this was a massive, heavily fortified site near Jerusalem. It may be that this is why the Beth Shemeshites wanted the Ark sent here, or why later writers would have thought that this was a plausible place for the Ark to be sent. Kiryat Yearim was a border town straddling the traditional land of the tribes of Benjamin and Judah, and a location of conflict between the northern and southern kingdom. Does the story of the Ark being transferred to Kiryat Yearim reflect an historical circumstance when this site was extremely politically powerful, as its size and tactical position would suggest? Did the act of the Beth Shemeshites sending the Ark there reflect them acknowledging Kiryat Yearim as a center of power in the region?

THE ARCHAEOLOGY OF THE ARK AND IRON AGE RELIGION   41

And regardless of the dating, does the story of the transfer of the Ark from Kiryat Yearim to Jerusalem by David reflect a political situation in which Kiryat Yearim ceded its political power to Jerusalem? Is the story of David dancing in front of the Ark all through Jerusalem a story of him cementing his power over the region? Or, if Finkelstein and Römer are right, and we should date the stories surrounding the Ark and Kiryat Yearim later, was this city once an important cultic site, perhaps rivaling Jerusalem? They suggest that the story of the Ark being held at Kiryat Yearim was adapted from a tradition known in the northern kingdom of Israel, a kingdom for which Jerusalem was not the capital. While none of these questions can be answered with certainty, thinking about the Ark in relation to the archaeological and geographical realities of Kiryat Yearim suggests how the Ark functioned (historically, literarily, or both) as a symbol of power and authority in a context of political uncertainty.

The loss of the Ark, as detailed in 1 Samuel 4, can also be informed by archaeological and geographical considerations. There we are told that the Israelites camped at Eben-Ezer and the Philistines camped at Aphek. Scholars debate the exact location of Eben-Ezer and the battleground. However, we have a pretty good idea where Aphek was located. It was the location of one of the major Canaanite city-states, and its power was likely in part due to the strategic location of the site. In modern Israel, Aphek seems out of the way and somewhat hidden on the road between Tel Aviv and Jerusalem. But in ancient times, it was at a bottleneck on one of the most important corridors in the region—the *Via Maris* or Way of the Sea—the overland route that led from Egypt through the Levant. The bottleneck is now called the Afeq Pass and is about 2 km wide, with the Rosh Ha'Ayin Springs on one side and mountains on the other. This is a swampy area, near the Yarkon Stream, which is a beautiful area now and an important wildlife preserve but would have been impenetrable for armies driving chariots in the Iron Age.

These tactical reasons made it important for the Israelites to defeat the Philistines at this battle. In 1 Samuel 4:2, we are told that about four thousand Israelites were defeated in the battle. The Israelites could not afford to not take Afeq Pass, and so it makes narrative sense that they would bring out the big guns, that they would bring the Ark of the Covenant out from Shiloh in the hopes that it would give them an edge. Of course, it didn't, at least according to the book of Samuel, and the Ark was captured, and the Israelites experienced other heavy losses. So, while there is no archaeological evidence for the Ark at Aphek, and no one would expect there to be given the biblical

42 READERS OF THE LOST ARK

account, the consideration of archaeology and geography adds to our understanding of 1 Samuel 4.

Sometimes archaeological and geographical evidence immediately enhances our understanding of the Bible with little or no confusion. Other instances are not so simple, and that is certainly the case with the stories about the Ark and the Dagon Temple at the Philistine city of Ashdod, described in 1 Samuel 5. Perhaps most importantly, not only has no Dagon Temple been unearthed through excavations at Ashod, there has been little to no evidence for Dagon worship found at any Philistine site! And Philistine sites have been well excavated. My field school training was at two Philistine sites, first at the Philistine city of Ekron at Tel Miqne, and then at Ashkelon on the coast. Temples and religious items have been discovered throughout these Philistine sites, but Dagon worship is not attested archaeologically. However, this is a deity that is known from other archaeological discoveries. Dagon worship is well attested in the region now known as Syria, from before biblical times, and continuing afterward. The deities we do know from Philistia include a strange chair-shaped figure nicknamed Ashdoda by the excavators of Ashod who found a figurine of her (and we cannot be certain that this is a representation of a divine being) and a deity mentioned in an inscription from Ekron, whose name, preserved without vowels, is *ptgyh*, a deity who is otherwise unknown.

So how does this make sense with the story of the Ark's destruction of the Dagon temple? That is a difficult question. This is not the only way in which the biblical description of the Philistines seems to differ from the archaeological evidence. Indeed, the archaeological picture of the Philistines that has been painted by the archaeologists who have worked at these sites for the past fifty years or so is that this was a sophisticated, urban culture that migrated to the coast of the Levant from Greece, bringing that Greek culture with it. They are not the boors described by the Bible, and the contemporary slur to call someone a Philistine is, as the excavators of these sites argue, unwarranted.

So why the negative depiction? The Philistines were the enemies of the Israelites. Likewise, we would not expect Greek migrants to worship a Syrian deity, so why describe them as worshipping Dagon? Perhaps this was just part of the negative portrayal. The audience for the story in Samuel may have been expected to know who Dagon was, and that it was a deity that one should not worship, and so that was more evocative than *ptgyh*. Or perhaps the biblical writers just didn't know enough about Iron Age Philistia to draw a more reasonable description. Whatever the case may be, the story of the destruction of the Temple of Dagon at Ashdod needs to be read in the light of the Bible's explicitly hostile portrayal of Philistia.

The relationship between the Bible and archaeology is more complex than it may first appear. Both provide information about ancient Israel, but they both provide different kinds of information about ancient Israel and pose different problems for interpretation and evaluation. One cannot be used to naively check the other, as scholars had hoped would be the case in the nineteenth century. But that does not mean that archaeology cannot inform our understanding of the Ark. Archaeological and geographical realities that lay beneath or are presupposed by the biblical stories of the Ark can reveal new insights about the role the Ark plays in biblical narratives. Regardless of whether one takes the biblical stories as historical, the archaeological and geographical context illuminates these ancient writings.

Archaeological Analogues for the Ark

What about the archaeological evidence for the Ark itself? The Ark has not been found, and credible archaeologists do not expect it to be. Nor has there been any clear archaeological discovery of art that is contemporaneous with the Ark that depicts it. Despite this, there is still good archaeological evidence for religious equipment like the Ark, and it is clear that this would not have been an unusual type of religious object in Bronze or Iron Age religious practice in the Near East. Analogous equipment is known from Mesopotamia, but the most striking parallels are Ark-like boxes used in ancient Egyptian religion.

The idea that the Ark may be an Egyptian-inspired object has been percolating among academics for centuries. According to the book of Exodus, Moses grew up in Egypt and that has led to many traditions that he was trained in Egyptian religious practices. Part of the narrative thrust of the Exodus story involves a confrontation between Moses and Pharaoh, each harnessing the powers of their respective gods to battle with one another. Yahweh revealed himself to Moses in Egypt, and the commandment to construct the Ark was given immediately upon leaving Egypt. The Ark, then, has sometimes been situated within this historical context, and a tradition that Moses brought Egyptian thinking to the Hebrews has had a prominent place in European thinking about the Bible. European traditions have

44 READERS OF THE LOST ARK

long held that Egypt was a quasi-magical place and that the Egyptians held secret mystical knowledge. This was a vision of Egypt inherited from the ancient Greeks, and it has led to speculation that the Ark is a kind of hybrid of Egyptian and Israelite religious objects.

One of the most important proponents of this vision of an Egyptian-informed Mosaic religion was John Spencer (1630–1693), who struggled to understand Egyptian hieroglyphs long before the Rosetta Stone was discovered, which ultimately enabled their decipherment. Spencer, in examining Egyptian artifacts held in Europe, associated the images he saw in Egyptian art and writing with various descriptions of ritual objects in the Bible—the cherubim and the Ark the most important ones for our discussion. By situating the cherubim especially in an Egyptian context, Spencer was able to solve a problem he had long struggled with—why would God simultaneously command that cherubim be constructed while also demanding through the Ten Commandments that no "graven images" should be fashioned? Aren't these demands contradictory? His solution is that God wanted an Ark fashioned so that the Hebrews would have a visible form of Him for worship and that, since they came from Egypt, would be familiar with a form like the Ark, which he took as resembling an Egyptian sarcophagus. Later, Karl Leonhard Reinhold (1757–1825) took Spencer's idea even further. Reinhold proposed that God's revelation at Sinai was actually a secret Egyptian ritual service conducted by Moses, based on Moses's own knowledge of the mysteries of Egypt. However, Reinhold disagreed with Spencer in one key way. Reinhold believed that the Egyptian elements that Moses introduced were not intended as a means of conveying religious truth in a visual language that the Hebrews would understand. Rather, they were a set of spiritual truths already understood by the Egyptians and now being communicated to the Hebrews.

Now that scholars can read Egyptian hieroglyphs and are very familiar (through archaeology) with the religious practices of that region, such speculation on the origins of Hebrew beliefs within the secret knowledge of Egypt have mostly been abandoned. However, this same increase in our understanding of ancient Near Eastern religion means that we better understand the larger religious context of the Ark. And while earlier scholars like Spencer and Reinhold may have overestimated the importance of Egyptian religion specifically on Hebrew religion, the Ark bears striking similarities to religious equipment used in Egypt and the Near East more broadly.

Before we get into the equipment of ancient Egyptian (and to some extent Mesopotamian) religion, it is important to point out some differences between ancient Near Eastern religious practices and contemporary religious practices. Scholars refer to religious practices as "cultic," but this term does not have the pejorative sense that it has when talking about contemporary traditions. When used in the archaeological sense, scholars use it to refer to worship practices and activities. Even though the so-called religions of the book, Judaism, Christianity, and Islam, grew out of Near Eastern religion, the cultic practices of those faiths today are profoundly different from those of antiquity.

Monotheism is one of the major differences, of course. Judaism, Christianity, and Islam presume that there is only one god. That was not the case for the ancient Egyptians and Mesopotamians. And for much of the Iron Age, it was likely not the case for the Hebrews either. Note that the Ten Commandments do not say that there are no other gods. The Decalogue demands that no other gods be worshipped, which, in some ways, presumes that there are other gods, just ones that are not as powerful or worthy of worship. Otherwise, Yahweh would not be a jealous god. By the end of the Iron Age, scholars presume that most Judahites would have been monotheists, but the process of the emergence of monotheism is still something that scholars grapple with today.

It is not just monotheism that differs, however. The whole purpose of a temple in the Bronze and Iron Age was very different. These were thought of as the houses of the gods, where they lived, or at least where they would make their appearance on earth, and where humans could have contact with them. Statues of the gods were specific locations in these houses where the deities could manifest themselves. Artists sculpted statues, sometimes intending them to visually reflect what the gods were thought to look like and other times not. These sculptures were not immediately ready for the use of the gods, however. They required a ceremony to be performed first, one that we call an "opening of the mouth" ceremony, an abbreviated (and translated) form of the name the ancient Egyptians used for the practice. In the ceremony, a priest or some other kind of cultic specialist would ritually touch the eyes, mouth, and sometimes other body parts of the statue with some kind of ritual tool while reciting incantations. This prepared the statue to receive the deity and brought it to a kind of ritual life. The god could then inhabit the statue. This does not seem all that different from how the Ark is described as working, except for the fact that the Ark does not look like Yahweh. That

46 READERS OF THE LOST ARK

makes sense, given that one of the Ten Commandments forbade making graven images, such as these statues. And since the Ten Commandments were said to have been stored within the Ark, one would imagine that the Ark itself wasn't breaking a key commandment! While the Ark still functioned as a piece of equipment through which God could manifest His presence on earth, it was different from analogous cultic objects as it purposefully did not reflect the visual appearance of Yahweh.

Once these Mesopotamian and Egyptian cultic statues were brought to life, they needed caretaking just as any living being would. They needed to be fed, clothed, entertained, and generally treated as any living being would want to be treated. Offerings of food and drinks (beer especially in Egypt) were brought for the deity's consumption. Clothes were changed so that they were appropriate throughout the different times of day and for specific ceremonies. Musicians and dancers came and performed for the deities. The statues would be taken out of the temple for different rituals and holidays and sometimes paraded around to be viewed by the public and other times taken to different temples to visit with other statues of deities. Now, we don't imagine that the statues actually ate the food and drank the beer that was brought to them, so we presume that the priests themselves consumed it after a set time or threw it away. This was one of the ways through which temples became powerful economically as well as religiously. They gained resources through offerings and from lands that they cultivated to produce their own offerings. Temples were often independent economic entities, with full staffs of specialist workers like one might find in an agricultural estate or vineyard today.

The temple was a place to provide and care for the deity's manifestation on earth. Ancient temples were not places for regular people to come to interact with the gods. Unlike a synagogue or church, believers were not expected to come once a week to meet with one another and hear lessons from a priest, pastor, or rabbi. Believers might have gone to the ancient temple but likely would not have gone inside it. Instead, they would have paid a cultic specialist to offer a prayer or offering on their behalf. The everyday person would not have been ritually clean enough to even enter into the presence of the deity. This was left up to the specialists, the priests or other temple staff.

Thinking about the Ark in this context makes its description in the Old Testament seem less idiosyncratic than it might first appear. It was a cultic object created by humans (even though it was designed by God) for God to manifest His presence on earth. It was situated in the Tabernacle first and then the Temple, both of which functioned as homes for the divine presence. Everyday people were not welcome in God's home, however. They had to be ritually pure; even if they didn't intend any harm, touching the Ark while not ritually clean was a death sentence, as discussed in the previous chapter. The distinction between the sacred and the profane was often important in ancient Near Eastern religion, and the contamination of the sacred with something profane was a situation ancient religious practitioners worked hard to avoid.

The role the Ark seems to have played in the Bible fits very well with our understanding of ancient Near Eastern religion. But what about its physical appearance? As already mentioned, it might not seem so typical of the ancient Near East, since it was not a cultic statue like those found in Mesopotamian and Egyptian temples. The Ark was, however, very similar in appearance to a distinct form of Egyptian religious equipment, equipment that, like the Ark, was made of wood inlaid with gold and carried on palanquins during celebrations. These were simple box-shaped objects that were used for storage, for seating, and in processions, all functions ascribed to the Ark.

Archaeologists have recovered many wooden boxes plated with gold and other materials from Egypt. Perhaps similar objects would have been common in Mesopotamia, but here, what archaeologists call "formation processes" impact the types of evidence that are available. There are two types of formation processes, natural and cultural, and both may be at play here. Natural formation processes are those environmental conditions that mean some things survive archaeologically and some don't. Organic materials survive better in extreme environmental conditions, and so the very dry climate of Egypt means that wood survives very well there, much better than elsewhere. Cultural formation processes may also have led to archaeologists finding far more wooden boxes in Egypt than elsewhere. These are things that people do that impact what archaeologists find. Normally, a wooden box inlaid with gold would never have been thrown away by ancient people (they would use it until it could no longer be used or strip the gold for reuse). The idiosyncrasies of Egyptian funerary customs, however, have meant that this kind of furniture was placed carefully in tombs and some items were not disturbed for thousands of years. Furthermore, ancient Egyptian artists depicted such objects on the walls of tombs and temples, so those pictures provide even more evidence for this kind of material. Those who want an

48 READERS OF THE LOST ARK

exhaustive list of all remotely "Ark-like" Egyptian furnishings should read David Falk's book on the topic.

Perhaps the most "Ark-like" of these Egyptian furnishings are the elaborate wooden boxes used for carrying images of deities between and within temples. The story of David's procession of the Ark into Jerusalem in 2 Samuel 6 well matches the Egyptian-style processions with similar equipment that are well known from Egyptian art and written descriptions. Many of these boxes had rings for poles just like those described by the Ark. They were carried palanquin-style by porters bearing the poles on their shoulders. Imagine Cleopatra being carried while sitting on her royal chair (but in this case, instead of the queen, it would have been a sculpture sitting there). Some of these cultic boxes were quite large, and some that have been preserved seem unlikely to have been able to be moved, but many were intended for processions. The positioning of the poles on the boxes tells us that the objects or people born atop the palanquin were meant to be seen by onlookers. The poles were located lower than the centers of gravity of the boxes themselves, making it more difficult for the porters to carry because it forced them to hold the boxes in a higher position. Clearly the ability of crowds to view such objects while they were carried was more important than the comfort of the porters who had to bear them.

The image of the deity would have been visible to the crowds that may have lined the Egyptian procession ways, hoping to get a rare glimpse of statues that were normally hidden deep within the recesses of temples that an everyday person would not be allowed to visit. Is this a difference from the Ark of the Covenant, with its mercy seat and cherubim? We will return to a discussion of the cherubim shortly, but in some ways the cultic statue riding atop the Egyptian boxes is more analogous to the Ark than it may seem materially. For the theology of Yahweh forbade the depiction of a cult image. Yahweh himself was thought to sit or stand atop the Ark, and so space needed to be left for Him, but no image of him would have been appropriate. Indeed, the cult images from Egypt were materially separate from the boxes upon which they were carried and so the similarities between them and the Ark are relatively striking.

Like the Ark, these Egyptian boxes also bore blankets or screens. David Falk compares the coverings for the Ark with the coverings used when similar Egyptian ritual equipment was carried between locations. With the Egyptian examples, we know that the coverings were designed to keep these sacred pieces of Egyptian religious equipment separate from the profane

THE ARCHAEOLOGY OF THE ARK AND IRON AGE RELIGION   49

space that they were being brought into. This was likely the case for the Ark, too, which needed to be covered when it was not in the Tabernacle or Temple. These instructions are given in Numbers 4:5–6, where Aaron and his sons are told that when the Tabernacle is to be moved, they must take down the screen that separates the Ark from the rest of the Tabernacle and cover the Ark with it. The covering for the Ark is described there, although the meaning of some of the Hebrew is uncertain. Certainly, some of the screen is made of scarlet cloth, but there is also some kind of leather (*tahash* תַּחַשׁ) that translators have variously taken as badger or dolphin over the years. It does not seem reasonable that people dwelling in the Sinai Desert used either badger leather or dolphin leather, although perhaps the dolphins would have been caught in the Red Sea. In any case, it seems more likely that *tahash* refers to something else. One candidate, based on similar words that we know in the Mesopotamian language of Akkadian, is that it is orange-colored dye. Mesopotamian terminology also suggests that it could be a kind of beadwork. It may also refer to an Egyptian word for a particular process of stretching out hides when tanning skins. No one knows for sure anymore, as these kinds of words for equipment and technical processes are often the most difficult to translate. We can figure out roughly what is being referred to, but the specifics have been lost to time. Whatever *tahash* means exactly, the point here is that just like in ancient Egypt, a screen or blanket was laid over the Ark when it was transported.

The Anubis shrine found in King Tutankhamun's tomb (Figure 2.1) is evocative of the Ark of the Covenant in many of the ways described so far and is itself representative of such equipment in Egypt. When Howard Carter opened King Tutankhamun's tomb in 1922, most of the funerary equipment was untouched in a way that was atypical of the tombs of Egyptian kings that had been plundered in antiquity. The Anubis shrine was found as it had been left when it was interred. A wooden sculpture of the god Anubis, in recumbent jackal form, sits atop a box staring straight ahead. Anubis was found wrapped in a linen shirt with fine gauze around its neck. He sat atop a trapezoidal shrine, also made of wood but covered in a gold leafing. Howard Carter described it as pylon-shaped, believing that the shrine was purposefully shaped like an Egyptian temple, with a cavetto cornice running along the upper edge, flaring out slightly. The shrine is covered with hieroglyphs and typical Egyptian imagery, like Djed pillars that reference stability. The shrine opened and contained within were numerous cultic objects, objects associated with different Egyptian deities and with funerary practices. The

Figure 2.1 The Anubis Shrine from KV 62 (King Tutankhamun's Tomb) (photo by Aidan Dodson)

shrine was fastened to two large carrying poles at the base. Behind Anubis was a chest that contained the canopic jars of King Tutankhamun. Canopic jars bear the internal organs of the mummy of the tomb, and their preservation was quite important in Egyptian theology, so it is likely that Anubis was placed in this position to guard these parts of Tut's body. I am not saying here that the Ark was modeled after this particular shrine and Anubis statue. But it does bear similarities to biblical descriptions of the Ark and shows how an analogous piece of religious equipment was used in a culture contemporary with the Israelites.

There is another element of the Ark that seems to reference Egypt that has only been referred to in passing so far—the cherubim that sit atop the Ark. Returning to Exodus 25:18–20, the New International Version translation reads:

> And make two cherubim out of hammered gold at the ends of the cover. Make one cherub on one end and the second cherub on the other; make the cherubim of one piece with the cover, at the two ends. The cherubim are to have their wings spread upward, overshadowing the cover with them. The cherubim are to face each other, looking toward the cover.

That these are winged beings is made explicit in Exodus. And as I have already mentioned, the medieval vision of cherubim being fat, winged babies

THE ARCHAEOLOGY OF THE ARK AND IRON AGE RELIGION   51

does not match the Bronze or Iron Age understanding of cherubim. We will talk about where the fat, winged baby idea came from in Chapter 4.

The word *cherubim* likely comes from the Mesopotamian Akkadian language, a language which shares a number of cognate words with Hebrew. Both are Semitic languages, and in Semitic languages, words usually consist of three-letter consonantal roots, which carry the basic meaning of the three consonants. By adding different prefixes and suffixes, and changing the vowel patterns, one gets different but related words. We do this to some extent in English. Take, for example, the consonants "rn." *Run, ran, running,* and *runner* all use those same base consonants, but these minor alterations change verbal tense or turn the word into an adjective or noun. The same is true in Semitic languages but to an even greater extent. So the Akkadian word that is likely related to cherubim is *karābu,* which is a verb related to prayer or blessing, and *kāribu,* which describes an individual (human or deity) making a gesture of prayer. Based on this comparative analysis, one would presume that the cherubim were anthropomorphic (humanlike) figures posed in supplication. But it isn't that simple. The Ten Commandments prohibition against graven image manufacturing may suggest that this is problematic.

Many scholars of the ancient Near East take the cherubim as winged, hybrid creatures, like sphinxes. That they have wings is obvious from the biblical description, but the rest of the description is vague because the biblical writer likely presumed that the reader would know what cherubim were. Here, archaeology can help us to some extent because we can look to see what kinds of winged figures appear frequently enough in Iron Age art for such a reference to make sense to an ancient reader. Unfortunately, there are a few too many winged figures in Iron Age Levantine art to solve this problem to the satisfaction of all: birds, snakes, scarab beetles, lions, bulls, people, and discs. Perhaps the Ark's cherubim would have been like the sphynx depicted as part of an ivory furniture decoration recovered from Tel Megiddo in Israel. What is perhaps difficult here is that the wings are said to be pointing toward one another, a pose that is atypical of sphinxes. More often, sphinxes are depicted with their wings pointing behind them. The ivory from Megiddo, however, does show that the wings of such creatures varied in position. They could also have been bulls (instead of lions), like such creatures in Mesopotamia, although this seems very unlikely given the incident of the Golden Calf, which suggests a prohibition against the use of bovine imagery.

52   READERS OF THE LOST ARK

Personally, I vacillate between thinking that they are humanlike or sphinxlike. Ranaan Eichler provides a detailed discussion of the major scholarly views over the past two thousand years, and so that information need not be repeated here. Eichler contends that they must have been human figures. Because of the European tradition of reading the word *cherubim* as angels, the vast majority of Ark depictions over the past two thousand years have included winged humanlike creatures on top. However, there is little evidence that the Israelites conceived of beings such as angels back in the Iron Age. The word usually translated as angels in Hebrew is actually better read as messengers. In any case, the archaeological and philological evidence gives us possibilities to choose from but does not provide a clear answer as to what the cherubim were.

Such is the case with archaeology in general, as regards the Ark of the Covenant. Despite the promise of answers that it offers, the actual practice of archaeology leads to further questions. In part, that means it is a productive type of scholarly activity. Scientific investigations should open up new questions to be asked, not bring an end to questioning. What becomes apparent though, when thinking about how archaeology sheds light on the Ark, is that it provides us better evidence for the context in which the Ark stories were told and provides us with analogues in ancient material culture that help us better understand the Ark as an object. As we shall see in Chapter 8, there are some quite compelling resemblances between the cultic practices described in this chapter and those still practiced in Ethiopia today, and so the comparison of similar activities in different contexts can be revealing as well. Short of actually finding the Ark of the Covenant, a hope that no legitimate archaeologist working in Israel seriously holds, these are the interpretive interventions that archaeology can offer for the Ark. You might be surprised that this chapter has had no discussion of archaeologists actually looking for the Ark of the Covenant. There is a reason for that. No real archaeologists do this. In later chapters, I will talk about some of the explorers and pseudoscholars who have looked for the Ark, but this is not the work of professional archaeologists who take the field seriously in the twenty-first century. As we shall explore in the next chapter, ancient interpretations of the Ark grapple with the Ark's absence from Jerusalem. In the writings of early Judaism, there is a contemplation of its physicality, its theological meaning, and perhaps the recreation of new physical forms of the Ark as the historical situation of Judaism changed. For in a Judaism where the Temple has been destroyed and many Jews are now living away from Jerusalem, Zion and the Ark of the Covenant through which God manifests on Zion became potent metaphors.

3

Rethinking the Ark without the Temple

The Ark in Early Synagogues and Churches

Visiting the village of Capernaum is always something of a spectacle. Located on the north shore of the Sea of Galilee, it is the site of an ancient Jewish fishing village from the Roman era, but, more importantly for most tourists, a site in which many seminal moments of Jesus's life took place. Purchased by the Franciscans in the nineteenth century, the archaeological site is run by that order and not by the Israeli Park Service, as one might imagine of a site like this. Shawn and I have visited this site many times, and we visited it once again for this project, but this time without students in tow. We got stuck in a traffic jam created by a tour bus bearing South American Christian music students. They had spilled out of the vehicle to play music in a joyful reverie of faith, or in desperation for a break from historical and religious lessons. The first people we encountered once we got through this crowd were dejected tourists who were forbidden entry for wearing "immodest clothes." After paying the modest five-shekel entry fee (less than $1.50, the low cost a benefit of the site being operated by the Franciscans), we wandered into the main site of the complex, which was completely overwhelmed by tour groups. Despite the sheer volume of people, Capernaum was orderly, especially for Israel. Each tour group found a section of the site where the guide could lecture. The tourists themselves seemed almost universally bored, and you could see that only a few very devoted listeners were paying attention, as most seemed to doze off in the sun or gaze listlessly into space waiting for the spiel to end. I often wonder if the guides care. As a university professor, I'm pretty used to trying to wake up the hungover students in the back row of my morning classes. But I wonder if the tour guides are happy just to run down the clock, since the sooner they get through their spiel, the sooner they get back on the air-conditioned bus, and home.

Shawn and I had come to see one specific piece at Capernaum, a common subject of one of these tour group spiels. As luck would have it, none of the tour guides (or their groups) seemed interested in it today. It is a carved

Readers of the Lost Ark. Kevin M. McGeough, Oxford University Press. © Oxford University Press 2025.
DOI: 10.1093/9780197653913.003.0004

frieze on a stone from the synagogue at the site (Figure 3.1). There are lots of carved stone friezes at Capernaum, from the synagogue and from other buildings there. In fact, there are so many that there is a whole section of the site, now roped off to tourists, that has them piled up in a systematic fashion. This frieze, though, is stationed in a place of primacy in the main courtyard where one first enters the site, along with an information plaque that explains why it is so interesting.

The image on the frieze is unusual. It shows a seeming box on wheels. The long side of the box has five Ionic columns holding up the roof. The shorter side is divided into four sections, looking like a stylized doorway with a rosette on the arched lintel above. The top of the structure is a curved arch, matching the lintel. This looks like a building on wheels. Ionic columns are typical of Roman buildings. Wheels are not. Tour guides often tell tourists that this is an image of the Ark of the Covenant. Yet it is hard to imagine why since this looks nothing like the Ark described in the Bible, except maybe that it is vaguely box-shaped. Yet as will be discussed in Chapter 4 regarding medieval Christian art, fidelity to scripture does not necessarily mean fidelity to physical descriptions found in scripture. The Capernaum frieze bears some similarities to the visual depictions of the Ark elsewhere (such as at the Cathedral in Chartres, France), even with its wheels. There is little evidence that artists who depicted the Ark in the first thousand years or so of the Common Era read the Bible or were concerned with fidelity to the text. There is little reason to think that the sculptor of this image would have

Figure 3.1 The "Ark" Frieze from the Synagogue at Capernaum

RETHINKING THE ARK WITHOUT THE TEMPLE   55

the biblical literacy (in a period and theological environment where not everyone was meant to read the Bible) necessary to depict the Ark according to Exodus 25. If he or she were told to depict a box on wheels, this seems like what one would have come up with.

Despite the divergence from the description in Exodus, the object on the frieze from Capernaum may in fact be the Ark. There is an easy explanation for the wheels. The story of the Ark is one of movement and while the Israelites usually carry the Ark on poles, 1 Samuel 6 describes an historical moment when the Ark is carried on an ox cart. This is the story of the Philistines sending the Ark back to Israel, and it was depicted relatively frequently. We have an ancient painting of the Ark from the synagogue at Dura-Europas in Syria where it is on a wheeled cart, for example. So the wheels are not as completely out of place as they may at first seem. The Capernaum frieze is also out of context from the rest of the artistic sequence. So we don't really know if this is part of a larger scene depicting events from the book of Samuel, or from some other story. If it is supposed to be the Ark of the Covenant, where are the cherubim and why is the mercy seat rounded? As shall be discussed in Chapter 4, later Christian art frequently depicts the Ark as a kind of treasure chest on wheels, without accurately representing the cherubim or mercy seat. Even if one imagines that the wheels are part of the wagon, it still does not look very much like the Ark of the Covenant as described in Exodus.

I think that the comparison with other ancient art is convincing enough to show that the Capernaum image is an artist's rendering of the Ark. There are further clues that I think make this argument compelling. One is that it was found in the context of an early Galilean synagogue, and for archaeologists, context is always important. This is the largest ancient synagogue so far discovered in the Holy Land. Excavated and partially restored by the Franciscans, scholars disagree on its dating (the third or fourth century CE) and whether it was built on the location of a much older synagogue that would have dated to the time of Jesus. Crafted from beautifully hewn limestone, the Capernaum Synagogue seems monumental in ways that other early synagogues do not.

The second clue that this strange, wheeled box on the relief may be an artist's vision of the Ark of the Covenant is that there are five Ionic columns on the side. In a Roman context, Ionic columns would be expected in architecture. But this is a Roman-Jewish context and the five columns in a synagogue are compelling. Does this mean there are implied to be ten in

56 READERS OF THE LOST ARK

total, if one imagines the other side had such columns, thus signifying the Ten Commandments? Or perhaps the viewer is only meant to think of five, which is the number of the books of the Torah, the first five books of the Bible. Perhaps this means that I am wrong, and that this is not the Ark. It may actually be a depiction of a piece of furniture for storing Torah scrolls. Those types of ancient furniture may also reference the Ark of the Covenant, since this symbolic connection has been drawn in present-day synagogues.

Torah Arks and the Architecture of Ancient Synagogues

After the destruction of the Jerusalem Temple, the reading of the Torah becomes one of the main activities that take place in a synagogue, an activity that is functionally embedded in the architecture of the synagogues. A "Torah Shrine" is built into the side of the synagogue that faces Jerusalem, so that worshippers can direct their prayer activities facing the location of the former Temple. These vary in shape and design, but most if not all of the ancient synagogues that have been excavated that postdate the destruction of the Temple bear evidence of such a niche oriented toward Jerusalem. Associated with this shrine was the storage location for the handwritten scrolls of the Bible (the Torah scrolls) that was read at different times in the liturgical year. Some of these were portable containers, and some of these were built directly into the synagogue architecture.

The relief from Capernaum may not be a depiction of the Ark of the Covenant directly but one of these containers, a Torah Ark (also known as an Ark or the Law of Ark of Scrolls). In contemporary Judaism, the Torah Ark of the synagogue is conceptually connected to the Ark of the Covenant. The similarity in name—that is, both are referred to as "arks" and the fact that a Torah Ark is a container for storing the words of God—are convincing as popular etymologies. That is to say, centuries later, not knowing why tradition holds that the Torah Ark came to be called an ark, the connection with the Ark of the Covenant seemed logical. Both Ashkenazi and Sephardic traditions in twenty-first-century Judaism use terms for the Torah Ark that reference the Ark of the Covenant. Ashkenazi Jews, Jews from central Europe who traditionally spoke Yiddish, call the Torah Ark the "Holy Ark" (ʾārōn qōdeš), which is a clear reference to the Ark of the Covenant. Here the difference is that the Torah Ark is "a Holy Ark" and the Hebrew expression for the Ark of the Covenant that it references is "the Holy Ark." Sephardic Jews, Jews who lived on the Iberian Peninsula until they were driven out of the region during the Spanish Inquisition, call the Torah Ark a *hēkal*, which is related to the Hebrew expression for palace or temple. This is less clearly a direct reference to the Ark of the Covenant but rather to the Temple, and perhaps the Holy of Holies where the Ark was stored.

A further contemporary custom involving the Torah Ark of a synagogue that references the Ark of the Covenant is the use of a *parochet*. This is a curtain that either covers the Torah Ark or is found within the Torah Ark covering the Torah scrolls. It is a response to Exodus 40, where Moses is instructed to bring the Ark of the Covenant into the Tabernacle and shield it with a curtain. The ritual curtains in twenty-first-century synagogues vary in decoration or design, and some communities have a special *parochet* for use during the High Holy Days (like Rosh Hashanah). Many designs reference the Ten Commandments visually (by depicting the two stone tablets) or the Jerusalem Temple (especially through images of the two named pillars from the Temple, Boaz and Jachin). However, *parochet* designs are not solely devoted to the Temple or Ark by any means. Often, they are decorated with images typically symbolic of Judaism, such as a candelabra. Sometimes they are aniconic and feature only Hebrew words and nonfigural designs. Still, their use in contemporary times is inspired by the screen that God commanded be used to shield the Ark in the Tabernacle.

Scholars are divided, though, about whether there was an early conceptual, theological, and/or architectural relationship between a synagogue's Torah Ark and the Ark of the Covenant. This is a common concern in the study of ancient Judaism. How much do contemporary traditions actually relate to really ancient ones? Of course, the question isn't that simple because there have been multiple different traditions in the history of Judaism and multiple different understandings of those traditions. So this question of the early relationship between the Ark of the Covenant and the Torah Ark may not be as simply resolved as discovering that there was or was not a relationship. It is possible, and perhaps more likely, that there were multiple and competing views on this in ancient times. What perhaps offers more interesting evidence for the question of the relationship between the Ark of the Covenant and the Torah Ark, even if at the outset we acknowledge that this problem may not be able to be resolved, is the art from some of the most ancient synagogues. To get at this evidence, however, it is necessary to understand some of the transformations Judaism underwent at this time, and the context from which these synagogues emerged.

58 READERS OF THE LOST ARK

Indeed, part of what makes the study of Judaism complex in this period following the destruction of the Second Temple by the Romans in 70 CE is that new traditions were created as a response to this event. This was a transformative period in Jewish history. The destruction of the Temple in 70 CE was a key moment in the Great Jewish Revolt against Rome (66–73 CE). At the time, Judea was a province of Rome, and the Judean population found itself at odds with Rome over a number of issues. Disputes over taxation, however, led to widespread anti-Roman riots that led the Roman governor of Judea to seize assets from the Temple and arrest a number of senior Judean officials. The response to this was violence, and Judean rebels initially forced the Roman military into a defensive position as a Judean government was formed in Jerusalem. Emperor Nero's response to this was to send troops to subdue the rebellion and so started a long war that led to the destruction of the Temple and the eradication of a Jewish religious authority centered in Jerusalem.

This was not the last revolt of Judeans against Roman rule. The second war is usually called the Kitos War (115–117 CE), and it mostly involved Jews living outside of Judea. It is the third war, the Bar Kokhba Revolt (132–136 CE), that had a more lasting impact on Roman–Judean relations. Named after the leader of the revolt, Simon Bar Kokhba, the conflict flared up as a continuation of tensions between Roman authorities and local Judeans. The immediate causes of the revolt were Roman plans to build a new city on the location of Jerusalem, and a temple to Jupiter on the Temple Mount. While the Great Revolt in 66 CE carries more resonance today because it led to the destruction of the Temple, the long-term consequences of the Bar Kokhba Revolt were perhaps more significant. After the Bar Kokhba Revolt, the Judean population was devastated, although scholars disagree to what extent. The Jewish presence in and around Jerusalem, however, was significantly limited and the center of Judaism moved north to the Galilee region. There Jewish life continued on and new traditions, not centered on a physical presence in Jerusalem, but memories of that presence, emerged.

Judaism in the Galilee region after the Bar Kokhba Revolt provides an interesting window into thinking about the Ark of the Covenant. While the Ark had long been taken as physically absent from Jewish life, now there was no longer even a Temple in Jerusalem. Religious authority was no longer centered on Jerusalem and the religious elites there. Rather, this authority shifted to the written traditions about Jerusalem, and new institutions emerged to facilitate the continuity of Judaism. One of these institutions was the synagogue and the varieties of early synagogues known from the Galilee region of Israel speak to the complexities of the emergence of a new tradition without a central authority. What, then, did the Ark of the Covenant mean, if anything, to these new communities?

Two Galilean synagogues from this period after Bar Kokhba may shed light on not just the role of the Ark of the Covenant in the Jewish traditions that emerged at the time but also on its relationship to the Torah Ark. The synagogues at Beit Alfa and Hammat Tiberias both feature what may be Arks of the Covenant or Torah Arks as part of remarkably similar mosaics. The mosaics from both synagogues have relatively secure dating. The Beit Alfa mosaic has an Aramaic inscription that dates it to the reign of Justin the Emperor (517–528 CE). That from Hammat Tiberias bears a Greek inscription mentioning "Severus the pupil of the most illustrious patriarchs," and stratigraphic analysis shows that there was at least a period when both were in use contemporaneously.

We know that Hanina and his son Marianus crafted the mosaic at Beit Alfa, as they are mentioned as doing so in an inscription there. They are also mentioned at the synagogue in Beth Shean, where a mosaic of fruit, floral, and geometric designs was discovered. Given the errors in Hebrew in the Beit Alfa mosaic, Hanina and Marianus may not have been able to read that language. Some of the artistry of Beit Alfa looks somewhat unsophisticated, suggesting that perhaps the artisans were just starting out as mosaic artists when they crafted it. Their design choices seem to deviate from styles more typical of Roman artists.

Similarities in mosaic designs and artwork throughout Israel suggest to some scholars that there may have been set patterns that customers would choose from a book when hiring the craftsmen. The artistic programs at Beit Alfa and Hammat Tiberias are remarkably similar, perhaps suggesting that the Beit Alfa artists copied the mosaic at Hammat Tiberias. However, they may have selected the patterns from a pattern book or copied the design from another synagogue for which a mosaic has not been recovered archaeologically. Whatever the case may be, the similarities are too striking to be coincidental. Both contain images of nude figures, zodiacal wheels, and the Pagan sun god, Helios, all images that seem out of place in a synagogue. Scholars are divided on how to make sense of this. Do the zodiacs at these two synagogues reflect Jewish communities that were heavily Hellenized? Do they reflect Jewish efforts at fitting in with the surrounding Greek population? Does this reflect a Jewish tradition from the period that is at odds

60   READERS OF THE LOST ARK

with later traditions that would have been normative for the Galilee at the time? Would Galilean Jews not even have noticed this imagery as pagan and thought of it in terms of their own traditions only? Was this just one of the cheaper patterns available for the space apportioned for the mosaic? It is impossible to know for sure. Whatever the case may have been, this may have been distinct to the Galilee because the synagogue at Ein Gedi in the south from roughly the same period has inscriptions mentioning the signs of the zodiac but lacks the figural images.

Yet what is really of interest for the discussion of the Ark of the Covenant are the top panels of both mosaic schemes, nearest the *bimah* or central apse of the synagogues, where one would expect the Torah Arks to be positioned. Both top panels feature a structure that is very likely a Torah Ark, potentially meant to be reminiscent of the Ark of the Covenant. These are artistic depictions of this part of the synagogue, with different symbolic elements complementing the main design. While neither looks much like the relief from Capernaum, there are shared elements, and it makes sense that there would be various conventions for depicting them given the differences in the media. In mosaic art, the Torah Arks consist of the two elements already mentioned as typical of the period. There is the Torah Shrine, which is the architectural feature, usually with a pediment (triangular-shaped structure) on top and columns on the side. Then there is the Ark of Scrolls, which is, in mosaic art, usually rectangular in shape and divided in different geometric patterns.

At Hammat Tiberias, the Torah Ark is flanked by two Ionic columns with an upper pediment bearing a rosette or conch design. There is also a piece of cloth hanging from the lintel, tied in a knot in the middle, reminiscent of a *parochet*. The structure is surrounded by equipment associated with the Jerusalem Temple that came to be symbols of Judaism in the art of the era. Flanking the structure are menorahs, shofars (ram's horns used as a kind of bugle), incense shovels, and two plants associated with Jewish festivals. There is a lulav, which is a bound cluster of palm frond. There is also an etrog, a citrus fruit that is usually depicted in an ovular shape with a stem, which is carried in some festivals. The references to the Temple are clear, and this mosaic gives us not only a sense of what a Torah Ark would have looked like, but the conceptual associations that it bore for synagogue members.

The top panel from Beit Alfa seems more rudimentary, but that is in keeping with the rest of the mosaic. Here there are columns, but not Ionic ones. The roof looks more gabled than pedimented, although the conch is more clearly a conch. The conch comes to be an important symbol in Judaism, but in these early stages, it may not "mean" anything. The conch may just be a convenient shape to fit in the blank triangular space of a pediment, and be an easy enough thing to design in different media, explaining its frequent appearance. The conch eventually comes to be so common in relation to Torah Arks that it starts to symbolize them. The Torah Ark in the Beit Alfa mosaic is also flanked by the same kinds of Temple equipment as at Hammat Tiberias, but at Beit Alfa there are also lions and birds bordering the structure. Both the figures in the binding of Isaac scene, and the lions from Beit Alfa are not depicted through expected Greco-Roman mosaic conventions. They are schematic at best, perhaps reflecting the still-developing skills of the mosaic artists.

A similarly ambiguous kind of structure is depicted at Beit She'arim, a site in the southern hills of the Lower Galilee. At Beit She'arim though, the depiction of interest is not part of a synagogue mosaic but rather is a carving inscribed into a tomb known to archaeologists and tourists today as the "Torah Ark Cave." This is just one of the many tombs found in the necropolis of Beit She'arim. The site consists of a network of around thirty underground catacombs and numerous tombs carved into caves, many of which have yet to be excavated. The catacombs are quite large and often multistoried. Each usually has a large main gallery to which access could be gained through an open courtyard. Hewn into the stone at the entrances were depictions of architectural flourishes, resembling monumental doors to houses. Inside, bodies were placed into a variety of receptacles, running the gamut from simple pits, to rock-hewn bunks, to massive limestone sarcophagi set along the walls. The main phase of use of the cemetery at Beit She'arim was from around 220 CE, when Rabbi Yehuda Ha-nasi was buried here, until the necropolis was destroyed toward the end of the fourth century. It was really the Rabbi's internment here that made Beit She'arim a prominent cemetery. It was not merely a local cemetery; Jews from as far away as what is now Yemen chose this as the final resting place for their loved ones. The art and iconography at the site reflect the same moment in Jewish history as the synagogues so far discussed.

The so-called Torah Ark Cave is what interested me on my most recent visit, however. This is a cave in the section of the site known as the "Menorah Caves Compound" in the southwest part of the site. It has four main chambers and could have held around one hundred burials. This particular cave bears inscribed symbols typical of Judaism, like the menorah and lions found

62   READERS OF THE LOST ARK

in the synagogue mosaics. The Torah Ark is a large carving that resembles but is not identical to the images from the mosaics. Here the door is flanked by four columns, two on each side, and sits on a platform with what may be stairs. Above the door is an arch with a conch. Why depict this in a tomb context? Given the other images from this tomb, the artists who decorated it clearly chose symbols reflective of Judaism. Nearby figures are not so clearly religious. Most noteworthy is the so-called Jewish Gladiator, which is a schematic image of a man in a gladiatorial outfit and who is presumably Jewish because of the context. Throughout the site's tombs, however, is a curious blend of Hellenistic and Jewish motifs, with quotations from Homer written on the tomb walls being more common than quotations from scripture. Just like the synagogue mosaics, the tomb complex of Beit She'arim bears more Greco-Roman references than one might have imagined for Jewish religious sites.

That these Torah Ark depictions are found alongside such Greco-Roman motifs perhaps speaks to the new form of Judaism that emerged in the aftermath of the Bar Kokhba revolt. This was a new Judaism centered not on Jerusalem and the Temple, but on local communities, in which Jews were consciously attempting to retain a distinct identity among a larger Hellenized population, who had embraced Greek and Roman culture. If the Torah Ark was meant to reference the Ark of the Covenant, it did so in a way that both recognized the importance of the Jerusalem Temple in Jewish tradition but was offering a new path for Judaism that was not centered on the Temple. The new law did not reside in the Ten Commandments stored in the Ark of the Covenant but in the Torah scrolls stored in the Torah Ark. While Torah Arks may have been oriented so that synagogue members faced Jerusalem, the presence of a symbol of the Ark in the synagogue actually reoriented the community locally.

The evidence from the mosaics is evocative, but other types of evidence shed further light on ancient Torah Arks, such as an architectural fragment from the ancient synagogue at Nabratein, just north of the town of Safed. There, found in a reused context, was the upper lintel of a pediment stone from a Torah Ark. Just as at Beit Alfa, lions flank the gables of the Ark, but here touch it directly. The typical conch shell design sits just under the gable, as at Beit Alfa. There is a hole in this conch from which, presumably, a lamp was hung. The rosettes are another flourish, identifiable from the different synagogue sites as typical of this era of art. This seems to have been part of an actual Torah Ark, not just a depiction of one, and if this is the case, it is the oldest known.

The images at Beit Alfa, Tiberias Hammat, and Beit She'arim, and the lintel from Nabratein are all clearly representative of Torah Arks. Whether these images reference the Ark of the Covenant cannot be proven, I must admit, although I am convinced of this. Where we have a representation of the Ark of the Covenant without a doubt is at the synagogue at Dura-Europas in Syria. This is one of the oldest synagogues in the world, with an Aramaic inscription in its final phase of use dating to 244 CE, meaning that it must be older than that. Excavations at the synagogue began in 1932, where, unlike the other synagogues so far discussed, this one had been preserved mostly intact. That it survived for almost two thousand years in such good condition makes its current state so much more tragic, having been destroyed in 2015 by the Islamic State during the Syrian Civil War.

Dura-Europas was a small town right on the eastern edge of the Roman Empire, bordering Persia, whose Sassanian Empire destroyed the site around 256 CE. As a frontier town, Dura-Europas had a mixed population who followed the eastern religions that were popular among the Roman military. Along with a clearly Jewish population were people of diverse faiths, among them Hebrew-literate Christians, proponents of Mithraism, and worshippers of Greco-Roman deities like Zeus. These and other "foreign" traditions were practiced along with more local Syrian religious traditions, such as devotion to the god Bel, known in the Old Testament as Ba'al.

The synagogue was built up against the city wall, preserving what the excavator Clark Hopkins has called a forecourt and house of assembly. On the wall facing Jerusalem was the Torah niche, where the Torah Ark would have been and where worship would have been focused. The Torah niche here bears similarities to the other depictions discussed so far. Columns flank the sides, and the upper section is arched. Here the conch is obviously such, with a three-dimensional modeling that captures the seashell qualities dramatically. Curiously, above the Torah Niche is a painting of a similar structure, except with four, not two, columns flanking. Is this an image of a Torah Ark above the niche? Or does this suggest that the niche is referencing something else, like the Ark of the Covenant?

There are two certain paintings of the Ark of the Covenant at Dura-Europas, and neither looks like what one expects of the Ark based on the description in Exodus. They are found in wall paintings of scenes of the Bible and are part of the artistic program that makes Dura-Europas so remarkable archaeologically. Not only are wall paintings like this rarely preserved in ancient Jewish contexts to such a significant degree, they are unexpected given

64   READERS OF THE LOST ARK

the aniconism that is often presumed. It perhaps suggests that the less well-preserved synagogues in the Galilee may have had similar artistic schemes, since the mosaics make clear that aniconism was not a tenet of the Judaism in that region.

One scene shows the Ark of the Covenant being carried at the Battle of Eben-Ezer, the battle in which the Ark is lost to the Philistines. Here the Ark is carried by four priests, differentiated from the others in the scene by their lack of battle armor and weapons. They carry the Ark with the poles expected from tradition. But the Ark itself looks more like a beehive or gravestone. It sits upon a two-tiered foundation. It does not match the dimensions of the Ark of Exodus, being much taller than it is wide. It has an arched top, without cherubim, but various designs along the visible side. It looks similar in the other panel, a scene of the Ark on a wagon being sent away from the Philistine Temple of Dagon, where the damage it has wrought is clearly visible. The Ark is resting on what appear to be pillows or cushions on top of wheels and covered by some kind of canopy.

What is perhaps striking about these images of the Ark from Dura-Europas is how much they differ from the description in Exodus. Yet the context of these paintings makes it clear that these two items were meant to be the Ark of the Covenant, showing that Jewish artists of the era were not constrained by an urge to be faithful to the book of Exodus in their renderings of the Ark. Perhaps they would only have been aware of the stories of the Ark, and not had access to the biblical text. Or perhaps these artists were not Jewish at all and had no religious or cultural connection to the stories of the Ark and were merely attempting to illustrate something described by the individuals who had hired them. Yet there are consistencies between these Dura-Europas paintings and the Torah Ark images and the Torah niche, suggesting that the choices made cannot simply be explained through recourse to artistic license.

Comparing the frieze from Capernaum with the Ark depicted in the panel of the Temple of Dagon sequence makes the identification of the object in the Capernaum frieze as the Ark seem more reasonable. But the Dura-Europas images also suggest that both kinds of Arks can be referenced simultaneously. The paneled door and the conch shell above the door at Dura Europas are reminiscent of a Torah Ark. Similarly, the dimensions of the Ark from Dura-Europas are more similar to the dimensions expected of Torah Arks. Maybe it does reference both. While the story of the Ark being stolen by the Philistines offers the kind of kinetic narrative that makes for an interesting relief, perhaps why it is meaningful in the synagogue is that it shows how the Ark functioned as a portable shrine for God. In the absence of the Temple, such portable or mobile shrines were needed again and so emphasizing these aspects of the Ark justified the new status quo. So while I cannot say with certainty that the twenty-first-century tradition that links the Ark of the Covenant with the Torah Ark found in a synagogue reflects ancient beliefs, it seems more likely than not that at least some ancient Torah Arks explicitly referenced the Jerusalem Temple.

Ancient Commentary on the Ark

Art and architecture are far from our only evidence for how the Ark of the Covenant was understood in early Judaism. Various authors wrote about the Ark, preserving traditions rooted in biblical studies, but reflecting the interpretive approaches of their current communities, interpretive approaches that have remained important in Jewish culture to the present day. Mirroring early synagogue art, these writings reflect the emergence of Judaism in new contexts. We see the tensions between traditional Judaism and the Hellenistic-Greek culture that gained traction in the Levant after Alexander's conquests. We see struggles between the authority of the Jewish leadership and the Roman state. And as the Roman state becomes a Christian one, we see Judaism transformed into a diaspora community, separated from its traditional homeland. The Ark remains an object of historical memory, but that memory holds metaphorical truths that continue to resonate with the community and inspire new ways of thinking of the Ark beyond the strictly historical.

One of the earliest nonbiblical commentators on the Ark of the Covenant is Philo of Alexandria, a Jewish philosopher who wrote in Greek and lived in Roman Egypt from around 20 BCE to 50 CE. His writings are voluminous. Of interest to us here is how he attempted to merge Jewish traditions with Hellenistic philosophy, often using allegory as a means through which to do so. He took scripture literally and as historically accurate but also believed that there were deeper meanings and lessons to be learned from thinking about the Bible. Philo scholars debate how much of his writing reflects Jewish thought and how much reflects Greek thought. Since Philo wrote in Greek, he was certainly attempting to reach readers who primarily worked in that language. Yet that does not mean that that was not a Jewish audience, for

66 READERS OF THE LOST ARK

Greek was the more common spoken language of the time. However "Greek" one takes Philo to have been, he certainly knew the Bible well. Some of his works are verse by verse exegesis of the Bible, offering substantive commentary merging Jewish and Greek thinking. Other works operate on a larger interpretive level, beyond textual analysis, ruminating on questions not even touched on by the Bible.

Philo's treatment of the Ark exemplifies the confluence of these two cultures. It is a serious application of traditional Jewish interpretive techniques informed by philosophies that were popular in Greek intellectual currents. Philo was especially concerned with the physical nature of the Ark, but not because he was really interested in what the Ark looked like. For Philo, the materiality of the Ark had allegorical and symbolic implications. The physical descriptions in the Bible were not intended to be merely descriptive of the Ark's appearance. Rather, they revealed more significant truths about the universe. These truths are explored in his *Questions and Answers on Exodus*, where he offers verse-by-verse commentary on the instructions for the construction of the Ark. He is not concerned with the practical components of constructing the Ark, how the materials were put together, or what the materials were, like modern archaeologically informed commentators are. Instead, Philo offers an explanation of the allegorical meaning of these verses. He applies a dualistic Greek philosophy that distinguishes between a material and spiritual world to the Exodus instructions for the construction of the Ark. Here the influence of Plato and later Platonic thought is apparent, with the emphasis on separate physical and spiritual worlds that exist alongside one another. This dualistic philosophy is at the heart of most of Philo's interpretation of the Ark.

A few examples show how Philo applies these Greek dualistic sensibilities to his interpretation of the Ark. For Philo, the materials and components of the Ark are not just physical things. Their descriptions in the Bible have deeper meanings. To start with, Philo ponders why the Ark needs to be made of wood that cannot decay. It is partially, he explains, because God's law was kept inside it and that law is incorruptible. So the container that held God's law had to be equally incorruptible. Yet Philo notes that all things of this world do eventually decay and so when the Bible describes material that cannot decay, it must be referring to something else. He concludes that it is really referring to the soul and the intangible elements of the world that bind all things together. The Ark is not an object but the rational human soul that the laws of God are to be stored within. The instructions on how to construct the golden box are more importantly the means God uses to describe this rational soul. Philo extends his consideration of the materials of the Ark to its gold plating. That it must be plated with gold inside and out reflects the dual nature of the universe. Both the exterior world of the body and the inner world of the mind need to be treated with care, and in Exodus, God is instructing us to do so. He is not just commanding that metal plating be added to the Ark.

Now most readers take the instructions in Exodus 25:11 as straightforward. The artisan was simply commanded to add four rings on the Ark that the carrying staves would be inserted through. It makes functional sense as a means of transporting the Ark. But such an explanation is too simple for Philo. For him, the fact that there are two rings on each side of the Ark is meaningful. In his dualistic Greek vision of the universe, there are two sides to everything: those that can be perceived by the senses and those that can only be understood through reasoning, those of the material world and those of a higher order. These ring poles are not described to explain how to carry the Ark but to explain the fundamental ordering of the world, in Philo's reading of the text.

Another early Jewish commentator who wrote about the Ark in conversation with Greek and Roman worldviews is Josephus (c. 37 CE– 100 CE). Josephus is often referred to as an apologist since he tried to make Jewish culture understandable and sympathetic to a Roman audience. Around 93 CE, he wrote *Antiquities of the Jews*, where he lays out Jewish history, partly based on scripture. He blends his paraphrasing of scripture with his own arguments about the importance of different scientific and philosophical traditions within Judaism, attempting to demonstrate the sophistication of Jewish thought to non-Jewish readers. His treatments of the Ark mostly paraphrase those accounts in the Hebrew Bible, but with additional commentary to explain things for his Roman audience. He tells them that it is called "Eron in our own language" and that the cherubim are "flying creatures but their form is not like to that of any of the creatures which men have seen, though Moses said he had seen such beings near the throne of God."

What has excited many later Ark enthusiasts, though, is Josephus's description of a Samaritan, who claimed to know where the sacred vessels deposited by Moses were located. Josephus describes how the Samaritan attempted to take a group to view the sacred vessels on Mount Gerizim, the location of the Samaritan Temple. According to Josephus, the Samaritan was executed by Pontius Pilate before he could bring the group to see

68   READERS OF THE LOST ARK

Moses's vessels and so the knowledge of their hiding place was lost forever. What Ark enthusiasts tend to ignore is that not only is there no mention of the Ark, but this references vessels Moses deposited, not vessels from the Temple. Likewise, Josephus's evaluation of this Samaritan is also usually ignored. He describes the Samaritan as a man, as translated by William Whiston, "who thought lying a thing of little consequence, and who contrived everything so, that the multitude might be pleased." In other words, Josephus did not think that he was a trustworthy source. So, despite not referring to the Ark, and despite Josephus's belief that the man was a liar, this story has still inspired searchers for the Ark, reading what they want to read into the text.

There is more to this story than Josephus's account, however. Medieval and modern Samaritan traditions preserve beliefs that the entire Tabernacle was concealed, which was more important to them than the Temple in Jerusalem that they rejected. The Tabernacle and its furnishings (potentially including the Ark), it is believed by Samaritans, will be revealed again when the Messiah arrives. Scholars debate how these traditions relate to the account of Josephus and other ancient writings. For Ark enthusiasts, this is enough to suggest a potential location where the Ark may be, and as we shall see in Chapter 5, people have gone looking for it based on these ideas.

Perhaps just as influential for later Ark hunters has been the account found in 2 Maccabees 2:4–5, which situates the disappearance of the Ark with the actions of the prophet Jeremiah. The book of 2 Maccabees is one piece of literature in a group that has come to be called "apocrypha." Some Christians (such as Catholics) will recognize these books as biblical, since they are considered canonical in their traditions. In Protestantism, these books are deemed "apocryphal" and, if included in a Bible, are included in a separate section between the Old and New Testaments. When Martin Luther published his Bible in 1534, he separated out any books, and portions of books, that did not exist in an original Hebrew or Aramaic form. This is in keeping with Jewish tradition in which these books are not considered biblical and they are not included in Hebrew bibles. Regardless of whether one takes these books as scripture, these are ancient Jewish writings that give us insight into some of the traditions during the Second Temple Period and after about the location of the Ark.

The subject of 2 Maccabees is not Jeremiah but the Maccabean revolt and was perhaps written sometime between 125 and 163 CE. However, in the opening sections, the author highlights the prophet Jeremiah's heroic work to preserve the First Temple. The verses in question read, according to the New Revised Standard Version (NRSV) translation:

> It was also in the same document [one that records the deeds of Jeremiah] that the prophet, having received an oracle, ordered that the tent and the ark should follow with him, and that he went out to the mountain where Moses had gone up and had seen the inheritance of God. Jeremiah came and found a cave-dwelling, and he brought there the tent and the ark and the altar of incense; then he sealed up the entrance.

This document that is cited in 2 Maccabees, whatever it may have been, preserves a tradition that Jeremiah removed the Ark from the Temple and buried it in a cave likely somewhere in Jerusalem, before Jeremiah himself was exiled by the Babylonians. The context of 2 Maccabees is to highlight the heroic actions of Judahites in response to external threats. But ever since, it has captured the imagination of Ark seekers. A similar tradition is recorded by Eusebius (c. 260–339 CE), a Christian Greek historian, whose written works are an important source on the early Church. In his work *Preparation for the Gospel* (*Praeparatio Evangelica*), he quotes an earlier Hellenistic Jewish historian, named Epolemus, as having said that Jeremiah took the Ark and the tablets.

An alternate tradition is that Nebuchadnezzar took the Ark as well as the other Temple treasures when he sacked Jerusalem, destroyed the Temple, and took the Judahites into exile in Babylon. This perspective is preserved in the book known by the names of 2 Esdras, 4 Ezra, or the Apocalypse of Ezra. Written as early as the last decade of the first century CE, this is a pseudepigraphical text, meaning that is a text that is attributed to someone who did not actually write it, which was very common in Greek literature. Ezra (Esdras in Latin) was a high priest who returned with the Judahites to Jerusalem after the exile and is credited with the canonical book of Ezra in the Old Testament. The book of 2 Esdras was written much later and records a supposed apocalyptic vision that came to the high priest. In the context of his vision of the destruction of Jerusalem and the Temple, the book contains a passage (10:20–22) that clearly states that the Ark was carried off by Nebuchadnezzar. Verse 22 reads, in the NRSV translation, that "the ark of our covenant has been plundered." The plunderer here is Nebuchadnezzar. What complicates the text, however, is that this is the fourth of seven visions the scribe Ezra writes about, and so it is not meant as a straightforward

70 READERS OF THE LOST ARK

historical record. Having been written so long after the destruction of the Temple, it was not meant as an eyewitness account. The vision suggests that Zion will be restored eventually, but the fate of the Ark is not made clear.

The fate of the Ark is also discussed in another pseudepigraphical text, the book of 2 Baruch. This work is attributed to the prophet Jeremiah's scribe, Baruch, to whom many ancient writings were credited in the first few centuries of the Common Era. This particular manuscript is preserved in the language of Syriac (although this was likely translated from Greek) and describes Baruch's apocalyptic vision just before the destruction of Jerusalem by the Babylonians. Among other things, Baruch sees heavenly figures remove the Ark and other Temple accoutrements just as the Temple is about to be destroyed by the Babylonians (2 Baruch 6–7). These heavenly figures proclaim that the objects from the Temple, including the Ark, may be restored to earth again at a later time. So, while both 2 Esdras and 2 Baruch record visions of the restoration of Zion, 2 Baruch makes explicit that the return of the Ark will be part of that restoration.

Early Christian and Jewish interpretations of the Ark have much in common, which should not be surprising, given the shared origins of these traditions. The treatment of the Ark in the book of Revelation from the New Testament offers a vision of the Ark, like 2 Baruch, literally and figuratively, being restored in the end days. This is the final book of the New Testament and one which offers an apocalyptic vision of the future and Christ's return to earth. Credited to John, but not the John who wrote the Gospel, Revelation is one of the key books in Christian theology and reflects an important trend in Roman-era Judaism. It is a difficult book to understand, rich in vivid descriptions and symbolism, simultaneously leading to multiple and conflicting interpretations.

The Ark is mentioned in Revelation 11:19, just as the final stages of the second coming of Christ begin. This is after the Seventh Trumpet has sounded, which means that the Seventh Seal has been broken and Heaven and Earth have become one, forever. It reads (New International Version):

> Then God's temple in heaven was opened, and within his temple was seen the ark of his covenant. And there came flashes of lightning, rumblings, peals of thunder, an earthquake and a severe hailstorm.

The Ark here, just as it was at Sinai, is seen alongside of God's appearance. But here the Ark is not an earthly vessel for God's manifestation but a sign from above as the two worlds, heaven and earth, come clashing together. The Ark which had been the axis mundi (where heaven and earth meet) has, in Revelation, become a visual cue that the realms of the sacred and profane are no longer separate. This is the climax of Revelation.

Rabbinic Literature on the Ark

Philo wrote in a time when the Temple still stood in Jerusalem and a Jewish state still existed, even though it was within the Roman Empire. Josephus and the authors of 2 Esdras, 2 Baruch, and Revelation wrote in a different context. After the Great Jewish Revolt (66–73 CE), and the destruction of the Jerusalem Temple in 70 CE, as has already been discussed, the focus of Jewish religious life shifted to the synagogue. The leadership of that religious life came to be vested in the rabbis (teachers), who emphasized the importance of prayer and biblical study, now that the rituals of the Temple could no longer be practiced. What emerged in this context was rabbinic literature, which came to be fundamental to Jewish life. Rabbinic literature is very distinctive in style and interpretive approach. The arguments shift between very close, almost legalistic readings of the Bible to longer digressions on many other elements of life. For novices jumping into these writings, it can be quite disorienting, but there is a consistent logic to this literature.

One of the most important approaches to understanding the Bible that can be found in rabbinic literature is called *midrash*, and sometimes the literary output of this activity is referred to by the same name. Midrash was one of the major methods for biblical interpretation common until around 500 CE. It was not confined to Jewish interpreters; some of the writings of the New Testament and the early Christian church could rightly be classified as products of this method. It involved very close reading of the ancient text, as a means of better understanding its literal meaning, making sense of seeming contradictions, and identifying the textual basis for laws and customs. As preserved in rabbinic literature, *midrash* treats the Bible as a perfect document and any seeming contradiction was actually a hint that further interpretative work needed to be applied. Sometimes this involved attempts to understand the "real" meaning of the text, treating what was written as cryptic or allegorical for other truths, and oftentimes prophetic. This interpretive approach helped make the Bible meaningful in new historical contexts, because it allowed the rabbis the freedom to draw out connections

72   READERS OF THE LOST ARK

between their lives and the Bible that are not necessarily self-evident in the ancient text. The manner in which these interpretations have been collected as literature that we have access to today is through the citation of different rabbinic authorities in relation to specific passages.

Perhaps the oldest of this rabbinic literature is the Mishnah, the collection of Jewish teachings that tradition holds was also granted to Moses on Sinai when he received the Ten Commandments. Tradition holds that the Mishnah was conveyed in oral form, and hence it is often called "Oral Torah." It was written down sometime at the end of the second century or beginning of the third century CE. This was not the end of the development of the Mishnah, however, and further commentary came to be called Gemara. The combination of these two texts, the Mishnah (the main text) and the Gemara (the analysis), came to be known as Talmud. There are two Talmuds, the earlier Palestinian Talmud and the more influential Babylonian Talmud. The Babylonian Talmud came to be the central text of Judaism and an important source for rabbinic law. There are also interpretations of the biblical texts called Targums, which are interpretive translations of the Hebrew Bible into Aramaic. These are not literal translations of the Bible but rather are expansive explanations of the biblical text.

Rabbinic writings are not always in agreement with one another, which gives these collections multiple and different meanings that hold authority in different ways. The rabbis ponder why the Bible does *not* explain everything and attempt to fill in those gaps. The disagreements within rabbinic thought show how important close reading was in the biblical exegesis of these scholars. Within this rich body of literature, the Ark is a subject of intermittent concern, and while it is not possible to give an encyclopedic treatment of rabbinic views here, some main themes can be drawn out. Rather than presenting a systematic treatment of the Ark in this literature, I want to illustrate the kinds of interpretive strategies that were enacted to understand the Ark, and what elements of rabbinic interpretation of the Ark continue to be influential.

As I have mentioned, one of the hallmarks of rabbinic thought is the close reading approach taken toward the biblical text, and especially efforts to harmonize inconsistencies between different parts of the Bible. As discussed in Chapter 1, nineteenth-century German scholars took these inconsistencies as evidence that the Bible was written by different sources. For the rabbis, these seeming inconsistencies were interpretive challenges, parts of the Bible that were simply not understood well enough. One of the inconsistencies the rabbis identified about descriptions of the Ark was its size in comparison to the dimensions of the Holy of Holies. The metrological descriptions in the Bible are not consistent, which was noticed by the rabbis. Various explanations are offered, but never that there was a scribal error. Rather, the suggestions that are made usually imply that divine measuring schemes are more complex than those available on earth, or that earthly rules do not apply in divine space like the Temple.

Similar types of logic are employed in rabbinic discussions of what the Ark contained, or how, exactly, it was constructed, inspired by noticing disparities between the different biblical sources about the Ark. Even differences in pronouns were noteworthy. The rabbis noted discrepancies between Exodus 25:10 and Deuteronomy 10:1. Deuteronomy 10:1 commands: "And make *you* an Ark of wood." Yet Exodus 25:10 states: "And *they* shall make an Ark of acacia wood." For modern readers these two verses don't seem to be all that different. In Deuteronomy it seems that Moses is commanded to make the Ark, whereas in Exodus, it seems that the whole community is commanded to make it. This observation leads to further philosophical discussions on community obligations, related to issues like who should supply materials for sacrifice or how Torah scholars should be supported financially.

The rabbis also ascribe various powers to the Ark that are different from those described in the Bible. What seems to have been especially of interest to them, at least in terms of the Ark, were its abilities, and by extension, God's demonstration of His abilities. In some of the rabbinic treatments, the Ark displays seeming supernatural powers, although these should presumably be credited to God. One power that deviates from biblical accounts is the Ark's seeming ability to move by itself, by flying or levitating. Rabbinic treatments of the Israelite sojourn in the wilderness describe the Ark rising up itself and flying to the next camp spot, each camp spot a three-day-walk away, leading the way for the Israelites. The Ark is also said to have moved of its own accord to lead the Israelites across the River Jordan. In the book of Joshua, the Bible describes the miracle of the waters parting so that the people could cross on dry land. Midrash on Joshua expands on this miracle by describing an Ark that moves of its own volition, dragging the priests with it.

Rabbinic literature treats the Ark as both a metaphorical foundation for investigating theological truths and a quasi-magical object, through which God's powers could manifest on earth. The allegorical types of interpretations well reflect the richness of rabbinic and, as we shall see, medieval treatment

74   READERS OF THE LOST ARK

of biblical subject matter. For theologians, rabbinic allegorical reflections about the Ark have been most influential. Yet these allegorical interpretations have not been central to how later Ark enthusiasts have read these texts. For those who are mostly interested in the Ark, rather than theology, it has been the rabbinic- era claims about the current resting place of an historically "real" physical Ark, an Ark of wood and gold not of metaphor, that have had more of an impact. Some rabbinic traditions hold that the Ark, along with other sacred vessels hidden before the destruction of the Temple, will be revealed again in Messianic times. As we shall see in Chapter 5, this belief has had a significant impact on policymaking surrounding the Temple Mount in Jerusalem.

The rabbis discuss the Temple in depth, but where their discussion differs from the Bible is in their interest in the Shettiyah (also known as the Noble Stone or Foundation Stone), which is located where the Temple once stood. This is the rock that is the focus of the Dome of the Rock (discussed in more detail in Chapter 5), the golden shrine erected in the seventh century CE, although since rebuilt. It is now one of the most sacred locations for Muslims. Rabbinic understanding of Solomon's Temple situates the Holy of Holies as having been directly above the Shettiyah, an argument that many still accept. For the rabbis, this rock was the foundation upon which the creation of the earth began. Thus, the Ark was installed directly where God began creation, a place of primordial importance. For Ark enthusiasts, this means that rabbinic tradition might describe the exact place where the Ark was once located. In the Talmud, the Shettiyah stands as a kind of ghostly reflection of the Ark. It was there before the Ark was installed in Jerusalem, and it remains there now that the Ark is in exile.

Perhaps the most influential story of the Ark's location that is found in the Talmud is that the Ark was hidden in the Temple itself. There is a story from the time before the Second Temple was destroyed, that a priest wandering in the Temple courtyard noticed a stone that was different from the others. He reported to a companion that he had found a spot where one of the flagstones was different from the others. Suddenly he died, struck down before he could explain to his companion where that flagstone was located. God had killed the man rather than let him reveal the hiding place of the Ark beneath the Temple.

How much did the rabbis care about where the Ark was in their day or what happened to it? Probably not too much. This never seems to be a major concern of the rabbis, but a few of the stories of the location of the Ark are

RETHINKING THE ARK WITHOUT THE TEMPLE 75

particularly provocative. Nineteenth- and twentieth-century readers, however, have made much out of sorting through these voluminous writings looking for clues as to the location of the Ark. Those Ark explorers are the subject of Chapter 5. The more immediate impact of rabbinic treatments of the Ark was to provide a foundation for thinking about it metaphorically. Until the nineteenth century, these metaphorical and allegorical approaches come to dominate European thinking about the Ark. That is not to say that European interpreters of the Ark did not believe in an historical Ark. Rather, they believed that there were significant truths that could be understood through contemplating the Ark and what was written about it. In the next chapter, we will leave these ancient interpretations but also return to Kiryat Yearim, to the site where the Ark was thought to be kept before being transferred to Jerusalem. We will consider some of the medieval and early modern traditions about the Ark of the Covenant and what the Ark comes to mean in Europe then. We will see that medieval interpreters of the Ark embraced the metaphorical approaches that were favored by the Rabbis but that they also read these metaphors in light of the theologies of that era.

4

Medieval Theology

The Ark as Metaphor

We drove up the windy road of Abu Ghosh, ancient Kiryat Jearim, the Arab-Israeli town located on the highway between Jerusalem and Tel Aviv. This is where the Ark had been sent after the people of Beth Shemesh became afraid of it but before David brought it to Jerusalem, or so the tradition goes. The small rental car was having difficulties with the steep slopes of the Judean Hills, and my already bad sense of direction was being confused by the various roundabouts that usually provide forgiveness in Israel for lost travelers. You can usually drive around and around until you figure out where you need to turn off. We pulled onto Notre Dame Street, but something wasn't right. Almost immediately we hit a large green gate that prevented us from going further. We were trying to get to the Church of Our Lady Ark of the Covenant, which was supposed to be open. But it wasn't. Instead, there was a large, locked gate bearing the sign "Monastery Sisters of St. Joseph of the Apparition." Not wanting to bother the nuns who resided here, I thought we should leave.

I was quick to give up, but my long-time colleague Shawn forced me to get out of the car and try the call box. Reluctantly, not wanting to seem like a harassing tourist, I touched the button and listened to the ringing. A quiet, female voice answered and said, in a questioning voice, "Yes?"

I stammered in response, "Uhm, shalom, uh, can you let me in to see the Ark of the Covenant Church?"

She responded, in the same quiet and completely unsurprised voice, "Yes."

But then she continued, "You cannot go inside right now. You can only look from outside."

"Uh. Ok. That's fine."

She told me that she would open the gate. So I got back in the car, where Shawn and I watched the gate slowly slide open. She put the incredibly tiny, Nissan Micra into first and the car, which really seems too small for any Israeli highway but the perfect size for the narrow and congested streets

Readers of the Lost Ark. Kevin M. McGeough, Oxford University Press. © Oxford University Press 2025.
DOI: 10.1093/9780197653913.003.0005

of Jerusalem, chugged up the hill to the parking lot. We got out of the car and walked up to the courtyard between the church which we wanted to visit, Our Lady Ark of the Covenant and the convent where the Sisters of St. Joseph of the Apparition reside. The courtyard was incredibly tranquil, with no hint of the noise and excitement of Abu Ghosh on the other side of the fence. Large trees provide shade for a garden-like space, dotted with ancient column bases atop of which sit flowerpots and planters filled with flowering greenery. Most of the ground consists of the gray gravel typical of the region. The buildings themselves are constructed of large limestone blocks, also typical of the region, at least for those structures built before World War II. The site is at the top of a hill, with views of the suburbs of Jerusalem and the Jerusalem hills in the distance, as well as the terraces of olive trees along the lower edges to the north, east, and south. The whole complex feels like an oasis, and the sisters clearly work to maintain this as a place of quiet contemplation. All of this is built atop ancient Kiryat Yearim.

What brought the nuns to Abu Ghosh was a vision that came to Sister Joséphine Rumèbe in 1900. She was a member of a religious order who had come to the Holy Land in 1848 to assist the Franciscans working in Jerusalem, especially with responsibilities related to education. Their name, Sisters of St. Joseph of the Apparition, refers to the revelation that was given to Joseph in Matthew 1:20, in which he is told not to be afraid to take the Virgin Mary as his wife. And just as Joseph's vision led him to take action, Sister Joséphine's vision led to the construction of the basilica Our Lady Ark of the Covenant. She had been stationed at the base of the hill to work with the impoverished, especially helping to supply them with food. There she had a vision of a mountain of fire and a voice spoke to her, instructing her that she needed to purchase the site at the top of the hill. This was not her first vision. When she was five, she claimed to have seen Jesus, and at eight, her mother and her both saw the Virgin. Throughout her life she was plagued by what she claimed were invisible stigmata, especially manifest as leg pains. Still, the vision she had at Abu Ghosh compelled her to act. After she purchased the land, work began on the basilica that stands there today, as does the convent that was originally constructed as a medical facility for long-term physical illness (in those days called a sanatorium).

The Sisters of St. Joseph of the Apparition is an order that is particularly open to visions and revelations. One corner of the grounds outside of the church is currently dedicated to Our Lady of La Vang, an apparition of the Virgin Mary that appeared in 1798 to Catholics who were being persecuted in

78   READERS OF THE LOST ARK

Vietnam. Pilgrims from Vietnam now routinely visit the church. These were the only other tourists we encountered at the site. Visions of the Virgin are referred to by the Catholic Church as "Marian Apparitions," and while claims of such appearances are common, it is very uncommon for the Church to authenticate them in the twenty-first century. Now, the Church tries to show that these were imagined experiences. What constitutes a Marian Apparition today is very specific. It cannot be a dream, and it cannot be an interior voice (so Sister Joséphine's voice telling her to buy the land would no longer count as one). The viewer actually has to see Mary, and usually the reason that Mary has appeared is to give some kind of message about the Church.

The nun with whom I spoke over the intercom was from Vietnam. When she came out to greet me, however, she did not come out to talk about Our Lady of La Vang or apparitions of Mary in general. Rather, she wanted to let me know why we could not go into the church. She explained that it was because the church was no longer safe to enter as it had fallen into such bad condition. The nun explained that cracks and fissures in the ceiling had spread so much that materials were starting to fall from above. Pictures of the damage were set up outside the church, and these cracks seem pretty significant. Certainly, my desire to sneak into the basilica was cured by looking at these pictures. Still, I assured the nun, I was mostly wanting to view the grounds and especially the statue of Mary that stands atop the building. The nun left us to our own devices and told me that we could find her in the gift shop should we need her.

Of course, why I had dragged Shawn here was so that we could see the Ark imagery at the church (Figure 4.1). To the right of the main entrance of the church was an icon featuring the Virgin Mary holding Jesus set into a niche with a table for prayer candles in front. Mary stands in front of the walls of the Temple, above which are a rainbow and two angels. Beside her, two men kneel, one holding aloft a chalice and the other a harp. Below her, eight men carry the Ark of the Covenant, which is depicted with angel-like cherubim using their wings to embrace each other atop the mercy seat.

Much more impressive is the large, strikingly white concrete statue of Mary that is set atop the basilica and is visible throughout Abu Ghosh today (Figure 4.2). Mary holds Jesus in one arm and stands atop a large Ark of the Covenant. Its cherubim are babies with faces looking down at the landscape over the edge of the Ark. They face the opposite direction from the cherubim in most Ark depictions. Only one wing of each is visible from below, each pointing up to form a triangular shape in front of the Madonna's

MEDIEVAL THEOLOGY 79

Figure 4.1 Icon of Mary and Jesus at the entrance to the Church of Our Lady Ark of the Covenant

legs. A blanket lies across the mercy seat of the Ark, but one corner is visible, showing the everted rim of the lid and the hooks for the poles on that side. It is a curious depiction of the Ark in how it deviates from standard expectations yet is still readily identifiable as the Ark.

Figure 4.2 Statue of Mary standing on the Ark of the Covenant atop the Church of Our Lady Ark of the Covenant

Yet this is not really the Ark for which the church was named, even though the church is supposedly set on the hill where the Ark was kept until brought to Jerusalem. The name of the church is "Our Lady Ark of the Covenant," not "Our Lady *of the* Ark of the Covenant." For it is not the Old Testament Ark that is celebrated here but Mary in her role as the new Ark of the Covenant. In some Christian theologies, much of what is described in the Old Testament is taken to be typological for the New Testament. People, places, and things in the Old Testament are taken to foreshadow the New Testament. The Ark of the Covenant, in this kind of reading, is the dwelling place that God had built to house his words, the Ten Commandments. The Gospel of John (1:14) in the New Testament reads, according to the New International Version (NIV) translation: "The Word became flesh and made his dwelling among us." Here is a reference to Jesus as the Word. The location where God fashioned the Word into flesh was the womb of Mary. Just like the Ark had functioned as a space for God's commandments to come to earth when Moses had put the Ten Commandments inside, so, too, did Mary's womb act as the location through which God's Word could come to earth. Jesus's appearance replaced God's commandments according to this interpretation. In this theology, then, Mary is the *new* Ark of the new covenant. The basilica of Our Lady Ark of the Covenant, while standing where the Ark of the Covenant was once thought to be present, is more a celebration of Mary as the new Ark than the Ark of the Covenant from the Old Testament. And while tourists come here because of the association with the Ark of the Covenant (and because it is an easy place for tourist buses to stop just outside of Jerusalem), pilgrims, like those Vietnamese pilgrims of La Vang, come here to celebrate this Ark of the New Covenant.

The Ark in Medieval Theology

Understanding Mary as the "new Ark" is not an unusual Christian reading. Christian interpretations of the Old Testament vary considerably, but an important element of many is what can be called "supersessionism." That is to say, Jesus and Christian practices replace the rules and laws of the Old Testament. Paul's Epistle to the Hebrews from the New Testament lays this out, and it is worth quoting it in length to see how the Ark informs Paul's interpretation of the Old Testament. Hebrews 9:1–12 (NIV) reads:

Now the first covenant had regulations for worship and also an earthly sanctuary. A tabernacle was set up. In its first room were the lampstand and the table with its consecrated bread; this was called the Holy Place. Behind the second curtain was a room called the Most Holy Place, which had the

82 READERS OF THE LOST ARK

golden altar of incense and the gold-covered ark of the covenant. This ark contained the gold jar of manna, Aaron's staff that had budded, and the stone tablets of the covenant. Above the ark were the cherubim of the Glory, overshadowing the atonement cover. But we cannot discuss these things in detail now. When everything had been arranged like this, the priests entered regularly into the outer room to carry on their ministry. But only the high priest entered the inner room, and that only once a year, and never without blood, which he offered for himself and for the sins the people had committed in ignorance. The Holy Spirit was showing by this that the way into the Most Holy Place had not yet been disclosed as long as the first tabernacle was still functioning. This is an illustration for the present time, indicating that the gifts and sacrifices being offered were not able to clear the conscience of the worshiper. They are only a matter of food and drink and various ceremonial washings—external regulations applying until the time of the new order. But when Christ came as high priest of the good things that are now already here, he went through the greater and more perfect tabernacle that is not made with human hands, that is to say, is not a part of this creation. He did not enter by means of the blood of goats and calves; but he entered the Most Holy Place once for all by his own blood, thus obtaining eternal redemption.

The laws of the Old Testament, concerns for ritual purity, and access to God's teachings are all made to seem mundane and unimportant, not sacred at all, just the simulacra of the sacred. For Paul and the Christians that follow Paul's teachings, the Temple, the Ark, and the sacrifices made by the priests were temporary measures until the coming of Christ. Here, unlike elsewhere in the Bible, the Ark of the Covenant is described in mundane terms, although, ironically, Hebrews 9:4 has excited Ark enthusiasts for centuries, offering an idea that the gold jar of manna, Aaron's budding rod, and the Ten Commandments were literally stored in the Ark and might still be inside it today.

Not all Christian theologians see Mary as the Ark of the New Covenant, nor do they all ascribe to this metaphor. There are other metaphorical Christian Arks. Especially prominent in medieval theology was the idea that Christ's physical body was the new Ark, because it was the actual flesh of Christ through which God's Word became manifest on earth. Just as the Ten Commandments and the Mosaic laws were held in the Ark, the "Word" as understood through the theology of John in the New Testament was held in the physical body of God's son. Salvation in Mosaic times came through the law, the vessel of which was the Ark. Salvation in Christian times, according to this logic, came through the body of Christ.

Thomas Aquinas was one such theologian who argued that Christ was the new Ark. In his commentary on Hebrews 9:5, Aquinas explicitly draws the connection between the wood of the Ark and Christ's flesh. For him, the descriptions of the Ark in the Bible do not just explain what it looked like. Similar to Philo's approach discussed in the last chapter, Aquinas's approach understands that the visual description of the Ark as well as its actual physical form expresses God's message. The gold plating of the Ark, according to Aquinas, prefigures Jesus's wisdom. The mercy seat is the place where God sits and the two cherubim gaze directly there. They are always contemplating God, just as, Aquinas argues, all believers should. Elsewhere, in his *Summa Theologica*, Aquinas argues that the wood of the Ark is significant. It and other wooden objects are important in biblical history, like Noah's Ark, and the staff that Moses used to split the waters of the Sea of Reeds. Thus, for Aquinas, it was fitting that Christ should die on a wooden cross as wood is the material of all of these sacred objects. In Aquinas's writing, the concern with the materiality of the Ark and other Old Testament relics reflects his thinking about the physicality of Jesus as an expression of God's message.

Some Christian medieval theologians saw a connection between the Ark of the Covenant and the church as a whole. Such an argument is laid out in *De Tabernaculo* by the Venerable Bede (672/673–735 CE). Bede was an Anglo- Saxon monk best known for his work *Ecclesiastical History of the English People*. He wrote on numerous subjects, especially historical issues, from the exegesis of ancient texts to the computation of early chronology. *De Tabernaculo* and its companion work *De Templo* provide commentaries on the sections of the Bible dealing with the construction of the Tabernacle and Temple respectively. Through these commentaries, his vision of their relationship to Christianity is made explicit. Take, for example, Bede's discussion of the dimensions of the Ark, here translated by Arthur Holder. After referring to Josephus to understand how big a cubit actually was, Bede draws his allegory about the Ark:

> Mystically, however, the length of the ark suggests the long-suffering patience with which our Lord and redeemer lived among humankind; its width suggests the amplitude of that love with which He was willing to come to us and dwell among us; its height suggests the hope of future

84 READERS OF THE LOST ARK

sublimity, in which He foresaw either that He Himself would be glorified after His passion or that we shall be glorified.

The allegories continue:

The Ark, therefore, was two cubits long because when the Lord appeared in flesh, he was brilliant both in word and deed, and it was a half cubit more because of the long-suffering with which he bore the slowness of the disciples who could never perfectly grasp either his words or deeds.

This is typical of Bede's approach, to paraphrase a passage from the Bible and use that as a jumping off point for theological allegory. Bede takes the dimensions of the Ark as literally accurate, but symbolically meaningful at the same time. Unlike rabbinic interpretations that allow that the measurements of the Ark may not be understandable to humans, Christian interpretations have tended to take them literally. Bede's allegorical approach to the descriptions of the Ark is very similar to that of the ancient interpreters. God's message was made manifest through the physical expression of the Ark; it is up to the theologian to decipher these messages. The Tabernacle and Temple are, in Bede's theology, allegorical of the Church at different stages, with the Tabernacle reflecting the Church as it is present in the world today and the Temple allegorical for the Church that is yet to emerge. In both of these, the Ark is a kind of mediator between Jesus and the Church.

Bede continues his verse-by-verse expansion on Exodus, offering allegorical readings of the physical description of the Ark. Like Philo of Alexandria, Bede also interprets these verses allegorically, and under the influence of Platonic philosophy that distinguishes between the earthly and the spiritual. But unlike Philo, he takes the different components of the Ark to represent Christ or the Church. The Ark is overlaid with gold, for example, because Jesus's body was filled with "the full power of the Holy Spirit on the inside, and on the outside it openly displayed the words of the Holy Spirit." The four rings for the poles of the Ark signify the four gospels. The poles themselves are the "holy teachers" who preach the word of God. The mercy seat is both the savior Himself and his heart of compassion. The cherubim, however, represent real angels, but the two facing each other "signify the peaceful fellowship of the angels." It is Bede's summation of the Ark in his comments on Exodus 25:22 that draw his allegories to completion, where he explains that: "The ark can also be taken figuratively as the Holy Church which is constructed from incorruptible wood (that is, from holy souls)." While the Ark was taken to have been an actual physical object that existed historically, in the typological theology of Bede that was common in medieval thought, messages about the future redeemer and church could be identified. The Ark represented the Church and various elements of church theology simultaneously.

This concern for the physicality of biblical traditions remained and remains a contested theme in European Christianity. For many medieval Christians, influenced by Platonic thought, the physical and spiritual worlds were distinct, and the world of flesh was sinful and corrupt. From the moment of Adam and Eve's fall from grace, the earth has been, according to this theology, a world marked by sin. That sinful world, it was thought, will come to an end with the return of the messiah. One of the ways that these physical and spiritual worlds could interact, medieval theologians believed, was through angels, whose physicality (or at least appearance) was the subject of much medieval theological work. The cherubim on the Ark were understood within medieval contexts as angels, and the biblical function of the Ark as a location for the divine presence to manifest on earth encouraged these understandings of angels.

Medieval angelology was an important subfield of the theology of the era, and quite detailed categorizations of angels were produced, in some ways imitating the kinds of Aristotelian taxonomical approaches used to understand the natural world. The most influential of these taxonomies was that offered by Pseudo-Dionysius the Areopagite, sometime in the late fifth or early sixth century. In his *De Coelesti Hierarchia* ("On the Celestial Hierarchy"), he divides angels into three distinct orders or choirs (highest, middle, and lower) based on their proximity to God. Thomas Aquinas adapted this taxonomy, giving it an almost official status within Christian thinking. The cherubim were classified in the highest order, the angels closest to God. Among the highest order, the seraphim were the closest to God. But the cherubim were closer to God than the ophanim (also called throne angels). Despite the differences in proximity, all of the angels of the highest order were believed to see God directly. In the Renaissance, this group of angels came to be depicted in the form of the "putto," chubby, winged babies. This was itself a motif from classical art resurrected by the Renaissance artists, but instead of using it to represent the Greek divinity Eros or the Roman version Cupid, the winged baby was used to represent this order of angel. This is how we have come to think of cherubim as cute, chubby, winged babies, not sphinxes or winged adults. The Ark was very

86 READERS OF THE LOST ARK

important in medieval angelology because the most significant discussion of cherubim found in the Bible related to the Ark. Understanding the cherubim as types of angels meant that God must have wanted angels on either side of him and atop His Ark. Following this logic, angels deserved to be figures of devotion. Since they are attached to the Ark, they were seen as aids to human understanding of the divine. Perhaps because of their position in relation to the Ark, Thomas Aquinas and others associated angels with knowledge.

Medieval theologians saw the Ark as a place where humans could come into contact with God within the sinful physical world and so they associated it with one of the most important gifts God could give humans: grace. The medieval concept of grace differs from how the term tends to be used in the twenty-first century, which is usually taken as a kind of favor from God given to undeserving humans. While theologians were not necessarily consistent in their understanding, grace was something tangible that could actually be fused with the soul. Working with notions that grace was a palpable gift from God, one that was transferred from the supernatural realm to the worldly realm, the Ark of the Covenant was conceptualized as an example of or allegory for this grace. The Ark is contemplated in such a fashion in *The Cloud of Unknowing*, an anonymous fourteenth-century document that gives instructions for prayer and for gaining a knowledge of God. In the seventy-third chapter, the author explains how the different approaches Moses, Bezalel, and Aaron took to the Ark offer different examples of how one can attain grace and better knowledge of God, as "grace is figured in that ark." Moses learned about the Ark directly, but he did not learn about it from his own work, even though he had to climb a mountain. Rather, he learned of the Ark because God chose to teach him. However, Bezalel fashioned the Ark himself, with his own hands. He did not learn about it from God directly, but he attained grace by the practical application of this knowledge. Aaron's grace came entirely from the teaching and work of other men (Moses and Bezalel). Yet he had access to the Ark in the Temple whenever he wanted it. The author ends by recommending that the student be like Aaron, since the author of this work (and by extension the teacher of the reader) does not have the skills of Bezalel and so cannot offer practical instruction.

Other theologians had different ideas about how the Ark could lead to the attainment of grace. Contemplating the details of the Ark of the Covenant, such as the consideration of the cherubim (here understood as angels), was one method Richard of Saint Victor (d. 1173) suggested for gaining access to heaven. In his *The Mystical Ark* (also known as *Benjamin Major* or *The*

Grace of Contemplation), Richard offers a theology related to the efficacy of prayer and the nature of the mind. He makes explicit what his goal is in relation to the Ark. He wants to unlock the moral sense behind the allegorical and mystical meaning of the Ark, which he takes to represent Christ. By contemplating the Ark, Richard expounds, one can purify oneself and experience God's grace. In the Bible, valuable things are placed in the Ark. What is valuable in this allegorical Ark is God's grace. Richard offers a number of instructions on contemplation and describes six types, describing how they relate to contemplation of the Ark. The physical attributes of the Ark, which are so emphasized in scripture, were intended to assist in meditation on theological truths, even if it was believed to be impossible to fully understand these truths. Contemplation of the physical can lead to contemplation of the otherworldly. Richard uses his discussion of the Ark, just as Philo of Alexandria did, as the theological justification for a philosophical investigation.

At a smaller scale, various church practices were also understood through analogic reasoning associated with the Ark. In these cases, it was not the Ark's function as a repository of knowledge that was invoked but rather how it facilitated God's communication with humans. Some theologians felt that the Ark prefigured the sacraments of the Church, especially the Eucharist in which the body and blood of Christ are made manifest physically for communion with Christians. Holy relics functioned similarly by giving people the opportunity to experience the divine through material objects that facilitated contact between the sacred and profane worlds. The Ark was invoked as evidence in controversies among medieval theologians about these kinds of religious practices. One such point of contention was the debate on the appropriateness of the use of images in worship. For those who argued that the use of images for veneration was appropriate, the Ark provided good evidence that this was the case. Since God had commanded the construction of the Ark, explicitly and undoubtedly according to scripture, God clearly, according to this theological reading, desired the use of images in His worship. Opponents to this view, those who believed that images should not be used in worship would cite other parts of scripture to support their claims, especially the Ten Commandments, which were also associated with the Ark, because of their prohibition against graven images. The Ark, then, was invoked to some degree on both sides of this theological debate.

Medieval Jewish readings of the Ark also treat it as both a physically "real" ancient object and a larger metaphor or symbol for knowledge. This is

88 READERS OF THE LOST ARK

apparent in the first sections of the *Mishneh Torah* compiled by the Sephardic scholar Maimonides (also known as the Rambam) between 1170 and 1180 CE. There he lays out the relationship between Oral Torah, as discussed in the preceding chapter, and the Ark of the Covenant. Maimonides references an older tradition that all of the commandments given to Moses at Sinai were written down by Moses and placed beside the Ark of the Covenant (quoting Deuteronomy 31:26). However, other interpretations of the commandments were also given at Sinai, and these were not written down. They passed down orally through the generations, first to Joshua and from him to other biblical figures. Thus, the Oral Torah is presented as complementary to the Torah, which was preserved in the Ark, and just as significant. Maimonides explicitly evokes the Ark in his justification for the authority of the Oral Torah that he is now passing down in writing.

Jewish commentators also continued to attempt harmonizations of the Bible in keeping with the traditions described in the previous chapter. These new readings reflected their different intellectual and social milieu. For example, the discrepancy in grammatical number between Exodus 25 and Deuteronomy 10, described in the previous chapter, was also of concern to the Ramban, also known as Rabbi Moses ben Nahman or Nachmanides (1194–1270), a Sephardic rabbi who wrote about the Bible. To reiterate the problem here, Exodus 25 states "*they* will make an Ark," but Deuteronomy 10 commands, speaking to Moses, "*you* will make an Ark." In Ramban's commentary on Exodus 25:10, he explores this difference in grammatical number and interacts with older arguments about the discrepancy. His conclusion is that these different verses record that God wants all of Israel to participate, in some fashion or another, in the construction of the dwelling of God. Whether through material contribution or physical action, all those who participate will be deserving of learning of Torah. The Ark stands as a symbol for Torah.

Similar methods of interbiblical readings were used for understanding morally complicated sections. For example, Maimonides discusses the death of Uzzah, the man who tried to stabilize the Ark as it was being sent by wagon to Jerusalem on David's orders. He argues that Uzzah's death was in fact caused by David. David had ordered the Ark to be placed on a wagon, when really the Ark was supposed to be carried directly on the shoulders of humans using the attached poles. This is akin to the rabbinic approach discussed in the previous chapter, where two different sections of the Bible are read very closely and then compared. Here the problem is not that the two sections of the Bible don't agree. Modern scholars might presume that the verses preserve two different memories of how the Ark was carried at different times. For Maimonides, there is more that can be taken from these verses. David has not followed rules described elsewhere in the Bible, and he should have known better. Thus, interbiblical analysis is used to expand on the story of Uzzah's death.

Such discussions illustrate how medieval theologians were aware of inconsistencies within the Bible and attempted to harmonize them. Like the rabbis, they used typological readings to help solve these problems, but unlike the rabbis, Christian theologians applied supersessionist logic. One of the key inconsistencies related to the Ark that needed to be harmonized stems from the passage from Hebrews cited earlier in this chapter. It was problematic as it seems to directly contradict the books of Kings and Chronicles. In 1 Kings 8:9 and 2 Chronicles 5:10, it is stated that there is "nothing in the Ark except the two tablets that Moses had placed in it at Horeb." Yet Hebrews 9:4 adds that it also contained a golden jar of manna and Aaron's staff that had budded. Sometimes historical explanations were offered. One argument explains the discrepancy as due to the fact that the Kings/Chronicles passage and the Epistle to the Hebrews describe the Ark at different times. The contents of the Ark shifted, and the Bible is simply mute about when the contents shifted or why. A more distinctly Christian explanation was also offered to the problem. The reason that the rod of Aaron had budded was because something new had started to grow on it. This new growth reflected the changes to the world brought by Christ, and so the rod and golden pot of manna were put inside the Ark in response to this.

The Medieval Ark in Rome

In medieval times, the European church most associated with the Ark of the Covenant was the Basilica of St. John in Rome, better known today as Saint John Lateran's Basilica (Lateran refers to the part of Rome in which the church is located). This is the church that was founded by the Roman Emperor Constantine after his conversion to Christianity. Before the Vatican became the seat of papal authority in Europe, it functioned as the home of the pope. Even after losing its primacy to the Vatican, St. John Lateran's has remained a church of central importance and remains the pope's cathedral to this day. Of interest here is how it was presented as the new, Christian version

90 READERS OF THE LOST ARK

of the Temple of Jerusalem and for a period was believed to hold the actual Ark of the Covenant.

How the Ark was imagined to have come to Rome was through Titus's sacking of the Second Jerusalem Temple. The Arch of Titus in Rome depicts Roman soldiers hauling out Temple treasures, like a menorah. The Ark is not depicted on the arch, and Titus never claimed to have seized it. Still, that was enough of a visual cue to suggest that the Ark had been brought to Rome. By medieval times, an "Ark" had come to be part of the Church's relic inventory, and perhaps symbolically the most important of these relics. It was claimed that the Ark survived the sacking of Rome by barbarians, and the supposed Ark was incorporated into the liturgy of the church.

Eivor Anderson argues that the Ark came to be important for this church, because unlike other churches, St. John Lateran's was not founded on the remains of any known saints. Its association with Constantine was insufficient to make it *the* holy space in Christendom according to the mores of medieval Europe, and so the treasures of the Jerusalem Temple, and especially the Ark, came to justify it as the preeminent church. He reads the *Descriptio Lateranensis Ecclesiae*, a piece written around 1100 CE to describe the Temple treasures, like the Ark, held by the church, as an argument justifying the importance of St. John Lateran's. The church is treated as the Temple of the New Covenant, which would have resonated with people after the First Crusade, when Christians had once again come to be interested in Jerusalem.

The Ark held by the church has not survived, and descriptions of it are fairly laconic. It was a decorated wooden box, carried by two long rods, and covered by a silk *parochet*, reflecting the idea from the Old Testament that it should not be seen by the laity. The Ark was not on display, however. It was hidden within an altar, which was the same size as the Ark. Contained within were typical treasures associated with the Ark, such as Aaron's budding rod and the tablets of the Ten Commandments. It was also said to contain a seven-branched menorah, likely inspired by the menorah depicted on the Arch of Titus. Various New Testament relics were also kept there, according to the *Descriptio Lateranensis Ecclesiae*. That the Ark was in the altar, the center of the church, symbolically imitated the Ark's position in the Holy of Holies in the Jerusalem Temple. That it now contained New Testament relics helped make the divine presence even more potent. The church was thus sanctified both through Iron Age and medieval theologies.

Pope Innocent X inaugurated a series of renovations on the church, putting Francesco Borromini in charge with the express order that the basilica would still evoke the Temple of Jerusalem. It was to reflect a Christianized version of the Temple's function, as a place to hold treasures like the Ark. Allusions to the Temple can be seen in the many images of columns, referencing the columns Boaz and Jachin mentioned in the book of Kings that were integral enough to the Temple to be given names. Still, the baroque remodeling of the church has meant that there are only a few hints that remain of the cathedral's association with the Ark. Near the sacramental altar, on the far left-hand side of the church, farthest from the entrance, a 2-m-high model of the Jerusalem Temple stands above the ritual table. Given our knowledge of Iron Age architecture now, the model is difficult to recognize as Solomon's Temple. Sculptures of four Old Testament figures stand installed beside the altar piece: Melchizedek, Elijah, Moses with his typical Latin-inspired horns, and Aaron in his priestly vestments. A gold image of the Last Supper stands above the Temple model, illustrating that Jesus has replaced the Temple as the point of contact between God and humanity. Other minor flourishes make allusions to the Ark. Sometimes these point to the tradition of the cathedral being the new repository of objects from the Jerusalem Temple, sacked by Titus, including the Ark. Other times they reference the kinds of metaphorical uses of the Ark discussed in this chapter, such as Mary being the new Ark (Figure 4.3). In 1745, Pope Benedict XIV had the Ark and its rods removed from display. He likely saw them as obvious medieval forgeries and an embarrassment to the church. The sacramental altar and model of the Temple were allowed to stay, since those were legitimate pieces of art on their own and still seemed stylish in the eighteenth century.

Our Lady Ark and Byzantine Pilgrimage

The interpretations of the Ark discussed in this chapter embrace both a physicality of the Ark and a metaphorical treatment of it. Typological theologies have not been the only driving force of Christian interest in the Ark, however. When Our Lady Ark of the Covenant was built in the 1920s, a mosaic and numerous ancient column bases were uncovered. The discovery of these archaeological materials changed the plans of the sisters. Initially there had been no intention of building a church (just the convent and sanatorium), but discovering these remnants of early Christianity brought the significance of the site to light. In the words of the booklet that can be purchased at the church gift shop, "It became imperative to build a church in order to sanctify

Figure 4.3 Mary as the New Ark in the ceiling decorations at Basilica of St. John Lateran

the site once again." In other words, realizing that the site had once been holy, the sisters decided to make the site holy once again. Indeed, the possibility that biblical artifacts are buried underground excited their imagination just as the possibility that there are buried biblical artifacts throughout Israel does for many today. As we shall explore in the next chapter, once Europeans and North Americans gained direct access to the Holy Land, their interest in the physical realities of the Bible grew dramatically.

The ancient church that was discovered during construction of Our Lady Ark of the Covenant was built around 450 CE and destroyed in 610 CE, in the early part of what scholars call the Byzantine Period (c. 330–1453). The Byzantine Empire was the Christian empire that emerged out of the eastern part of the Roman Empire. Whereas the western half of the Roman Empire is typically taken to have collapsed in 476 CE, the reasons for which are heavily debated, the eastern half continued on for another thousand years or so until it was finally conquered by the Ottoman Empire. This was a seat of significant Christian thinking and because the Holy Land was within the Byzantine Empire, the most important sites of Judaism and Christianity still have a Byzantine flavor today.

For pilgrims and tourists to the Holy Land, it is Empress Eudocia (c. 401–460 CE) who had the most important impact on biblical sites. She was the wife of Emperor Theodosius II (r. 408–450 CE), but this was not a marriage that went well. Eventually Eudocia left the court in Constantinople to take up residence in Jerusalem. Why exactly she left remains debated by scholars; some presume she had an extramarital affair, while others suggest some kind of power struggle at court, perhaps with her sister-in-law. Whatever the case may have been, Eudocia had visited Jerusalem previously and had returned to Constantinople with numerous holy relics. After being banished from court, she spent the rest of her days in Jerusalem. There she followed in the footsteps of Constantine the Great (272–337 CE) and his mother, Helena. They had already identified many of the locations of important biblical events, engaging in a kind of historical geography like the nineteenth-century explorers discussed in Chapter 2. Perhaps best-known today are the Church of the Nativity in Bethlehem, where it was believed that Jesus had been born, and the Church of the Holy Sepulchre, where it was believed that Jesus was crucified.

Eudocia identified other sites, like Kiryat Yearim, and had churches built as locations of veneration and as stops for pilgrims. For pilgrims, actually being present in the location where biblical events transpired was meaningful and deeply moving (and still is for pilgrims today). One of the major motivations for such pilgrimages was medical treatment. Sister Joséphine's work at Kiryat Yearim, and the sanatorium that was built there, reflects a continuity of that tradition. These holy sites were thought to offer miraculous

94   READERS OF THE LOST ARK

cures to otherwise untreatable illnesses. Many travelers likely never intended to return home but rather to die in the Holy Land. Those that did return home likely took with them souvenirs of various sorts, such as flasks of holy water from the Jordan River or medallions of stamped earth from the ground of the Holy Land. What exactly they may have acquired at Kiryat Yearim is not clear, but the types of souvenirs were fairly standard. By the time of the Persian Sassanid invasion of the Holy Land in 611 CE, the area around Jerusalem was connected by a network of pilgrimage sites and established routes, including Kiryat Yearim. Being physically in the same space where the Ark of the Covenant once stood would have been deeply moving experience for many pilgrims, just as it still is today. That experience of space and geography remains an important element of some Christian theologies. While the Persians only held the area until 629 CE, many of these pilgrim sites were destroyed during that time, including the church at Kiryat Yearim where pilgrims would have contemplated the Ark of the Covenant. Unlike other pilgrimage sites, this one was not rebuilt.

While Kiryat Yearim is very interesting, the ultimate pilgrimage site for Christians and Jews is Jerusalem. The next chapter will show how thinking about the Ark has long been entangled with thinking about Jerusalem. For European and North American explorers, the increasing ease of travel to Jerusalem in the nineteenth century led to a new interest in looking for the actual, physical Ark. The Ark, and much biblical interpretation, moves out of the realm of metaphorical interpretation and into the realm of historical interpretation. Archaeology seemed to offer biblical scholars the possibility of confirming the biblical text and experiencing the places and artifacts of biblical times through a new kind of scientific style of pilgrimage. As we shall see in the next chapter, visions of a treasure buried in a secret vault beneath the Temple inspired and continue to inspire treasure hunters and those who imagine that they can be the ones who will find the lost Ark.

5

The "Real" Raiders of the Lost Ark

From Jerusalem to Japan

I love Jerusalem. I have been lucky to be able to visit this city often since my first time working on an archaeological excavation, back in 1994. The COVID-19 pandemic had interrupted the regularity of my visits, and there had been a few stretches where I had remained away for extended periods. Shawn and I had both last been there in 2019, taking our students touring through the city as part of our international archaeological field school after the excavation work was finished. We couldn't resist visiting Jerusalem now that travel restrictions had eased and life there was returning to normal, or as normal as life can get in Jerusalem.

On this trip, we made a special point of visiting the City of David excavations, on the edge of Jerusalem's Old City, where archaeological work has been conducted for decades. There, thousands of tourists flock to see the most visible remains of Iron Age Jerusalem. Shawn in particular was desperate to go with me because, while she had been visiting the City of David on an almost annual basis, it had been years since I had been there. She knew I was in for a shock. And while I had been keeping up with the reports of the excavations there, seeing the scale of the work, and how different the archaeological park now looked from when I had last visited, was as much of a shock to me as she thought it was going to be. The excavations had expanded significantly, and the whole site had become much larger, at least in terms of what there was for visitors to see. It is set up so that tourists can walk beneath the modern roads of Jerusalem, seeing the remains of the buildings from thousands of years ago that lie buried beneath the city. One can walk through the new tunnels built by archaeologists and the ancient tunnels built for Jerusalem's water systems.

These tunnels lead beneath the walls of the Old City, and one route allows visitors to exit the archaeological park, right by the Western Wall and the Temple Mount, where Solomon's Temple likely once stood. Walking around this area, one finds a confusing array of structures, some still in use, some

Readers of the Lost Ark. Kevin M. McGeough, Oxford University Press. © Oxford University Press 2025.
DOI: 10.1093/9780197653913.003.0006

96   READERS OF THE LOST ARK

with pieces seemingly abandoned at random, dating to radically different time periods. Ottoman period architecture intermingles with Roman. Even the names used here are palimpsestic. Many of the architectural pieces are named after nineteenth- century British explorers. Others bear different names that had come into use through different languages over the past two thousand years. This part of Jerusalem and these tunnels have long captured the imaginations of Ark enthusiasts, for, if there really was an Ark, it would have been here at some point. Some speculate that these labyrinthine tunnels are where it resides today.

The Temple Mount and Ancient Jerusalem

Visitors to Jerusalem today will spend much of their time exploring the Old City, wandering among shops and historical sites crowded inside its imposing walls. These walls and its gates were built in Ottoman times, during the reign of Suleiman the Magnificent (1535– 1542 CE). From this period until the nineteenth century, this was the main part of Jerusalem. Now it is a predominantly tourist and religious area, consisting of four main quarters (although it isn't a perfect square): the Christian Quarter in the northwest, the Armenian Quarter in the southwest, the Muslim Quarter in the northeast, and the Jewish Quarter in the southeast.

The extreme southeast is the location of the Temple Mount. This is where it is thought that Solomon's Temple once stood, and it is the last certain location of the Ark mentioned in the Bible. When the Judahites returned from exile, the Second Temple was built on this location and was later expanded by King Herod. Herodian-era elements of the Second Temple complex still exist as the Western Wall, also known as the Wailing Wall, built directly on bedrock. The Herodian bricks are very distinctive, with their large size and very flat margins surrounding the edges of each block. For Jews today, this is the closest location to the original Temple where they are allowed to pray. It is, as one would guess from the name "Western Wall," located at the western edge of the Temple Mount.

Today the Temple Mount is also known as the Haram as-Sharif ("Noble Compound"). It is now a plaza that holds both the al-Aqsa Mosque and the Dome of the Rock (although the name al-Aqsa is sometimes used to reference the whole area). The Dome of the Rock is a shrine or pilgrimage site and is the third most holy site in Islam. Within the Dome of the Rock is a massive stone, the *Shettiyah* (also known as the foundation stone or noble rock) from which the Prophet Muhammad began his night journey, one of the most important moments in the origins of Islam. The possible relationship between the Dome of the Rock and the Ark of the Covenant continues to be evocative for scholars. As discussed in Chapter 3, some of the ancient rabbis believed that the Ark sat directly upon the *Shettiyah*, and this was the location from which creation emerged. Some modern scholars hold the same view, at least that the Ark was located on the *Shettiyah*. Leen Ritmeyer even believes that he has identified the exact spot in the Dome of the Rock where the Ark of the Covenant had once been installed. He argues that a rectangular depression on the *Shettiyah* once held the Ark. The coincidence of the size of the depression, which would fit the Ark and other materials, its location in relation to his reconstruction of where the First Temple was located, and the continuity of the rock in religious practice after the Temple was destroyed all lead him to make this claim. Whether he is correct is unlikely to be proven at any point. However, it is also a potentially inflammatory claim, as it makes a direct Jewish claim to one of the key monuments in Islamic tradition. As we shall see, the contested rights over the Haram as-Sharif make explorations for the Ark complicated, leading such ventures to have political implications beyond simple historical interest.

The Old City of Jerusalem is not exactly the same location as Iron Age Jerusalem. Excavations to the south of the Old City have shown that the oldest inhabitation of the city was on this ridge. Many of the important features of the Iron Age city lay outside of the current Old City walls, including the main features of the Jerusalem water systems. The names used to refer to these parts of Jerusalem are a blend of names referencing historical personages and events as well as the nineteenth-century British explorers who mapped and identified them. Visitors to the City of David archaeological park in Jerusalem are able to enter what is called "Warren's Shaft," named after Charles Warren (1840–1927), an officer in the British Royal Engineers who was one of the first explorers of Jerusalem and who became infamous later as the London police chief who was unable to solve the mystery of the Jack the Ripper murders. Warren's Shaft refers to both a water complex and a very long, natural vertical shaft that allowed access to the Gihon Spring. The Gihon Spring was one of the main water sources for Jerusalem, and it used to regularly pulsate water. Different ancient water systems took advantage of this natural water source, diverting the water from the Gihon Spring to other catchments. One of the most important of these was the Shiloah (Siloam)

98 READERS OF THE LOST ARK

Pool, which in the Iron Age would have been within the interior of the walls of the city. These water systems were important in the Iron II period for they allowed residents of Jerusalem to gain access to water without leaving the safety of the walls of the city.

The water systems of Jerusalem inspired some of the first major scientific archaeological investigations of the city. By the middle of the nineteenth century, hygiene in Jerusalem had become quite bad (with cholera especially prevalent), in part due to outdated water systems and the unsystematic treatment of the mostly private cisterns that collected rainwater. British missionaries wanted to overhaul and install a modern water system and, under the auspices of the Jerusalem Water Relief Society, sent the Royal Engineers (of the British military) to produce a topographical map of the city. So what do these water systems have to do with the Ark of the Covenant? In some ways, nothing. Yet in the history of exploration for the Ark, they have been central because archaeological investigations are completely restricted on the Temple Mount, the last known location of the Ark of the Covenant. The various water systems and, as we shall see, the tunnels running in association with the Herodian Western Wall have tempted the imaginations of explorers looking to find a secret tunnel that runs beneath the Temple Mount. Inspired by pseudobiblical accounts that suggest that figures like Jeremiah may have hidden the Ark deep beneath the Temple, the possibility that one of these tunnels may lead to a secret passage has seemed plausible.

Many people believe that the Ark must still be present in Jerusalem. That the Ark could have been destroyed or even misplaced is for some an unacceptable idea, since this was the object through which God appeared on Earth. How could He Have let it be destroyed unless He wanted it to be destroyed? As discussed in Chapter 3, since Roman times, there has been speculation on what happened to the Ark, despite the striking lack of biblical interest in the subject. For Second Temple Period writers, the figure of Jeremiah seems to have been the most likely candidate for shepherding away the Ark. As a prophet active from the reign of Josiah until the fall of Jerusalem and a figure reputed to have written much in the Bible, he seems the most logical person to have known what happened to the Ark. Jeremiah's own references to a future time when Israel would no longer need an Ark seemed, to some ancient authors, to hint that he had spirited it away. As discussed in previous chapters, the Apocryphal book of 2 Maccabees and the writings of Eusebius both preserve traditions that Jeremiah hid the Ark. That it could be found somewhere in Jerusalem seemed most likely, but

THE "REAL" RAIDERS OF THE LOST ARK 99

Mount Nebo in Jordan and various even less likely locations have also inspired Ark hunters.

The Parker Expedition's Psychic Quest for the Ark

The idea that Jeremiah had hidden the Ark beneath the Temple Mount inspired Lt. Montague Parker to put together an expeditionary force to search for the Ark. The expedition, which came to be known as the Parker Expedition (1909–1911), did not just involve him, but rather a group of men who had fallen under the sway of a Finnish mystic named Valter Henrik Juvelius. Juvelius had written a doctoral dissertation on how ancient Judean conceptions of time were based on Solomon's Temple and secretly coded in the Bible. He was, remarkably enough, granted a doctoral degree for this work, and so Juvelius applied this same methodology, based on numerology, Kabbalah, and astronomy, to the issue of the Ark of the Covenant. In 1906, Juvelius gave a paper where he presented his "decoding" of the secret messages embedded in the books of Jeremiah and Ezekiel. The secret message detailed a hidden chamber beneath the Temple Mount, with enough specific information that, Juvelius claimed, an expedition could discover it. The Ark, according to Juvelius, had never actually been in the Temple. It was first installed in a hiding spot constructed by David, where Solomon installed the Ark after the construction of the Temple, rather than in the Holy of Holies. Later it was moved to an even more secret location, when King Hezekiah built his new Jerusalem water system. This location, within that water complex, was described in cypher in the Hebrew Scriptures. Through cracking the coded message and corresponding with another mystic, Henning Melander, who had his own equally spurious theories about the location of the Ark, Juvelius determined that the final location was to the south of the al-Aqsa Mosque. Conveniently, this was in the vicinity of the excavations that had been conducted by Charles Warren.

Secret Bible codes and Jewish artifacts hidden beneath Muslim monuments made for exciting news at the time, just as they still do today. Most of the members of the team that Parker put together were well-to-do British upper-class men who, for various reasons, were taking breaks from their military service. Parker himself was on medical leave, likely experiencing posttraumatic stress syndrome after his military ventures in South Africa. These men had enough money not to need regular jobs but

100 READERS OF THE LOST ARK

wanted something interesting and vaguely athletic to fill their time. Perhaps more important in enticing investors to put up funds for the expedition was that Juvelius estimated that the Ark could likely be sold for about 100 million British pounds. Similar claims likely also inspired the Ottoman government to grant this team that had no previous archaeological experience a *firman* (permit) to excavate in Jerusalem. Given his connections, Parker found the fundraising for the project relatively easy, and he had soon amassed a fortune to conduct this work, with a formal syndicate offering funds in hopes for a share of the rewards. Parker's expedition was more of a business venture than an academic one, although neither the scholarly nor financial reasoning behind it was in any way sound.

The expedition traveled to Jerusalem in 1908 and began where Warren, and other explorers left off. However, what differed in their planning is that, rather than bringing with them the tools and skills of military surveyors, they brought with them a clairvoyant (called a "thought reader" at the time), who would speak directly to the dead to advise them on where to tunnel. This was Otto von Bourg, who had previously used his "skills" to solve murders and later founded the First Spiritualist Church of Minneapolis. Having two mystics on the team was somewhat problematic, as Juvelius and von Bourg found themselves at odds with one another. Juvelius had his cypher to explain where the Ark was, but von Bourg claimed to be communicating directly with the spirits. Juvelius would often go off on his own, supposedly searching for the Tomb of Moses, gradually losing interest in the Ark quest. Eventually, Juvelius was forced to leave Jerusalem, reportedly due to contracting malaria. The real reasons, however, were his alcoholism and complaints that he sexually assaulted local women.

With the help of Ottoman authorities, Parker purchased land near the entrance to the Gihon Spring, pretending that he was engaged in the charitable building of schools and hospitals. But in 1909, when the Parker Expedition began work, his team was really just engaged in unsystematic excavations of the area, looking for a way to connect to the underground tunnel system in order to find the secret chamber. Digging where Warren already had, they were guided by the clairvoyant and the secret code reader, presuming that this would lead them to discover something Warren missed. Unsurprisingly, their mystical methodologies did not help them, and the team was not successful in finding the Ark. The excavation work did, however, attract the attention of the *École Biblique*, the French archaeological institute in Jerusalem. Father Louis-Hugues Vincent joined the team to record their archaeological discoveries, probably completely unaware that the expedition was really just searching for the Ark and other Temple treasures. A legitimate scholar, Vincent actually published the real discoveries made by these excavations.

Parker's expedition started off near one of the entryways to Hezekiah's tunnel, looking for the tunnel that had been previously discovered but filled back in. This was an ancient water system that allowed the inhabitants of the walled city of Jerusalem to gain access to water sources outside of the city, without having to leave the safety of the walled complex or navigate the crowded streets. The tunnels extend well south of the walled city of Jerusalem but are tied to more complex tunnels closer to the Temple Mount that in Parker's time were not well understood. They presumed that by exploring this tunnel system, Parker's team would be able to get at the hidden chambers that they were certain existed beneath the Temple Mount. Employing close to two hundred local workers to clear rubble, the team worked day and night to achieve only meager results. Making it more difficult, they hadn't planned for Jerusalem's weather. They were excavating in an ancient water system, which, in the Iron Age, had been designed to collect the tremendous amounts of rainwater that suddenly fall in the city. No archaeologist would be shocked to learn that the fundamentals of the system still worked to some degree. Parker's excavations were completely overridden with flooding, the mud making excavations impossible. The team was forced to cease work for the winter but returned in 1910.

Parker had not done a good job of keeping a low profile. With lavish dinner parties and excavation techniques that made no effort to hide the lack of systematic approach, different groups worried that he was doing permanent damage to Jerusalem's heritage. In 1911, one of these concerned parties, Baron Edmond de Rothschild (1845–1934), decided to take action. A member of *the* Rothschild banking family, Baron Edmond was a committed Zionist (he would be a fundamental force in the establishment of the state of Israel) and had become gravely concerned that Parker would destroy the city of David and many of the Jewish monuments located in the vicinity. So he bought a section of land right next to Parker's excavations. Rothschild was deeply interested in the Temple himself, and it is still uncertain whether the rumors that he wanted to build a Third Temple were true. In any case, Rothschild also began searching for the Ark, hiring a French scholar, Raymond Weill, to look on his behalf. Obviously, Weill did not succeed, but on the land purchased by Rothschild, he did discover a number of tombs and some evidence for an early medieval synagogue. Rothschild

102 READERS OF THE LOST ARK

would play a further role in Israeli archaeology by funding an archaeology program at the Hebrew University in Jerusalem.

Rothschild's presence nearby was perhaps enough to make Parker nervous. On top of that, the Parker Expedition ran out of money, and so he left Jerusalem to raise more funds. When Parker returned, he decided to take a different approach. Juvelius had claimed that the cyphers described an alternative route to the hidden location of the Ark, the entrance to which was located in the Temple. So Parker bribed two officials to let his team work in the Dome of the Rock itself. One of these men was the governor of the city, Amzey Bey Pasha, who was notoriously corrupt. More surprising is that Parker was able to bribe one of the hereditary guards of the al-Aqsa Mosque and Dome of the Rock, Sheikh Khalil, who one would have expected to have taken his curatorial duties more seriously. These men allowed Parker's team to dig directly into the Haram as-Sharif, right near the al-Aqsa Mosque. The Parker Expedition members, all men of European descent, disguised themselves as Arabs and began conducting illicit excavations in the evenings and nights, when the Haram was mostly deserted.

After about a week without results, the Parker Expedition switched strategies. In April 1911, they began excavating *inside* the Dome of the Rock. Since even a non-Muslim presence in the Dome of the Rock could, at the time, have resulted in execution, this was an incredible risk. Now, the partially human-carved cavern beneath the Dome of the Rock, the Well of the Souls, has staircases and other facilities to allow authorized access. In 1911, it didn't and so the Parker team smashed large paving stones to get below the main floor of the third holiest site in all of Islam. They tied ropes to the *Shettiyeh*, the "Noble Rock" of the Dome of the Rock, the rock from which Muhammad is believed to have begun his Night Journey, one of the most important events in Islamic beliefs, in order to descend to the Well of the Souls. They may have been inspired by the Crusaders who believed that the Holy of Holies had been located in the Well of the Souls. More likely though, Parker had read Richard Burton's accounts of his explorations there in the 1870s and wanted to follow suit.

Parker's investigations were not very subtle, and he hadn't bought off all of the guards who had access to the Dome of the Rock. On April 12, 1911, the Parker Expedition was discovered. Accounts vary about how this occurred. Some suggest that a guard had unexpectedly arrived that night and investigated the sounds of the men working. Some suggest that this guard had become dissatisfied with the amount of his bribe. Whatever the case may have been, the Parker Expedition then made what was probably their first wise choice. They fled to their boat at the port of Jaffa. They escaped Jerusalem just before riots began and before Sheikh Khalil was attacked by the mob. Amzey Bey, recognizing the trouble he was in, ordered the treasure hunters be apprehended at Jaffa and their spoils confiscated. Luckily for the expedition, they had never found anything that even remotely resembled spoils. The officials let them go, and they were able to flee the country. This ended the Parker Expedition, although Parker did try, unsuccessfully, to raise funds for another venture.

Rabbi Getz and the Hidden Tunnels of the Temple Mount

Parker's amateurish fringe approach to biblical archaeology had a profound impact on Middle Eastern politics. Since the Parker Expedition, it has become a common-sense belief among Muslims in the region that Christian and Jewish archaeologists want to dig up the Dome of the Rock to find evidence for the Iron Age state of Israel. This fear is so hard-wired that visits by Israeli politicians can lead to rioting and political instability. And there have been a few instances since the Parker Expedition where these fears have been proven to be justified. Parker, Juvelius, and their financial backers were not the only ones who have been convinced that the Ark is hidden beneath the Temple Mount. Of those who were convinced, perhaps the most notable was a man who was Chief Rabbi of the Holy Places in Israel, in other words the Rabbi of the Temple Mount, for twenty-seven years. This was Rabbi Meir Yehuda Getz (1924–1995) who, in 1981, opened his own excavations beneath the Temple Mount, which again led to riots and the subsequent closing off of the area that had been tunneled into. Again, it was a search for the Ark of the Covenant that led another group, this time a group of rabbis, to enflame tensions and threaten the tenuous peace in Jerusalem.

To understand why Rabbi Getz's actions were so problematic, one has to understand a bit about the politics of the Temple Mount. The governance of the Haram as-Sharif can seem confusing to those who are new to the subject, and for that matter, to anyone. The area remained a flashpoint for hostilities between Jews and Muslims under the British Mandate; the discord surrounding the Parker Expedition was not an isolated instance. The situation was not simplified under Israeli governance. After the Six-Day War when the state of Israel took over Jerusalem from Jordanian control, General Moshe

104 READERS OF THE LOST ARK

Dayan recognized that the control of the Temple Mount by Israel would only increase hostilities with the Arab world. He believed that the Dome of the Rock was too central to Islam for other countries to tolerate Jewish regulation of the site. He decided that the status quo should be maintained, meaning that the same Palestinian authorities who had regulated the site under Jordanian rule, known as the *Waqf*, would continue to do so under Israeli governance. The agreement came to be known as "the status quo" agreement. The main difference was that Jews would now be allowed on the Temple Mount, but prayer would still not be allowed there. That meant that the Western Wall continued to be the focus of Jewish religious activity, since that was the closest location to the former Temple where Jewish prayer was permitted. As can be imagined, many religious Jews objected to the secular general's decision. Likewise, Muslims did not necessarily trust that Jewish aspirations to build a Third Temple on the location of the Dome of the Rock would remain appeased by this agreement. Muslim sovereignty over the Temple Mount is a meaningful concern to many in the Muslim world, and different groups make use of this issue to garner both popular and financial support.

Israeli archaeology near the Temple Mount (to the south) remains a contested activity. While it is one of the most excavated areas in the world and thousands of visitors tour the site each year, its extension into the Palestinian neighborhood of Silwan in East Jerusalem makes excavations there politically problematic, as does its proximity to the Temple Mount. Modern excavations began there in 1968, led by Benjamin Mazar, one of the towering figures in Israeli archaeology. His granddaughter Eilat led the twenty-first-century excavations of Jerusalem until her death in 2021, the excavations mentioned at the beginning of the chapter. Now known as the City of David excavations, the decades of work in the area have revealed much about Iron Age Jerusalem, that is to say, the Jerusalem of the era of the Ark. When archaeological work began in 1968, the scale of excavations led the *Waqf* to complain to UNESCO that Mazar's team was undermining the Haram as-Sharif and that the walls were being threatened with collapse. Specialists associated with UNESCO helped broker a kind of détente between Mazar and the *Waqf*, showing that Mazar's work was of no threat to the Muslim holy sites. They did, however, register complaints about how Israel had managed to seize private land in order to excavate it (but that's another story).

To return to the story of Rabbi Getz, he was not an archaeologist like the Mazars, and he was not conducting scientific excavations like those in the City of David. Unlike many of the other historical sites in Israel that are overseen by the National Parks Service, the area around the Temple Mount is overseen by the Ministry of Religious Affairs. Since the "status quo" was announced, this ministry had been trying to extend the religious space of the Temple Mount available to Jews by tunneling to the north of the Western Wall. While it is unclear whether these actions were harming the Temple Mount, this work was denounced by the United Nations in 1974, as it was clearly not of a scientific nature. Israel was even sanctioned because of this. Despite this, such work very close to the Temple Mount continued, and in 1981, a gate that had been lost since Victorian times was rediscovered by Rabbi Getz.

That gate was Warren's Gate, originally discovered by Charles Warren in his investigations of Jerusalem but his documentation of it was very vague. Another nineteenth-century explorer, Wilson, identified it and named it "Warren's Gate." It was covered again by the rubble of other explorations, left to be rediscovered by Getz and his team. Getz's team had been excavating north from Wilson's Arch, clearing out rubble and sewage that had blocked the nineteenth-century explorers. Warren had reached this gate earlier somehow, probably through his various climbing and clambering, the likes of which also led him to find the shaft that came to be named after him. Now Rabbi Getz's team had cleared a tunnel directly to it. The gate itself dated to the Second Temple Period, but Warren believed that this was the gate that Josephus said led to the tunnel that ran directly to the Holy of Holies, to the location where the Ark was kept in the Temple. Indeed, through the gate was a tunnel that seemed to lead under the Western Wall, and potentially, Rabbi Getz believed, to a chamber directly beneath the *Shettiyah*.

Rabbi Getz had long been motivated to find the Ark of the Covenant. He was a Kabbalist, a follower of Jewish mystical traditions, and spent much of his life in the tunnels of the Western Wall. He believed Maimonides's account that Solomon had built a secret chamber for the Ark, knowing that the Temple would eventually be destroyed. He was driven by a desire to hasten the arrival of the Messiah; and, for him, this could be achieved by finding the Ark. While ironically much of Getz's work has led to tourism into the tunnels, he would not have approved of this. He was against archaeological investigations and wanted the area reserved for religious observance, taking direct action to limit visitation to religious observance only. One of the ingenious ways he did so was to remove stone rubble from the tunnels and install Torah Arks. By doing so, he could explore as much of the Western Wall tunnel complex as possible and transform it into sacred space that would be

106   READERS OF THE LOST ARK

off limits to tourists. These Torah Arks were oriented so that worshippers would face the Temple. While clearing rubble in this fashion on July 22, 1981, his team stumbled upon Warren's Gate. This location is now the site of the Rav Getz Synagogue, and Warren's Gate is visible from within. When he removed the rubble from the gate, he discovered a tunnel and staircase, partially filled with water leading under the Temple Mount. In his diary, Getz wrote of his discoveries: "I was seized with joy and trembling and I felt deep down that the next step after discovering the tunnel would be the arrival of the Messiah and the redemption of the Jewish people.... I sat motionless for a long time, with hot tears pouring out of my eyes. I finally got up the courage and with God's help recited Tikkun Hatzot [a prayer over the destruction of the Temple], as is our custom."

Soon after, Rabbi Getz contacted Rabbi Shlomo Goren, an outspoken critic of the *Waqf*'s administration of the Temple Mount and a proponent of the construction of a Third Temple. Indeed, Goren's various efforts to find ways to get Jews into the Haram es-Sharif to pray led to an Israeli prohibition against Jewish entrance to the Temple Mount. The Chief Rabbinate of Israel issued a declaration written or endorsed by over 356 rabbis making it a sin to enter the area unless ritually clean. Citing Maimonides and other authorities who warned that ritually impure Jews should not enter into the space near the Holy of Holies, the Halakhic prohibition warns that since the exact location of the Temple is unknown, a ritually unclean person may accidentally walk over holy ground. And, to become ritually clean in the fashion required to safely walk in the area, one would need to have access to an unblemished red heifer born in Israel, something that had not happened for thousands of years. Some rabbinical authorities hold that all Jews had become ritually unclean with the destruction of the Second Temple, and this cannot be reversed until the coming of the Messiah. Rabbi Goren was not swayed by this ruling and continued to hold prayer services in relation to the Temple Mount and in support of Jewish claims to the site.

The pair of Getz and Goren was bound to cause trouble in this situation. For political reasons, Goren was keen to facilitate Jewish entrance to the area. For religious reasons, Getz was inspired to find the Ark of the Covenant and the Ten Commandments. The two assembled a team to work in secrecy, at night, just as the Parker Expedition had so many years ago. Fully believing they had found a tunnel that dated to the Iron Age, they cleared the mud and water out of its large, arched corridors. Meir Ben-Dov, who at the time led the Israel Antiquities Authority sanctioned excavations nearby, warned

THE "REAL" RAIDERS OF THE LOST ARK   107

them that nothing would come of their work. But rational archaeological expertise was not what was driving these excavators, nor was it informing their thinking about what they were looking for. Years later, Goren would tell Randall Price how they became certain that they were nearing the Holy of Holies. When they discovered a flooded staircase, they pumped the water out and discovered an insect. Now, as a field archaeologist, I wouldn't have been surprised to find an insect. Rabbi Goren, however, took this as a sign that the Holy of Holies was nearby. The Mishnah tells that a priest who is not ritually clean and gets trapped in the Holy of Holies must send an insect out. This, Rabbi Goren believed, was such an insect. Goren's feelings were similarly informed by mystical rather than scientific observations. His mapping of the various tunnels led him to believe that one particular wall was blocking the final stretch to the Holy of Holies. There, the team was convinced that they would find the Ark of the Covenant, the table that stood in front of it, a candelabra fashioned by Moses, and the rest of the treasures of Solomon.

They were so close, they claimed. But as we shall explore in later chapters, this is always where the story ends in pseudoarchaeological or amateur archaeological stories, whether it be the Ark of the Covenant, Noah's Ark, the Holy Grail, or some lost technology from the Atlantis. The government intervenes and investigations are stopped just before the momentous discovery can be made. In this case, a change in government personnel led to a change in policy toward the illicit work. On August 26, 1981, when a newly appointed head of the Ministry of Religious Affairs came to visit the site, the media came, too. The radio station Kol Israel broke the story that a group of rabbis were about to discover the Ark of the Covenant beneath the Temple Mount. What the *Waqf* knew and when is still unclear. But when this was announced on the radio, the usually unjustified paranoia that Israelis are digging beneath the Temple Mount to find the First Temple turned out to be justified. Violence erupted, but just as with the rioting surrounding the Parker Expedition, the exact details of what happened are not clear, perhaps because of the speed and intensity of the events. Whether the *Waqf* called for a riot then or whether the riot erupted spontaneously will never likely be agreed upon, but whatever the case was, a group of Muslims entered the area and a confrontation ensued between them and the group of excavators. Here again the accounts don't agree, even between Goren and Getz. Were innocent yeshiva students overwhelmed by a mob of angry Arabs? Or did the amateur archaeologists heroically get weapons and march to the Temple

108   READERS OF THE LOST ARK

Mount to protect the excavations? Did Getz pull out his gun like he reports in his diary? Did the police just let the Muslims attack the students as Goren suggests? As is the case with these kinds of events in Jerusalem, it likely involved a mix of staged actions and genuine emotional responses rising in the heat of the moment.

Regardless of exactly what happened, Getz's Ark story ended there. Prime Minister Menachem Begin, recognizing that this was a situation that could only get worse, ordered the corridor sealed. Riots were quelled before they could get out of control like with the Parker Expedition. Warren's Gate is now a sealed wall within the Rabbi Getz synagogue. Since the events of 1981, the figures involved in the excavation have occasionally announced that they actually saw the Ark of the Covenant, likely as a means of encouraging support to allow the tunnel to be reopened. In any case, both Rabbi Getz and Goren claimed to know exactly where the Ark was located, if only the government would let them find it. The Israeli government, according to them, knows where it is as well, and does not want it revealed to the public. As we shall see, this is the logic of pseudoarchaeology.

Ark Expeditions beyond the Temple Mount

There are other locations in and around the Old City of Jerusalem where semi- delusional explorers have sought the Ark, and these don't pose the same kinds of political concerns. One site of such activities is the Garden Tomb, a site that the British General Charles Gordon declared to be the actual site of Jesus's crucifixion, not the Church of the Holy Sepulchre. It is the location of an Iron Age tomb, and some claim, following Gordon, that this was the tomb in which Jesus's body was laid after being taken down off the cross. Now run by a Protestant Alliance, the Garden Tomb was the subject of investigations by a man named Ron Wyatt throughout the 1980s and 1990s. A nurse by training, Wyatt was a Seventh Day Adventist and was inspired by an Adventist teaching that the Ark had been sneaked out of the Temple and hidden nearby. The various underground passages that snake through the grounds of the Garden Tomb were good candidates, and he claims to have discovered the treasures of the Temple there. Unable to remove them himself due to their location in a narrow crevasse, he contacted professional archaeologists for help. Rather than help, however, the archaeologists were alarmed at what he was doing and attempted to put an end to his work.

THE "REAL" RAIDERS OF THE LOST ARK   109

The Israel Antiquities Authority did not agree with his identification of the materials as Iron Age, nor did they agree that this was a legal excavation. Wyatt remained convinced that he had seen the Ark and occasionally sought to restart his excavations. The relationship between Wyatt and the alliance overseeing the Garden Tomb waxed and waned over the 1980s and 1990s, although in 1991 they released a statement refuting his claims that members of their organization had seen evidence of the Ark on the grounds. Despite forming his own archaeological firm, Wyatt Archaeological Research, he was never recognized as a professional archaeologist.

The many stories about Jerusalem being the location of the Ark, the city's remarkable series of underground tunnels, and its very distinct religious history that prevents excavations from occurring will continue to inspire the imaginations of explorers. Jerusalem, however, is not the only place where explorers and those motivated by religious visions have searched for the Ark. An important folk belief that has inspired Ark hunters around the world is the notion of the Ten Lost Tribes of Israel. While not really a biblical idea, this tradition holds that when Assyria sacked and destroyed the kingdom of Israel in 722, the ten tribes that made up the northern kingdom migrated elsewhere (the two tribes that made up the southern kingdom of Judah were never lost). Stories of the Lost Tribes traveling far from the Middle East have provided the inspiration for some Ark hunters.

The possibility that the Lost Tribes traveled to Great Britain has ebbed and flowed in British thought, offering a direct connection between the islands and biblical history. In medieval times this idea was widely proposed by scholars and common in local traditions; by the nineteenth century the belief was mostly limited to fringe groups. Through arguments that connect political leaders or ethnic groups from the United Kingdom with Israelite genealogies, biblical history was claimed as European. In medieval times, such stories legitimated local leadership and traditions through biblical precedent, and emphasized the typological theologies discussed in the previous chapter. Later, such beliefs have offered justification for European political action in the Middle East. Arguments about shared European-Israelite genealogies facilitate the harmonization of biblical stories about the history of Judaism with what we would now call white supremacist beliefs. In other words, interpretations of the Bible that treat European Christians as the chosen people, and not the Jews, provide dangerous messaging. While very few people accepted this idea literally, a belief that Europe (and Great Britain) was the metaphorical, but more legitimate descendants of the Bible

110   READERS OF THE LOST ARK

than the people presently living in the Levant was very widespread, and it still is to some extent.

Toward the end of the nineteenth century, interest in the potential European location of the Lost Tribes of Israel reappeared in some pseudoscholarly societies. The most notable of these societies was the British-Israel Association of London, which believed that when Sennacherib destroyed the northern kingdom of Israel, one of the tribes of Israel fled to the British Isles. These were the Anglo-Saxons. Similar societies arose throughout the commonwealth. In the twentieth century, some of these groups joined, creating a larger British-Israel World Federation, bringing a level of standardization to the fringe perspectives of various local organizations. The British-Israel World Federation holds that the people of Great Britain and Ireland are the literal descendants of the Lost Tribes of Israel, and some members believe that, despite the well-known genealogy of the House of Windsor, the current British royal family are descendants of King David.

Most British Israelists probably only had some vague idea about how the lost tribes were part of British history but were rather just certain that it had to be the case. Some of the participants in the Association were Freemasons, seeking the Ark as part of their fraternal order's interest in all things related to the Temple in Jerusalem. The earlier British-Israel Association of London, which took the Anglo-Saxons as Israelites, was more extreme than the larger federation it later joined. That organization held that it was not just the Anglo-Saxons who were the descendants of biblical figures. Different groups within the United Kingdom each had their own biblical ancestors. Protestant or Ulster Irish were the descendants of the tribe of Dan. The Catholic Irish and Irish nationalists in general were thought to be the descendants of the Canaanites and the Phoenicians, the enemies of Israel and thus the enemies of Great Britain. The seeming similarity of the names "Fenian" and "Phoenician" seemed compelling, even though there is no actual etymological link between these words that come from two separate languages. They also believed that the Ark had been buried somewhere in Great Britain in antiquity. British Israelists wanted to find the Ark, not for financial gain, but rather to use it as the symbol for a unified Great Britain rooted in a renewed biblical history. This rebirth was understood in "millenarian" terms, the belief that with turning of the century to 1900, society would be fundamentally transformed as described in the book of Revelation. The British Israelists wanted to present the Ark to Queen Victoria just as the Messiah returned to earth.

Beginning in the 1880s, various fundraising ventures were successful in cultivating substantial financial support for excavations aimed at recovering the Ark of the Covenant. British Israelists believed that the most likely location of the Ark was Tara, located near Dublin, one of the most important sites in early Irish history. From 1899 to 1902, the British-Israel Association of London conducted excavations at Tara believing that the Anglo-Saxon Israelites had hidden the Ark there. While different members of the organization held different opinions, and none of the actual "excavators" published their results (not surprising, given that they lacked the ability to even understand what they were digging through), the most commonly cited belief was that the Ark was buried in the grave of Princess Tea Tephi. Irish tradition holds that she was born in Spain, the daughter of the last king of Judah (Zedekiah), and grew up to become a queen of Ireland. Some believed that she had traveled with Jeremiah to Ireland, but the medieval traditions about this vary.

The excavations of the British Israelists at Tara stirred considerable controversy. They were denied the right to dig by various scholarly organizations initially. However, since the land was under private ownership, they were eventually able to convince the landlord to allow them to work on the site. Their excavations were not illegal at that time, but they were also not sanctioned by the scholarly organizations of the era and in fact the excavators were castigated as vandals by legitimate researchers. Visitors to the site were horrified by the clear lack of archaeological skills demonstrated by the haphazard digging of the site. That these men had no archaeological training was widely reported and patently obvious to any visitors, and the press emphasized that idea that the Ark of the Covenant would be found at Tara was ludicrous. When Irish nationalists became aware of the digging at Tara, they fueled public outrage through letters to the newspapers and meetings with various organizations. The diggers were derided as lunatics in the newspapers, and eventually excavations were brought to a halt when the landholder was convinced that the British Israelists were doing irreparable harm to the site.

The site of Tara is something of a lightning rod of contested nationalist positions, like Jerusalem but to a lesser extent. The British-Israel Association of London believed that Tara was to become their "resuscitated Jerusalem," the center of a messianic and Christian British empire. Irish nationalists by the end of the nineteenth century saw Tara as the symbol of an independent and united Ireland. That an English team would be allowed to eradicate the

112 READERS OF THE LOST ARK

site through amateur archaeological vandalism was not taken just as a sign of a fringe group allowed to run rampant but as the desire of the English to destroy Irish cultural heritage. The protests of prominent public figures in the Irish nationalist movement, like William Butler Yeats and Maude Gonne, were not just expressions of concern over bad archaeology but arguments that the English were attacking the Irish culturally. Tara had already been invoked as a symbol of a free Irish state and the British-Israelist explorations were now invoked as a British protestant attack on that same state. By 1902, the British-Israel Association of London's quest to find the Ark of the Covenant in Ireland was brought to an end, but every once in while these claims are resurrected by amateur Irish historians and pseudoscholars.

Just as curious are the arguments that the Ark of the Covenant now resides on Mount Tsurugi in Japan. This high mountain on the island of Shikoku is one of the central holy sites of the Shugendo tradition, a tradition that emerged in the seventh century CE, blending elements of Buddhism, Shintoism, and other Japanese belief systems. Much of the current practice of Shugendo focuses on magical and divinatory practices, with the reading of omens, the casting of spells, and forecasting the future being key elements. Perhaps the sacred elements of the mountain and the syncretistic aspects of Shugendo as practiced there are what inspired Masanori Takane (1883– 1959) to identify one of Mount Tsurugi's caves as a possible location of the lost Ark. Takane engaged in a kind of research called "kotodama," which literally translates as "word spirit." The presupposition of kotodama is that there are powers invested in words, and by speaking those words aloud, it is possible to harness those powers. Takane's research led him to compare the Bible with the Japanese text *Kojiki* ("Record of Ancient Matters"), which preserves ancient traditions about Shinto deities and supernatural beings. While he identified many common themes in the texts, one parallel was particularly compelling to him. The parallel can be found in the book of Revelation (7:1), where John writes (New International Version): "I saw four angels standing at the four corners of the earth, holding back the four winds of the earth to prevent any wind from blowing on the land or on the sea or on any tree." Shikoku, the name of the island, means "four countries," and it is described as having "four faces" in the *Kojiki*. Further comparison, using similar kinds of logic, led Takane to identify Mount Tsurugi as a location where biblical and Shinto truths met, and specifically where the Ark of the Covenant had come to be buried.

In 1936, Takane led an archaeological expedition to find the Ark there. For twenty years, he and others excavated ancient remains from Mount Tsurugi. They made legitimate archaeological finds, although not excavated to the professional standards of archaeology as practiced elsewhere in the world at the time. They did not find any connection with the ancient Hebrews, however. Despite the failure to find positive evidence for a Japanese–Israelite relationship, others followed Takane's lead, including a navy admiral, Eisuke Yamamoto, who found a number of ancient mummies, and a treasure hunter, Yoshun Miyanaki. In 1956, however, excavations were banned from the mountain, when the Japanese government declared it a national park. For some, this government intervention has only fueled their imaginations that this may be the location of the Ark, a location that authorities want to remain hidden.

Why was the Ark, in particular, thought to be on Mount Tsurugi? It may be that Takane thought it was similar to portable Japanese shrines called *mikoshi*. These are brought out in ceremonial processions, carried like the Ark on poles and often with a sculpture of a bird on top. Priests who carry the *mikoshi* wear special clothes, and others dance and sing in front of them. Mount Tsurugi is one of the locations where such processions take place. For Takane, who was already convinced of parallels between Japanese and biblical culture, these similarities were compelling, suggesting some kind of early contact, where the ancient Israelites taught the Japanese to carry such ritual objects. Who were these ancient Israelites who traveled to Japan? For Takane and his later followers, they were likely the Lost Tribes of Israel, the usual suspects in such claims about ancient biblical connections to such remote places.

Takane may have been the most prominent, but there are other proponents of the idea that the Ark is located in Japan. One set of theories revolves around decoding the meaning of the traditional folk song *Kagome Kagome*. A *kagome* is a woven basket, and the song sings about birds coming out of the basket. The birds are associated with the cherubs of the Ark by these theorists, and the rest of the song, they believe, offers cryptic messages about where the Ark will be found. One theorist, calling himself "The Last Samurai" on his YouTube channel, compares the shape of the weaving of such baskets with the Star of David and notes that prominent Israeli officials have climbed Mount Tsurugi. He implies that they did so, knowing that the Ark is there, and perhaps intending to visit it.

114 READERS OF THE LOST ARK

Another "lost tribes of Israel in Japan" theory, laid out by Gene Jinsiong Cho, a music professor who worked at Detroit Bible College, holds that a group of Jews, heavily influenced by Persian Mithraism, left Babylon and traveled along the Silk Road. They brought with them a replica of the Ark of the Covenant that came to play an important role in Shinto traditions. This replica Ark was not the actual Ark from Solomon's Temple, but rather a model that was designed as part of the group's efforts to preserve Jewish heritage in the diaspora. Diaspora Jews then, contributed to Shintoism, which is the belief system of Japan that predates the arrival of Buddhism to the islands. The key figures of Shintoism are *kami*, supernatural beings who inhabit many things, especially landscapes and sacred objects. When the Jewish "lost tribe" entered Japan, their belief system was incorporated into Shintoism, and its Near Eastern origins were forgotten. The sacred landscapes of Sinai and Zion were incorporated into Shinto belief systems. The lost tribe was assimilated into Japanese society. The Ark that they brought with them was incorporated into Japanese religious life and remains one of the most important objects of veneration, with its Near Eastern origins forgotten. It is now, according to this theory, known as the *MiFune-Shiro*, a wooden chest located within the Ise Shrine (*Ise Jingu*) dedicated to the sun goddess Amaterasu and linked to the Japanese imperial family. The interior of the shrine is off limits to most people, making speculation about the religious items stored within possible.

As with most pseudoarchaeological arguments, which I will discuss in detail in Chapter 9, the "evidence" is unverifiable. The inability for people to see the Ark, even though its location is supposedly known, allows for such speculation. Why would it occur to anyone, however, that this central location of Shintoism should be tied to the Ark of the Covenant? Cho's theory was inspired by the arguments of Jenichiru Oyabe, presented in a book published in 1929. Like Takane, Oyabe was interested in the seeming parallels between Japanese and Near Eastern traditions. A Christian convert and graduate of Yale Divinity School, Oyabe wrote that the Japanese emperor was a descendent of the tribe of Gad. The name for the Japanese emperor is *Mikado* and so Oyabe claimed that the "Mi" was the honorary prefix" and "kado" was the Japanese language rendering of "Gad." He makes other etymological arguments using the coincidence of words in Hebrew and Japanese that both sound the same and have similar meanings as evidence for a genetic relationship between Japanese and Jewish culture. Likewise, similarities in ritual practices like those identified by Takane provide further evidence for the Jewish origins of Japanese culture. Such attempts to understand Japan's place in global history in relationship to the West were not uncommon in Japanese intellectual life prior to World War II, as part of Japan's modernization movement. Connecting Japan's imperial family to the West's biblical origin stories bolstered arguments about Japan's primacy of place in world politics, providing means for both celebrating traditional Japan and creating a new modern version of the nation which would stand at the center of global power. Now such ideas are resurrected by interested amateurs, such as Cho, who discovered a copy of Oyabe's book by accident and was inspired to do his own follow-up research.

More biblically justifiable arguments suggest that the Ark may be located on or near Mount Nebo. Indeed, Mount Nebo in Jordan has similarly drawn explorers who have dreamed of finding the Ark. This is the location where Moses looked upon the Promised Land but died before entering and so it has born significant interest since antiquity. It is likely this connection that led the author of Maccabees to suggest that the prophet Jeremiah hid the Ark here.

This reference in Maccabees led the Australian gold prospector and adventurer Antonia Futterer to search Mount Nebo for the Ark in the 1920s. After a near- death experience, the gold prospector gave up his efforts at mining and became a missionary and preacher. He left Australia in 1910 where he settled in the Bay Area and developed a number of tools for teaching Christianity. He called one of these tools the "Eye- Ographic Bible," and it originally consisted of ten large maps (not to scale) and a hardcover book that explained them. The explanations are a series of summary comments about the narrative events of the Bible keyed to the different maps. Using this "system" as it is described by later publishers of Futterer's work, a lecturer could pull out the map associated with the patriarchal traditions, for example, read his summaries of biblical events, and follow the instructions given for using the maps to illustrate scripture.

By 1926, Futterer's religious teaching in California gained him enough money to support a two-year expedition to the Holy Land to find the Ark of the Covenant. In his later accounts of these adventures, Futterer explained that, based on his understanding of 2 Maccabees, the Ark was hidden on Mount Nebo by Jeremiah, who knew that the Jews were soon to be exiled from Israel and that the land would be ruled by gentile empires for centuries to come. However, Futterer was convinced that, with the growing migration of Jews back to Palestine in the early twentieth century, the Ark would soon reappear on the Earth. God had purposefully hidden it but would reveal

116 READERS OF THE LOST ARK

the Ark as part of the reemergence of Israel. The reappearance of the Ark, according to Futterer, would benefit humanity by converting all people to Christianity, including Jews who would be convinced that they were breaking God's laws by not following the teachings of the Christian faith.

Futterer's Ark expedition was both a treasure hunt and a type of missionary work. When he arrived in the Holy Land, he applied for permission to explore Mount Nebo. While waiting for the authorities to respond, he toured the region, experiences he used as the basis for his guidebook and later tours. Permission was eventually granted, but only to explore Mount Nebo and not to excavate there. Futterer reported various versions of what happened during his visit to Mount Nebo. In most accounts, he discusses exploring the caves there. Sometimes he claims to have made a remarkable discovery: the cave where the Ark was buried. After being lowered into the cave, he found a wall inscribed with what was presumably a Hebrew inscription reading: "Herein lies the golden Ark of the Covenant." These walls flanked a long corridor that terminated in two sealed doors, akin to those described in 2 Maccabees. Although Futterer had become friends with the local sheikh, that sheikh did not allow him to tear down the doors and so he left the area, with only a story of his discovery to tell, not the Ark itself.

Futterer made good use of these stories in his later promotion of his work and the tours he and his family led to the Holy Land. After Futterer's death, these tours continued from 1954 to 1985, led by the Holyland Bible Knowledge Society. The tales about the Ark are not consistent in different accounts. Futterer started to refer to himself as "Ark Explorer" or "Golden Ark Explorer," often writing about himself in the third person using this name. That he hoped he would get permission to dig on Mount Nebo and be able to return to retrieve the Ark is clear in his later works. In his guidebook to the region, *Palestine Speaks*, he asks for donors, writing: "I may however appeal to some rich Jews to have the privilege of financing the next Ark search, so that the Ark may not be found without Jewish help nor would it be said by Jews that a Jew was not invited to help finance this expedition." Such donors never seem to have materialized. Still, Futterer is remembered as a curious character in the story of Ark seekers. There is currently a museum in Los Angeles where visitors can explore his collection of Holy Land relics and photographs—the Holy Land Exhibition in Silver Lake.

Tom Crotser claims to have followed in Futterer's footsteps and know where the Ark of the Covenant rests. Perhaps this should be taken with a grain of salt, however, as Crotser also claims to have found Noah's Ark, the

Tower of Babel, and even the stone with which Cain killed Abel. This would be quite the archaeological pedigree if there were any reason to believe him. Of course, there isn't. According to Crotser, in 1981 he led his organization, the Institute for Restoring History International stationed out of Wichita, Kansas, on an expedition to find the cave in Mount Nebo. Crotser claimed to have gained access to Futterer's notes about his expedition. After surveying Mount Nebo, Crotser and his team moved to a nearby location, conveniently not run by the Franciscans who were the operators of Mount Nebo. The Franciscans who oversee Mount Nebo are dedicated to archaeological work, and would not tolerate amateur excavations, and furthermore, have enough archaeological knowledge to be able to double-check his findings. On this other mountain, Mount Pisgah, such authorities are more distant. Crotser purports to have discovered a cave with an entrance covered by a sheet of tin. His team removed that and traveled farther into the cave, where they came to another wall. After taking down that wall, they found the Ark somewhat disassembled and took photographs. He exited the chamber with his team, told the media, and then never showed the photographs to anyone, even the media to whom he reported the discovery. There was one person to whom Crotser was willing to show his pictures, David Rothschild. Why Rothschild? Crotser seems to have fixated on this member of a prominent Jewish family, believing that Rothschild was a descendent of Jesus. As far as I know, Rothschild refused to meet him, likely somewhat used to attention from cranks like this, and probably somewhat concerned about meeting someone who thought he was the descendent of the messiah of a different faith.

Are any of these searchers for the Ark taken seriously by professional archaeologists? In a word, no. What Crotser, Futterer, Parker, and others like them were doing is not archaeology. It is treasure hunting. The question of whether these treasure hunts were based on plausible evidence is not all that important for determining that this work is not archaeological. Archaeologists do not seek out individual artifacts like Indiana Jones does. Rather, they seek to study the past systematically through controlled excavations and the analysis of material culture. The context of where the artifacts are found is far more important than any single artifact because it is that context which is the main focus of archaeological interest. As I tell my students, the Well of the Souls in which the Ark was found in *Raiders* (not to be confused for the Well of the Souls in the Dome of the Rock) is a lot more interesting than the Ark itself (like why was it filled with so many

118 READERS OF THE LOST ARK

poisonous snakes?). This may seem disingenuous coming from someone who has written an entire book on the Ark, but none of these Ark quests constitute archaeology. Even though these people might frame themselves as archaeologists today, what they are doing bears nothing in common with the academic pursuit.

In fact, what is apparent through these accounts of Ark seekers is just how destructive they are, both to archaeological heritage and to politically fragile situations. That these amateurs do not know what they are doing is not just comical, because what they have excavated cannot be undone. Once archaeological context is disturbed, most of the information that is of interest to archaeologists is destroyed. If excavators do not know how to excavate carefully, and are not able to report their findings, that information can never be recovered. These Ark seekers also seem to search for the Ark in locations of social and political fault lines. The Temple Mount in Jerusalem is one of the most politically fragile locations in the world. Tara at the turn of the twentieth century was a flashpoint for nationalism. As we shall see in later chapters, supposed locations of the Ark are often in political hotspots. At best, these amateurs are simply accidentally stumbling into problems that are more complicated than they understand. At worst, however, these Ark hunters purposefully use claims about the Ark to impact fragile political situations.

Yet I expect that we shall continue to see such self-proclaimed explorers, continuing to make claims that they know where the Ark is, but just are not able to retrieve it, for some reason or other. Despite the complex political situation in Jerusalem, there will likely be the occasional searcher, inspired by extrabiblical stories of the Ark hidden there and the seemingly suspicious lack of biblical information on its whereabouts. Jerusalem, and less so Mount Nebo, will continue to stand as candidates for its resting place. For documentary makers, Jerusalem provides a good location to frame quasi-journalistic pieces about the Ark, given the city's charismatic visual features that make it seem exotic and mysterious. These quests, and the reporting on them, inspired the most famous Ark story outside of the Bible— Indiana Jones and his pursuit of it in *Raiders of the Lost Ark*. The influence of this film on the reception of the Ark and the way it is depicted in other films is the subject of the next chapter.

6

The Ark of Indiana Jones and Other Cinematic Arks

I don't know how many times I've watched *Raiders of the Lost Ark*. It must be literally hundreds of times. In all sorts of formats (silver screen, pan and scan, widescreen, on my iPhone) and in all sorts of places (drive-ins, IMAX theatres, basement birthday parties). I even projected it at a buffalo kill site, at the archaeological field school Shawn and I run at Head-Smashed-In Buffalo Jump, a UNESCO World Heritage site. And there are some scenes I've watched even more than this and in all sorts of speeds, slow motion, and even frame by frame. One of these is the scene where Sallah and Indy, in the middle of an ominous thunderstorm, have descended into the Well of the Souls and braved the hundreds of asps and king cobras, the very embodiment of Indy's own snake phobia, to get to the rock-hewn structure that has housed the Ark since it was plundered by the Egyptian Pharaoh Shishak. John William's brilliant soundtrack makes it impossible to look away as the two men reveal the object of the quest. They insert wooden staves into the sides of the stone container which holds the Ark. Then, each taking one side, they slowly lift the Ark out, and its golden color seems to glow, bathing them in a gold light as well (Figure 6.1). The scene shifts, and now we see the Ark in shadow being moved through the hall of the Well of the Souls. Mirroring biblical prescription, Spielberg knows not to let the audience look directly at the Ark for too long. This is not for safety, as is the reason in the Bible, but to heighten the drama of the artifact, limiting the audience's view of it. We then see some close-up detailed shots of the Ark, as Indy and Sallah immediately put it into a crate. We won't see the Ark again until the climax of the movie.

Yet this is not quite the Ark of the Bible. The staves are not attached and would not have fit into the stone container from which Indy's Ark was drawn. Now, we can explain this away easily enough. Perhaps the Egyptians removed them as they would not have been concerned with God's commandments. Also deviating from the Bible is some of the ornamentation. The side of the Ark has a kind of brushed design, for example. Still, it is pretty faithful as a

Readers of the Lost Ark. Kevin M. McGeough, Oxford University Press. © Oxford University Press 2025.
DOI: 10.1093/9780197653913.003.0007

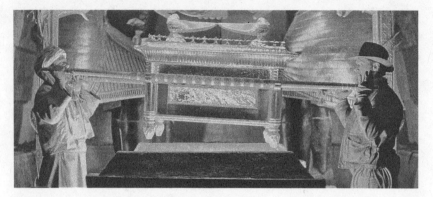

Figure 6.1 Indy and Sallah lift the Ark of the Covenant from its resting place in the Well of the Souls. Screenshot from *Raiders of the Lost Ark* (Paramount Pictures, 1981), digital enlargement

movie prop goes, much more faithful than, as we shall discuss shortly, some of the initial concept art.

The obsessive *Raiders* watcher can also find a favorite "Easter Egg" in this scene. An Easter Egg is something hidden in a film that should go unnoticed by most viewers but, especially now in an age of high-resolution digital images, can be found when one thinks to look. In this case, one needs look closely at the hieroglyphs. There, even if you have never formally studied ancient Egyptian writing systems, you may be able to identify something out of place. Between the seated scribes and the various animals are R2-D2 and C-3PO, of *Star Wars* fame. George Lucas, the director of *Star Wars*, was the producer of *Raiders* and one of the key creative forces behind it. The director, Steven Spielberg, the story goes, could not help but add this touch for his friend. We will return to how this relationship with *Star Wars* has influenced the reception of *Raiders* and the Ark shortly.

The Ark as MacGuffin

So why, narratively, does Indy want the Ark so badly? And why do the Nazis want it? And why do we as viewers get so emotionally involved in this chase? Partially it is an archaeological artifact, and that, we have been conditioned to expect, is something worth chasing. But there is another element that increases the urgency and that is the Ark's power as a weapon. The film

THE ARK OF INDIANA JONES AND OTHER CINEMATIC ARKS   121

situates the search for the Ark within the context of something viewers may have heard before, that Hitler was interested in the occult and sent teams out to recover artifacts like the Ark. Two men from the government appear at the college that Indy works at and explain that "Over the last two years, the Nazis have had teams of archaeologists running around the world looking for all kinds of religious artifacts. Hitler is a nut on the subject. He's crazy. He's obsessed with the occult." The concern is that the Nazis may find an ancient object that actually works as a weapon. The quest for the Ark is framed with a level of dramatic urgency that is plausible for viewers, even if the rest of the film is not so plausible. It establishes what literary scholars call a willing suspension of disbelief.

In real life, Nazi ideology was infused with and informed by many pseudoarchaeological and fringe beliefs. Hitler's view of the racial history of the world and Germany was based on fringe scholarship and some early, explicitly nationalist and racist scholarship on European archaeology. How important archaeology was to the Nazi program is exaggerated by the relentless number of documentaries about the Nazis that need a different angle to draw in viewers. Combining archaeology and Nazis brings together two of the most popular topics of channels like History and Discovery. The only thing missing is sharks. The Indiana Jones films have made the pseudohistorical aspects of Nazi ideology more prominent, and I imagine that many people having watched *Raiders*, assume that such German excavations were frequent in the years leading up to World War II.

Concerns about the Germans are what lead the American government to approach Indy. Military agents are confused by a Nazi communique that they have intercepted that mentions Indy's old mentor and an ancient artifact. As they talk to Indy and Marcus Brody, the museum curator with whom Indy works, it becomes apparent that the Nazis are looking for the Ark of the Covenant. Indy opens a Bible (conveniently sitting on the table between them already) and shows them an image of the Ark. Priests are holding it while standing on a rock in a valley, and some kind of beams are coming out of it, killing the soldiers surrounding them. Marcus tells the agents: "The Bible speaks of the Ark leveling mountains and laying waste to entire regions. An army which carries the Ark before it is invincible." This is why the Nazis want it and also why it is so important that the Americans find it before the Germans do. Now, it seems tough to imagine, from a biblical perspective, that God would use his power to help the Nazis, and of course, the Nazis who open the Ark at the end are all killed, so perhaps that could be understood

122 READERS OF THE LOST ARK

as God's wrath. That being said, God frequently punishes the Israelites in the Old Testament. Still, the logic of the film suggests that the Ark is some kind of weapon not specifically rooted in Old Testament theology, although it may still be supernatural. The story makes the Ark into a quasi-secular paranormal weapon.

At the climax of the film, the audience learns what powers the Ark holds. As Indy's evil counterpart, the French archaeologist Belloq dressed in the garb of the head Levite priest, recites an Aramaic prayer, the Ark is opened by Nazi attendants. The prayer is one that is actually spoken in synagogues today when the Torah Ark is opened. One of the Nazi officers puts his hand inside, and with disappointment pulls out, not the Ten Commandments or Aaron's budding rod, but sand, which he lets fall through his fingers into Belloq's. Then a strange noise begins, and all the electrical objects nearby begin to overcharge. In a bit of interbiblical interpretation, Indy tells Marion to keep her eyes shut and not look at what is in the Ark. In a "making of" documentary, the narrator explains that this was intentionally reflecting the story of Sodom and Gomorrah where Lot and his family were not to turn and look at what was happening to the cities behind them, lest they be turned into blocks of salt. The Nazis don't know not to look, and they watch as spectral figures begin to emerge. At first beautiful, the ghostly beings soon turn horrific, and various bodily tortures befall the Nazis. Some explode, some are burnt by energy rays, and some have their faces melt.

Treating the Ark as an ancient biblical weapon is not out of line with twentieth- and twenty-first-century media. The weaponized elements of archaeological materials are increasingly common in popular culture treatments of archaeology, in film, television, and especially video games. In such media, the past is often portrayed as dangerous. The inappropriate mixing of the past with the present and the blurring of those boundaries has the power to upset the normative social order. Here is the plot of the mummy films and mummy fiction in general. The archaeologist unearths something that should have remained underground. That ancient thing, a mummy, cursed amulet, or perhaps a Mesopotamian demon, like Pazuzu in *The Exorcist* (1973), cannot easily be defeated by the technologies of the present for they stand outside of our rational, mechanized world. Yet they usually are, and that defeat is reassuring, offering a vision of science, technology, and rationality trumping the unknown. Horror films involving archaeological materials show that modernity is a kind of triumph over our past selves, and that our rational approaches to the world are worth celebrating.

The Ark and other objects like it offer the opportunity for a technocratic variation on this theme. Artifacts are transformed into ancient weapons, often with a world-ending power mirroring that of nuclear weapons and probably resonating with audiences as a reflection of those fears. Our popular culture has conditioned us to the idea that the past was filled with ancient technologies that we no longer have and sometimes cannot understand (much more on this in Chapter 9), and these kinds of stories perpetuate that idea. They show technology to be something simultaneously celebrated and feared. Stories like this ease our worries about new technologies even if they start off by playing on our fears of them. Nuclear annihilation is perhaps less scary if one imagines that this threat was not new to the twentieth century, that people have had access to similar world-destroying technologies for thousands of years and managed not to bring about any major cataclysms.

The weaponization of archaeological artifacts through films and video games cannot be disentangled from how the mixing of archaeology with these media has been used as propaganda for the support of nation-states, contemporary political identities, and military activities. While Indiana Jones is an archaeologist, he is acting at the behest of the United States military, just as his rival, Belloq, is working for the Nazis. In both instances, the archaeological hero and villain stand as a proxy for a state military. Now, in part it is the context of World War II that allows this in *Raiders*, although the lack of anything resembling an Egyptian government is somewhat striking in the film (although historians debate how much Egyptian elites supported the Axis powers in relation to anti-British and Egyptian independence sentiments). And while Egypt was no longer under the formal control of the British at this time, it seems implausible that that nation would allow the Nazi military to operate unchecked within Egypt. Incoherent but imperialist political situations are typical of many other archaeological adventure films, set in different eras. The audience does not question the right of these Euro-American militaries to be operating in a Middle Eastern locale. It is not even taken as odd. If *Raiders* was the only instance of this, it probably would not matter. Audiences, however, see this again and again, in archaeological film after archaeological film. They don't question it in these movies. And so, their likeliness to question real-world military activities and real-world foreign policy is softened or undermined. The rights of Euro-Americans to world antiquities, which is presumed in these films, offers a kind of gateway logic for imperialist justifications at higher levels.

124 READERS OF THE LOST ARK

The military power of the Ark is not the only reason that audiences watching *Raiders of the Lost Ark* are willing to suspend their disbelief. As I have already mentioned, we have been conditioned by our popular culture, going as far back as the early nineteenth century, to accept that archaeological artifacts are something worth "chasing" and that archaeologists compete for them. Nineteenth-century readers thrilled to the exploits of Giovanni Belzoni, the circus strongman turned treasure hunter who wrote an autobiographical account of his own adventures seeking Egyptian antiquities and competing with other archaeologists in races to get to the artifacts first. Since his accounts, archaeology and treasure hunting have been entangled in popular culture, with the boundaries between these two activities blurred considerably. It makes sense for audiences, conditioned by over two centuries of popular culture, to accept that the Ark should be pursued like this. And stories of explorers like Parker (discussed in Chapter 5) actually having done so reifies this further.

This kind of popular culture conditioning has probably further influenced alternative interpretations of the Ark. As we shall explore in Chapter 9, media discussions of the Ark are often offered from pseudoarchaeological perspectives, the type of perspectives where ancient aliens and secret energy systems are invoked to explain different elements of antiquity. The weaponized ancient MacGuffins of archaeological films are explained, narratively, through the same logic as these pseudoarchaeological treatments. *Raiders* contributed to the Ark's adoption into this subculture, although as we shall discuss in Chapter 9, it was the subject of pseudoarchaeological works that predate *Raiders*. *Raiders* just made the Ark better known within this culture. The Ark's pseudoarchaeological status has increased with the more recent Indiana Jones films, especially the crystal skull of the interdimensional beings of *Indiana Jones and the Kingdom of the Crystal Skull*. The Holy Grail that Indy searches for in *Indiana Jones and the Last Crusade* could perhaps have a book similar to this written about it but is better known from Arthurian lore and pseudoarchaeology than any reasonable historical account. The Antikythera mechanism from *Indiana Jones and the Dial of Destiny* is an actual historical artifact, but it is one that is more likely to be discussed in a pseudarchaeological documentary than a college class on ancient Greece. The Ark, lumped in with all of these objects, seems less and less like an historical object and more the object of popular culture fantasy.

Other information that Indy and Marcus give to the government agents is a mix of real and imaginary. While most viewers probably do not pay all

THE ARK OF INDIANA JONES AND OTHER CINEMATIC ARKS   125

that much attention to the exposition here, this blending of historical and ahistorical has confused generations of viewers. Indy explains that the Egyptian pharaoh Shishak invaded Israel, and we have good historical evidence for this, both in terms of the biblical account and Egyptian historical inscriptions. That Shishak may have taken the Ark away with him is a theory that some Ark enthusiasts hold to, but the only evidence for this is coincidental. It is that the Ark no longer plays a major role in the biblical account of history after Shishak's invasion. Indy reports that Shishak was thought to have taken the Ark to the city of Tanis, which was covered by a sandstorm. There was a lost city of Tanis that was discovered by excavators long before the 1930s, when *Raiders* was set. Yet Indy and Marcus act surprised to learn that Nazi excavators have discovered the site. There is no historical reason to imagine that Shishak would have taken the Ark there anyways.

The Nazi communique mentions the headpiece to the Staff of Ra, which was an artifact that Indy's mentor had discovered. This is a golden piece of jewelry, with a crystal in its center, and instructions written on its edges describing the length of the wooden staff that it was to be placed upon. To learn the location of the Ark, one had to take this staff to a hidden map room in Tanis, put it in the right position, and wait for the right time of day for sunlight to pass through the crystal, which directs a beam upon a miniature model of the city built into the floor of the room. The light will illuminate the building in which the Ark is stored, revealing its location to the possessor of the Staff of Ra. This is one of the most dramatic moments in the film, one of my favorite movie moments of all time, and yet it makes no sense. Why would the ancients have created such an elaborate map system to record the location of the Ark? Who was supposed to have had this staff, why would there be a map room like this, and how did they know that the city would be buried by a sandstorm?

The logic of the Staff of Ra and map room is the logic of such media. Here is a common conceit in this kind of adventure fiction, whether it be film, book, or video game. The ancients embedded secret clues in different places to record where ancient treasures were located. Why they would do such a thing is often unclear. Sometimes it is explained that the person with the right knowledge will be able to decipher the code and, for some reason, will be deserving of the treasure. Sometimes it is suggested that these function like pirate treasure maps, where the pirates planned to come back for the treasure and had to create coded maps to help them find their hidden loot again. Yet really, with archaeology stories, these situations only make sense

126 READERS OF THE LOST ARK

because we have been conditioned to expect them in such fiction. Yet, as we shall see in Chapter 9, this presumption, that the ancients left codes in manuscripts and artifacts about where the Ark is located, is fundamental to much of the fringe theorizing about the Ark. People really believe that these codes hidden in artifacts actually exist. Once you have seen enough stories like this, or played enough video games, you are conditioned to accept the premises as reasonable.

All of these factors contribute to making the Ark one of the most note-worthy MacGuffins of the past two hundred years. Film fans know what the word *MacGuffin* means, which is "nothing." It is a word invented by Alfred Hitchcock as a nonsense word that specifically and intentionally refers to nothing in particular. Well, not quite. That's how he explained it in a famous conversation with the equally brilliant filmmaker François Truffaut. What he really meant though is that a MacGuffin is a thing that people chase in films. A MacGuffin, for Hitchcock, is something that audiences believe people will risk their lives to get, will kill or be killed to get, and is of the utmost importance that it does not fall into the hands of the wrong people. But if the filmmaker explains "why" in too much detail, according to Hitchcock, the effect is wrecked. The storyteller risks establishing reasons that are not important enough to justify people risking their lives for the quest, or, the stakes are set so high that the audience cannot accept that any character other than James Bond would be involved in such a venture. For Hitchcock, it was better never to explain what was being chased, because it was the chase that mattered, the action of the film, not the thing itself. When you watch a Hitchcock masterpiece like *North by Northwest* (1959), look for this. You never really care about what is on the microfilm that causes Cary Grant such headaches, and not caring doesn't take anything away from your enjoyment of the film.

This brings us back to the "thing theory" of the Introductory chapter, for the Ark is the perfect MacGuffin. It is a tangible object with an agreed-upon physical appearance. And it is a really important thing, but why it is important is a bit unclear. Likewise, it has some kind of power, and that power can be really dangerous, but that power is equally unclear. It can be built as a movie prop easily enough and look realistic. It has just enough of an ambiguous backstory and historical resonance to make it totally plausible that people would kill or risk dying to get it. This is the interpretive power of the Ark as explored throughout the book, but perhaps most clearly defined by its role in *Raiders of the Lost Ark*. The Ark of *Raiders* is not entirely an "empty"

MacGuffin, however. The film emphasizes its reception history as a biblical treasure and an object of power. Now, because of the film, people think of the Ark as a biblical treasure and possibly an ancient weapon.

Raiders of the Lost Ark did not invent the reception of the Ark as a kind of treasure and an object of unspeakable power. As should be clear from this book by now, these are both qualities of the Ark that have been part of its reception history since the Old Testament was written (and likely earlier). The Parker expedition discussed in the last chapter was a real-life version of this kind of quest, even including the use of supernatural forces to assist the explorers! The idea for the Ark's use as a MacGuffin in *Raiders of the Lost Ark* came to screenwriter Philip Kaufman from a different source. The dentist he visited in Chicago was obsessed with its supposed powers and this inspired Kaufman. He gave the idea to George Lucas, and the two of them played with the script early on, before Kaufman had to take other work. Later Kaufman would get credit as an original author of the story of *Raiders*. Nevertheless, the idea of using the Ark as a MacGuffin originated with people already treating it as an ancient treasure with supernatural powers, the pseudoarchaeological perspectives we will explore in Chapter 9.

Early treatments of the Ark suggest that the designers were not originally worried about fidelity to the biblical description. One set of concept art designs seems to be more inspired by William Blake, as suggested by J. W. Rinzler in *The Complete Making of Indiana Jones*. Most Blake-like are the designs for the side and end panels of the Ark. They depict what would have been scenes of Moses in various poses. In one panel he grapples with serpents, in one he is enthroned, and in one panel there are horses, winged beings, and Stars of David behind him. The only notes read: "carved wood finish in bas-relief antique gilded + aged." These are the most extreme variations from the Bible, but other images show boxes of different shapes, and the positioning of the cherubim varies considerably. I think that all of these designs would have undermined the impact of the Ark on the viewer.

Sound also influences how viewers understand what they are seeing, even if they are less conscious of this. As Belloq opens the Ark at the end of the film, the lid makes a metallic, grating noise. This is an effect created by the sound designer, Ben Burtt. It is actually a recording of him opening the lid of his toilet tank, a perhaps less dramatic reality that lies behind this climactic scene. He has said that when he replaced that toilet, he couldn't bear to get rid of the tank lid, which had become, to him, the mercy seat of the Ark of the Covenant.

128   READERS OF THE LOST ARK

The musical score that plays in scenes that feature the Ark also influences viewers in ways that they are not necessarily cognizant of. John Williams's approach to composing the soundtrack for *Raiders* was to create themes that reflect different characters, in a fashion that is similar to how opera works. If you have seen the film, then you are likely cognizant of the trumpet fanfare that represents Indiana Jones as a hero. You may also remember the romantic theme music for his leading lady, Marion, a soft, traditionally feminine score that neatly juxtaposes with her hard-edged character. The Ark also has its own music, varying in power depending on the circumstances of the Ark, but always vaguely unsettling.

When the Ark is not active, quiet trumpets and violins tell us that the object is dangerous and mysterious. The soft sounds of a female choir subtly hint at what will later emerge from the Ark, and the choir seems to indicate the Ark's responses to its environment, such as when it is put into a wooden crate after being rediscovered. These elements of the score hint that the Ark bears a feminine energy, just as was sometimes associated with the Ark in medieval and early modern theologies discussed in Chapter 4. When the female figures emerge from the Ark at the end, it becomes clear that the choir has foreshadowed these angelic beings seemingly residing within the Ark.

The fully realized power of the Ark, however, is reflected by the trumpets of the orchestra, perhaps alluding to the traditional Jewish horn, the *shofar* that represented God's presence in the Old Testament. The performance by Maurice Murphy (of the London Symphony Orchestra) for *Raiders* is powerful and bright and leads the viewer to think of the Ark as having agentive power, almost a character in its own right. At the climax of the film, the brass of the orchestra blows the viewers away as the ghostly figures transform from beautiful women into horrifying monsters and energy bursts forth from the Ark slaying the Nazis. Alternating between brass and choir, the music of the Ark theme tells the viewer about its characteristics and its powers—beautiful, feminine, and deadly. Perhaps the choir reflects the angels of the Ark and the trumpets the wrath of God Himself? Since the powers of the Ark are not explained in the film, this is left for the viewer to interpret.

However one understands the relationship between the choir and the trumpets, the musical theme of the Ark is unsettling and powerful. Its variations throughout the film help viewers understand the Ark and what is happening to it. Yet we can understand this because of our participation in a long tradition of musical reception. John Williams composed the Ark theme using the *diabolus in musica* interval as its central component. Also known as the

THE ARK OF INDIANA JONES AND OTHER CINEMATIC ARKS 129

tritone, or flatted fifth, it used to be uncommon in music because of its dissonant or discordant sound, which feels evil and foreboding. Heavy metal bands use it regularly now, as do composers of horror film soundtracks. The musical conditioning of audiences makes this interval very effective in stirring feelings of unease.

The visual and sound design that led to the onscreen Ark has left an indelible mark on how this ancient artifact is imagined. The Ark from *Raiders* is how I, by default, see (and even hear) the Ark. Now it may be because I am a film buff and an Indiana Jones fan that this is the case. But I'm also an expert enough on the Ark of the Covenant to write a book on the subject. I know better. It doesn't matter; this cinematic vision of the Ark remains, for me, the foundational image for what the Ark looked like and any deviation from this, no matter how historically grounded, seems wrong. This is a vision of the Ark that is rooted in cinematic history. In *Solomon and Sheba* (1959), for example, we see an Ark that is almost faithful to the description in the Bible used as a background set dressing. Yet interestingly enough, the designers did not bother being remotely faithful to the Temple's layout; otherwise the Ark would not be on view for the people. Nor were they concerned with anachronism, having a menorah, for example, feature as a key part of the Temple architecture long before this would have been adopted as a symbol in Judaism. To work as set dressing, the filmmakers had to fashion a recognizable Ark, and probably rightly presumed, that a Mesopotamian-like ziggurat could stand in for audiences as a Temple. So, while it may not be fair to give *Raiders* all the credit for designing how we imagine the Ark, that film cemented that vision for a new generation, and likely for generations going forward.

The power of contemporary visual culture to influence how we can imagine the past is well-studied. I think one of the best treatments of this is that of Jerry Mander, who was not an academic, an historian, or a Bible scholar. He was an advertising executive. He recognized that television advertising was having a profound impact on people, and in 1978 his book, *Four Arguments for the Elimination of Television*, was published. Now, obviously you can guess that I'm not a supporter of that proposition. But Mander's arguments are interesting, and they resonate with me in relation to historical imagination. He lists a number of historical circumstances and asks if the reader can imagine them *without* reference to cinematic images they have seen—the Old West, the American Antebellum South, a Stone Age Tribe, or ancient Greece and Rome. And I think he is right. While the same film may

130 READERS OF THE LOST ARK

not be evoked for everyone when gladiators are mentioned, the visual image one conjures is likely derived from film and television.

The Ark of the Biblical Epics

If *Raiders of the Lost Ark* has established what the Ark looks like to a generation, Cecil B. DeMille's 1956 version of *The Ten Commandments* has established a vision of the Exodus as a whole that has transformed our understanding of the story. DeMille's film is truly striking in how powerful it has been in shaping contemporary views of the Exodus, even if people have not seen the film in its entirety (which is most, actually). When I read Exodus with my second-year Hebrew students, many are surprised when the book deviates from the film, even those who have never seen it! It has become a baseline for how many imagine the Exodus. How many of us think of Charlton Heston (whether we want to or not) when we think of Moses? This, of course, is not all the time, but when you hear someone say "Let my people go," does Heston's dramatic, baritone delivery ring through your head? Maybe. Spielberg joked about this while working on *Raiders*, suggesting that when the Ark is opened at the end of the film, Charlton Heston should jump out wearing his Moses beard. Spielberg finally got his chance to make a gag like this when filming *Indiana Jones and the Kingdom of the Crystal Skull* (2008). It was supposed to appear in the opening scene in the government warehouse, where the heroes and villains are knocking over crates of mysterious objects and spilling artifacts out (including the Ark). Moses's wooden staff, modeled directly after Charlton Heston's, was filmed falling out with other artifacts. However, this didn't make the final cut of the film, so you can only see it if you watch one of the various "making of" documentaries.

While *Raiders* may have an outsized influence on our imagination of the Ark, DeMille has an outsized influence on our imagination of the context in which the Ark is said to have emerged. The advertising around the film emphasized the historical research that went into the film. It emphasized the accuracy of the sets, the props, and fidelity to the Bible. Yet the account in Exodus is not detailed enough to act as a sole source for a four-hour film. DeMille expanded the story of Moses and Pharaoh dramatically (and I mean that in all senses of the word). For me it is the personal relationships between the characters in the film that are most compelling, because we don't really learn about those relationships in the Bible. The complexities of the

THE ARK OF INDIANA JONES AND OTHER CINEMATIC ARKS 131

relationship between Charlton Heston and Yul Brynner is what really makes the film memorable to my mind, much more so than the elements of spectacle, like the parting of the Red Sea. And it is also much more compelling than the relationship between Moses and Pharaoh in the book of Exodus. That relationship has spawned an uncountable amount of art and interpretation, let alone three major world religions, because what is written is so ambiguous and leaves so much for the imagination. DeMille creates a completely relatable human story out of that relationship, adding so much more to the cryptic, repeated statements that Moses and Aaron appear before Pharaoh. DeMille's take on Exodus is so convincing that we can easily forget which elements are actually recounted in the Bible, and which were written for this movie.

One of DeMille's major visual sources for *The Ten Commandments* is Victorian painting. I think the most obvious of these is Edward John Poynter's 1867 *Israel in Egypt*. This is a masterpiece of a painting, capturing a biblical scene in an absolutely compelling fashion. It exemplifies Victorian historical-realistic painting because it is not at all historical, yet visually it is completely convincing in its authenticity. Leave aside the questions of the historicity of Israelite slavery in Egypt, the combination of architecture, art, and technologies in this painting is a complete mess of different time periods and places. Elsewhere I have argued that, in fact, this is what makes this painting brilliant. The hodgepodge of Egyptian things in this painting takes the scene out of an historical period and places it into a mythological time that has far greater resonance beyond an historically specific moment. Here I am not meaning mythological in the pejorative sense, but rather in the typological sense discussed in Chapter 4. It is akin to how Pharaoh is explicitly *not* named in the book of Exodus, which gives the story more power, because it is not tied to a specific historical Egyptian king. It is an event that can be reconstituted at every Passover seder in every Jewish house every year. The events of the Exodus stand outside of historical time and Poynter's painting captures this.

This is not, however, how the painting is used by filmmakers. They use Poynter's work as an historical reference piece for their own set, costume, and prop design. Because Victorian historical paintings were both visually realistic and seemingly accurate both historically and geographically (though not really), they are useful for filmmakers. They work as easily accessible reference materials for filmmakers who need to recreate such scenes visually and physically in a way that audiences will accept. Audiences may already be

132   READERS OF THE LOST ARK

familiar with famous paintings and have already been conditioned to accept that the ancient world looked like how it is depicted in these artworks. The use of such paintings is far from unique to DeMille. And this kind of eclecticism is far from unique to Poynter. Film ends up reifying many imaginative but visually realistic Victorian takes on biblical and classical times, because images that may be familiar to audiences (through these very well-known paintings) are made to come alive on the silver screen.

Seeing such seemingly historically accurate and plausible scenes on film impacts audiences in other ways as well. Filmmaker Paul Schraeder refers to one of these impacts as the "false syllogism" of film. A syllogism is a kind of logic where a conclusion is drawn from two premises or assumptions that are presumed to be true and bear a relation to one another. It's easier to explain with an example though, so let's use a popular one from first-year philosophy classes. The two premises are as follows: "All humans are mortal" and "Socrates is human." The conclusion, then, is that Socrates is mortal and the logic is sound. Schraeder's variation on this reasoning is that there are instances when the syllogism is false, meaning that at least one premise is actually untrue. He has identified one false premise that is commonly held by movie audiences. The false premise is this: "What one sees on film is real." The other premise is this: "An historical, biblical, or religious event has been shown in the film." Reasoning from these premises leads to a logically unsound conclusion, that the historical, biblical, or religious event depicted in the film really happened. It could be "real," but the fact that it was depicted on film is in no way evidence for this.

Perhaps it is easiest to explain this concept through the example of the parting of the Red Sea in *The Ten Commandments*. When DeMille used his special effects to make it appear as though the Red Sea was parting before Moses's staff, he created one of the most memorable scenes in cinematic history. People actually saw this happen before their own eyes, a miracle that people had been reading about for at least two thousand years. Yet now that they could see that DeMille made it physically happen, even if he used special effects, it meant that this miracle was something that *could* have happened. Because audiences saw someone part the Red Sea, it became plausible that the Red Sea was actually parted in antiquity. The logic, of course, is flawed because film uses special effects and other techniques to create the illusion that such a miracle has occurred. Seeing the starship Enterprise (of *Star Trek*) fly through space does not mean that this will happen, but, just in the same way, it is powerful because it not only suggests that it *could* happen but something

THE ARK OF INDIANA JONES AND OTHER CINEMATIC ARKS   133

akin to it is *likely* to happen. DeMille recognized this kind of power of film, although he would not have used the expression "false syllogism." He pushed this logic even further by starting his film with an introduction where he stands in front of a curtain, onscreen, and talks about the extrabiblical sources that he consulted to fill in the parts of the story of Moses's life that are not preserved in the Bible. He establishes that the film is historically accurate, somewhat apologizing for where he has had to add to the story. The power of this framing is profound, and even though the techniques for how DeMille parted the Red Sea are well-known, so well-known that they can be experienced directly by visitors to Universal Studios theme park in Hollywood, it does not matter. That the Red Sea could be parted by DeMille is proof that it could have been done by Moses. If the parting of the Red Sea could happen, the powers ascribed to the Ark are just as plausible. And so DeMille's film contributes to the reception of the Ark in the same way. It is well within the physical possibilities of the world that such an object could have existed and could have had the powers described in the Bible (although as I will discuss later, we don't actually see the Ark in this film).

DeMille's movie became a classic not just because of its qualities as a film, but because of some of the idiosyncrasies of television programming. It was licensed for television replay and became something aired on network television on Easter. This was a problematic holiday for television programming because viewing habits are not as predictable as at Christmas. It is expected that there will be a lot of potential television viewers because the holiday does not require as much socializing, but when exactly those viewers will watch television is not consistent. It is not a time to waste first-run content, not only because of the unpredictability of viewers, but because (at least up until the 1990s) it might come across as sacrilegious to broadcast nonreligious content. *The Ten Commandments* was perfect because it was very long, tremendously long when commercials are added in, and viewers can pop in and out of the film without being confused about what is going on. The presumed audience could tune in at any time and not be lost, and so could start watching whenever their own observances of Easter stopped. Watching it also seemed like an appropriately pious activity for a religious holiday. Every Easter this film was played on network television, at a time when there was only network television. Many people watched at least part of this film every year, and through repeated television viewings it became an unofficial part of nondenominational American liturgical life, for Christians who celebrated Easter and for non-Christians who watched it because there

134 READERS OF THE LOST ARK

was nothing else to do on Easter. This isn't the case anymore. Broadcasting mores have changed along with viewing habits, and now I cannot presume that the students in my class will know what I'm talking about when I mention it. But for the generations who birthed the baby boomers through to my generation (Generation X), this film has a unique resonance, even if unconsciously for those who never really paid attention to it.

Now, the Ark is never actually seen in *The Ten Commandments*. Perhaps I am cheating by including a discussion of *The Ten Commandments* in this book, which is perhaps a fair accusation, since I think it is really fun to write about this movie. But I don't really think I am cheating because the Ark plays a key role in the conclusion of this film. As Moses dies, the Ark, DeMille argues, is now how the laws of God will be carried forward. In this final scene, Moses passes his mantle of leadership to Joshua, signaling that this is a moment of transition. As the Israelite leadership looks down from Mount Nebo, they watch the procession of Israelites. Moses's wife Sephora says to him: "Look Moses. The People have come to the River Jordan. In the Ark, they carry the law you brought them. You taught them not to live by bread alone. You are God's torch that lights the way to freedom." While the movie is structured as a biopic of Moses's life, the name tells us that it is these laws that are the key point of the film, the story of their origin. The Ark, then, is what the film points to as the next bearer of the laws, what will continue to carry God's laws now that Moses cannot.

Cinematically the Ark fulfills another function in DeMille's biblical film. For DeMille's view of history is one in which events in biblical times began a movement that would culminate in the America of the 1950s. He saw the Ten Commandments as foundational for American democracy but also saw American democracy as the natural fulfillment of biblical processes. DeMille explains this in his opening introduction, that *The Ten Commandments* is the story of the birth of freedom. And this is how the film ends, with a fairly direct reference to American democracy. Moses sends Joshua, Sephora, and their attendants away so that he can die alone on Mount Nebo. He raises his arms and declares: "Go. Proclaim liberty throughout all the lands unto all the inhabitants thereof." Then he turns and walks away and the epic film has reached its dramatic conclusion with the end of Moses's story. Moses's final statement is a curious blend of the King James translation of Leviticus 25:10 and modern American democratic language. This command is inscribed on the Liberty Bell, and the significance of this would not be lost on DeMille's American audience. Yet the message to contemporary audiences is made

THE ARK OF INDIANA JONES AND OTHER CINEMATIC ARKS   135

even more directly than that. The translation of Leviticus deviates in an important place. In the Bible, liberty is to be proclaimed in the *land*. In the Cold War context of DeMille's argument, however, Heston as Moses demands that liberty be proclaimed through the *lands*. It is not just to the Promised Land or the United States that liberty should be proclaimed. This is a Cold War call to arms for Americans to spread democracy, and taken with DeMille's opening speech, it is an argument to spread democracy in the battle against communism and the Soviet Union. The end of *The Ten Commandments* is dramatically different from what is described in Deuteronomy, but fidelity to the text was not of great concern to DeMille. DeMille's vision of the Ark is that it plays a particular role in this type of history, what scholars would call "teleological," which sees historical events as moving toward a specific goal. The Ark, for DeMille, was one of the instruments that helped move history toward democracy, the next instrument for its transmission after Moses.

The 1956 version of *The Ten Commandments* was not DeMille's first attempt at filming the story of the Exodus. That came with his 1923 silent film of the same name. This film was not as epic in scope, and only the first part of the film deals with biblical times. Most of the film is a morality play set in the 1920s showing how the Ten Commandments had been abandoned in American society. The film offers a traditional Christian typological argument, just as discussed in Chapter 4, where biblical events stand as exemplars of things yet to happen. DeMille depicts the Israelites as displaying all the vices that he accuses Americans of displaying in the 1920s.

In other words, DeMille depicts the Israelites as engaging in sex, violence, and wild orgiastic partying. The great screenwriter Philip Dunne despised DeMille for many reasons, one being DeMille's active participation in the blacklisting of the McCarthy era and in his rabid support of the Republican Party. But in his autobiography, Dunne explains that his disdain for DeMille also stems from his perception of the director's hypocrisy. For he accuses DeMille of using the Bible and moralizing as a means of getting away with showing sex and violence on screen. Many artists have done that, including those Victorian painters who created seemingly archaeologically authentic biblical scenes of harems, nude bodies, and ultraviolence, allowing Victorian viewers to be titillated guilt-free. DeMille was caught out on this with his version of *The Sign of the Cross* (1932), which had been a moralizing play written by Wilson Barrett. DeMille transformed it into a vision of the debauchery of Rome (which is much more memorable than the original play), with some Christian moral messaging tagged on at the end. That film is often blamed as

136 READERS OF THE LOST ARK

the reason that the Hayes Code (also known as the Hollywood Production Code) was brought into effect, which censored the content of Hollywood films. While *The Sign of the Cross* was not the sole cause of imposition of the Hayes Code, DeMille's oeuvre to that point certainly contributed to the belief among some that such a code was needed. Despite DeMille's fashioning of his own self-image as a morally upright, conservative filmmaker, activist groups of the 1930s became outraged by his movies. The theophany at Sinai is truly the wildest scene in his 1923 *The Ten Commandments*, and while not shocking in its own right for viewers today, it is shocking that such a scene was filmed in the 1920s. The Israelites engage in hedonistic abandon, with, at one point, a woman seeming to erotically stimulate the Golden Calf. While we do not see the Ark in this film, we see the Theophany on Sinai, and it is juxtaposed with this sequence of debauchery.

Dunne himself tried his hand at writing a biblical movie, *David and Bathsheba*, which has mostly been forgotten today but was the top grossing film in 1951, the year it was released. Starring Gregory Peck, Dunne's film depicted a King David dealing with the posttraumatic stress of warfare, a theme that would have resonated with the many veterans of the era going through the same issues. Dunne was himself an atheist, and his take on the biblical events reflects those of a writer not constrained by an urge to depict the story with biblical fidelity.

Dunne's approach to miracles and miraculous objects in the Bible is thus agnostic. Unlike DeMille's films where the plots advance because of God's miracles, the miracles in *David and Bathsheba* are ambiguous. The characters in the film believe in the miracles of God, but it is left up to the viewers to decide whether these were really miracles. Secular and religious audiences can read the film differently. Dunne's agnostic filmmaking is apparent in his treatment of the Ark, in the scene when Nathan has brought it to Jerusalem and David is inspecting it. As he walks around the Ark, peering at it, David says to Nathan: "God's design is a strange one, Nathan. Consider how this box of wood has outlived the flesh that made it, and preserved it, and venerated it. A pity that it is mute and blind and cannot tell us of our ancient dead. Of Moses on the mountaintop. Of Miriam and Aaron. At Joshua at the walls of Jericho." Then David reaches out to touch the Ark, but Nathan stops him just in time, warning the king, "Do not tempt the thunderbolts of the Lord. His dwelling is not to be profaned by unconsecrated hands. To touch it is to die." David responds, but with Gregory Peck's disbelieving smirk: "As you say, Nathan." Would the thunderbolts have struck down

THE ARK OF INDIANA JONES AND OTHER CINEMATIC ARKS   137

David? We as viewers do not know, and Dunne has sidestepped the issue of its supernatural powers by acknowledging Nathan's belief that this might have happened, while the hero David, with whom the audience sympathizes, holds a more secular disposition. Dunne continues to straddle that line, for immediately following this dialogue, an Israelite rushes up in excitement to touch the Ark. The man immediately clutches his chest and dies. A heart attack from over excitement? Or the will of God? Or the will of God acting through a heart attack? Dunne leaves it ambiguous.

Dunne employs the Ark and the miracles of the Bible in a fashion that is almost directly oppositional to DeMille's approach, which makes sense given his generally oppositional feelings about DeMille. Dunne uses the Ark in a secular historically realistic fashion. His presentation of the Ark facilitates a reading of the Bible in which historical events were recorded, but the miracles of the stories can be rationalized through mechanistic explanations. Like some of the biblical archaeologists discussed in Chapter 2, Dunne wants to present a Bible that can make sense with twentieth-century conceptions of the world. Now, Dunne was probably most concerned with not alienating the middle-class Christian audience who would pay to see his film, but ironically, his atheistic approach to the Bible offers a powerful means of making the stories seem historically plausible for those in the audience who may be skeptics. As we shall explore in the next chapter, seeing a physical recreation of an historic-seeming Ark can be a powerful means for people to understand biblical events as historically plausible and meaningful for their own lives.

There is much more to this scene than Dunne's approach to miracles. Here the filmmaker offers a compelling reading of the Ark through David's soliloquy. The king ruminates on how objects carry the memory of the past but cannot recount those memories directly. The Ark offers a physical connection between David's Israel and the Israel of Moses. Moses, Aaron, Joshua, and other key figures in Israel's past have been in the presence of the Ark, and when David is near it, he can feel that presence. For David, that is the true value of the Ark, the social connections it bears that span the generations. It can survive far longer than a human lifespan. It links David to historical figures, but the link is limited because the Ark is only an object; it cannot communicate. As we shall see in the next chapter, objects mediate identities and memories in a complex fashion, just as suggested by David here.

The Ark's function as a means of communicating with God offers a solution to the awkward cinematic problem of providing exposition without seeming to do so. In *David and Bathsheba*, the Ark is used as a physical

138   READERS OF THE LOST ARK

object that is the focus of David's prayers, something that Gregory Peck can speak to onscreen. Dramatically this works well, as it conveys information that should be an interior monologue. David offers a soliloquy in the form of a prayer, where he expresses his despair at being the cause of Israel's current troubles. At this stage in the film, the kingdom is experiencing a major drought and the people are suffering because God is punishing all of them for David's moral failings. The king expresses his sorrow to the Ark, listing his sins, which are far less than those of David in the books of Samuel. David confesses: "I have been a faithless shepherd. I am dust in the sight of thine eyes. I am less than the meanest creature crawling on the earth. And yet, O God, I am also thy creation." David, in his state of despair and repentance, reaches out to touch the Ark, hoping to bring on his own death. As he does so, the lighting goes dark, and we hear a crash of thunder. The film switches to flashbacks of David's anointment by Samuel, his decision to fight Goliath, and the battle with the Philistine. Rather than David dying from touching the Ark, these memories coursing into his mind help him find clarity. Rain starts to fall outside, signaling the end of the drought that is beleaguering the kingdom, and so David believes that his act of repentance has worked. Again though, Dunne has written the scene purposefully so that audiences can decide for themselves if this is miracle or coincidence. David's prayer to the Ark is the dramatic conclusion to this film, where David gains redemption for himself and saves the kingdom of Israel.

David's redemption at the end of *David and Bathsheba* was a redemption that audiences of 1950s America could relate to. A similar relatability is much of the reason for the success of *Raiders of the Lost Ark*, where despite his seemingly superhuman action skills, Indy offers a character that viewers can see the best parts of themselves in or characteristics that they would like to emulate. Viewers like to imagine themselves as Indy, and this is readily apparent in the fan culture that surrounds the film. On every archaeological excavation that involves inexperienced volunteers, there is one poor soul who shows up with a brown fur felt fedora, thinking that it will be the right choice for doing heavy manual labor in oppressive heat. Well, I shouldn't say every excavation—I explicitly forbid my students from doing so in information sessions leading up to our field schools, promising them that they will earn an automatic "F" as a grade if they show up with a fedora, a brown leather jacket, or, especially, a bullwhip. Indiana Jones costumes are tremendously common, and at least a few "Indys" can be seen at any comic convention across North America or Europe. My hypocrisy is apparent in my

THE ARK OF INDIANA JONES AND OTHER CINEMATIC ARKS   139

chastising of students for dressing like Indy on an excavation, since I use this as my back-up "phoning it in" Halloween costume (when I don't have time to come up with something interesting). For those people who really love Indiana Jones, such embodied experiences are part of the fan culture, perhaps just as much as watching the films over and over again. These embodied experiences, fan cultures, and manufacturing of new Arks are the subject of the next chapter.

7

Toys and Teaching Tools

Models of the Ark in Communities of Faith and Fandom

Modern-day Jerusalem is filled with Arks, just probably not the one that used to be in the Temple. I went searching for some of these Arks in the Old City and knew exactly where to find them, at the shop of a friend of mine, a shop I've been visiting off and on since 1994. My colleague Shawn went with me, always happy to visit this store, and having visited it much more consistently over the years than I have. She has a much better sense of direction than I do and navigated us through the labyrinthine streets jammed with hurrying people, avoiding the occasional shockingly speeding motorcycle, while shopkeepers tried to get our attention, asking us where we are from and imploring us to look at their wares. The smells of spices and sweat permeate these parts of the Old City and the various bored-looking IDF officers stationed throughout suggest that there is an edge here that is atypical of other tourist destinations.

We stepped into Shop #14 on Christian Quarter Road. Unusually the shop was empty, even of shopkeepers. The décor of Shop #14 is a little different than the other stores in the Old City. While it has the same kinds of souvenirs for sale, it is not designed with the orientalist trappings that make tourists feel as though they are having an exotic encounter. There is even a sign stating that there is no haggling; all the prices are fixed and fair. That is perhaps one of the reasons that the rest of the décor is so different: most of the shop is filled with pennants from universities in the United States and Canada. We found the pennant from the University of Lethbridge, where Shawn had signed her name. And we found one from the University of Rhode Island, signed by our friend Will Krieger who had been coming to Shop #14 as long as I had been. This is the shop to which most of the North American archaeological field schools bring their students. Partially this is because of the set prices, but it is also because of the shopkeepers, who really look after the students and are completely trustworthy. And if they don't have something the students want, they help them get it from another store for an appropriate price.

Readers of the Lost Ark. Kevin M. McGeough, Oxford University Press. © Oxford University Press 2025.
DOI: 10.1093/9780197653913.003.0008

After spotting the pennants, we heard a surprised "hello." An older man with a big smile walked in, immediately shaking Shawn's hand and welcoming her back. This was Shaban. He hadn't noticed us come in at first, and Shawn was appearing a bit later in the season than usual. This was August and most of the North American field schools wrap up in July. Omar, who has taken over most of the day-to-day duties of running the shop, walked in and also greeted us warmly. Soon we were all discussing what our lives had been like through COVID-19, how the Old City had fared, and the differences between Israeli and Canadian responses to the pandemic. Shaban passed around Turkish coffee and then retired to a chair outside of the shop, while we continued chatting with Omar. While we know Shaban and Omar well, their treatment of us is not atypical of the Old City and Palestinian hospitality in general. There is often a frantic effort to get you into the store, but once you are in, you are seated and given coffee or tea to drink, and suddenly selling you something seems to be of no interest at all. It makes shopping in the Old City fun and more social than a typical souvenir shopping venture.

It was Shawn who first broached the topic of the Ark with Omar, saying that I was writing a book on it and that we had come to see their Arks. These were in a back corner of the second part of their shop (#19), across the street (Figure 7.1). Omar told me to spend as much time with the Arks as I liked, and he pointed out the one that he said was the most realistic. To my mind, he was correct. There were a number of miniature and not-so miniature Arks, fashioned to varying degrees of accuracy from the biblical description. Most were covered in a sheen of dust, suggesting that these are less popular items for sale than the t-shirts, silk scarves, inlaid wooden boxes, and chess sets elsewhere in the store. Still, I took them down to look more closely.

I inspected the one that Omar had chosen as the most visually realistic first. The base is imitation copper with a felt sticker on the bottom, with the label "Ark of the Covenant." Attached to this base is the die-cast Ark, painted a golden color, with the staves cast directly to the piece. Various tiny details add texture and design flourishes to the Ark. The mercy seat bears a circular pattern and a rosette in the interior. The cherubim spread their wings inward, following the biblical description, and while it is difficult to tell, the cherubim themselves seem to be the torsos of human-like figures clasping their hands in a gesture of prayer. To my surprise, however, the mercy seat and cherubim slid off, revealing that the Ark was designed to contain small things. I'm not sure what could fit, perhaps pills or stamps. A mirror in the bottom reflected my own scrutinizing expression back at me. I was drawn

Figure 7.1 Miniature Arks on the shelf of Shaban's shop in Jerusalem

to this particular one, and I decided that I'd purchase one for myself. I could justify it for research purposes, for science, even though I knew my wife will roll her eyes with annoyance at more junk to clutter up the house.

Similar renderings of the Ark were available in different sizes. The larger the model, the more care was put into the details, with the largest being close to half a meter in length. What was surprising to me were how many Ark "scenes" there were. These featured die-cast Levites and musicians carrying the Ark in some kind of procession, perhaps into battle, but since the figures seem more joyous and some hold musical instruments, they more likely depict the Ark's installation in Jerusalem. The turbans worn by the Levites and the sashes wrapped around their wastes add an orientalist flavor to the piece. All of these different types of Arks seem to be made of interchangeable pieces.

My archaeological urge upon closely examining these and other examples of souvenir Arks was to sort them into typological groups. This kind of thinking becomes hard-wired for archaeologists. The first kind of categorization that occurred to me was a functional one. What was somebody supposed to do with these Arks? Some functioned as a kind of container, like the one I had purchased. Yet some were dioramas, live-action scenes of the Ark in motion, suggesting another category of use. After dividing them by use, the second step in my classification was according to morphology, that is to say, based on the shape of the objects. The first class, the container category, shows a relatively standard morphology, with variation seemingly related to size. The second category, the procession scene, shows significant stylistic variations and could be categorized into much more discreet groupings. Each, however, shows orientalizing male figures bearing the Ark, its staves on their shoulders, with variable numbers of musicians in front. Now, for any archaeologists reading this, the logic I am using will be familiar but also likely induce disagreements about the appropriateness of the groupings. Some, for example, may start with material or color. Regardless, it is really hard for archaeologists to *not* think like this after a certain point in their careers.

I don't think the typological categorization gets us too far in this case. More important is to figure out what meanings these commodified and endlessly reproduced Arks hold. Why did even I buy one, someone who at this point should be relatively jaded about such items? Maybe it helps to start thinking about what I will do with mine. I wondered if my then seven-year-old daughter would just decide that it is hers. She loves little boxes like this, and so I thought that she may just take it away and put it with all of her other small boxes. She didn't take it. Instead, she made a bunch of paper ghosts to put inside, like those that come out of the Ark at the end of *Raiders of the Lost Ark*. Since my daughter didn't confiscate it, perhaps it will now just collect dust on my desk at the university. Perhaps it will act as a conversation piece with students who have awkwardly come to talk to me in my office hours but don't know what to say. It may signal certain elements about me that articulate my identity in different ways. Perhaps it will act as an excuse for me to tell people about this book that I have written. I imagine that students will want to talk to me about Indiana Jones when they see this and that it will signal my Indiana Jones fandom. It may also lead to conversations about where I purchased it.

Do We Control Our Objects or Do They Control Us?

Most purchasers, I would imagine, treat these as travel souvenirs— as material evidence of a visit to the Holy Land. The souvenir Ark helps make the ephemeral moment of travel have a durative power. Memories of a vacation remain more vivid through the assistance of a material reminder of the trip. Likewise, the object also helps tell the story of the travel event to others,

144 READERS OF THE LOST ARK

perhaps as a means of showcasing the expense of wealth that is necessary for such a trip or perhaps indicating the worldliness of the owner as a global traveler. Religious purchasers may also use the Ark to signal the piety of their voyage, showing that they had engaged in a pilgrimage. In these cases, the Ark symbolizes Jerusalem as a religious destination and certifies that the owner was there. The famous French theorist of objects, Jean Baudrillard, has shown that what collectors collect is themselves. The Ark objects likely evoke something comforting or satisfying in the individual, whether it is something specific to the Bible, *Raiders of the Lost Ark*, or the constellation of tropes to which the Indiana Jones films or scripture make reference.

These kinds of articulations of identity are studies in a branch of anthropology called "thing theory." This vaguely named theory is an approach that looks to see how people's lives are mediated by objects. Objects, in this kind of theory, become "things" when they are seen to assert their own agency. Now, throughout this book we have discussed different instances when the Ark of the Covenant has seemed to assert its own agency. Biblical instances of people dying from touching it or the Ark helping to knock down the walls of Jericho are all examples of this. Yet imagining such agency in modern times might seem like insanity and often my students are completely puzzled when we first start talking about thing theory. But we are not really talking about objects in an anthropomorphized sense here. We are talking about the pull they have on people and how they seem to be more active participants in our lives than they might first appear. Think of all the explorers of the Ark who were drawn to search for it. The imagined "thinginess" of the Ark has led people to change careers and sometimes literally risk their lives, even starting actual riots in Jerusalem. These souvenirs can also be compelling in this fashion, but not enough to cause riots. Something about them compels a person to purchase them. I am particularly susceptible to such object agency. I would say that the Ark I purchased drew me to it, much in the same way that vinyl records compel me to search for them and find them in dusty record stores, to bring back to my house and listen to once. My wife doesn't subscribe to my arguments about thing theory and the records having agency over me. She thinks I make my own choices and just make bad ones (because I don't need yet another version of *Sgt. Pepper's Lonely Hearts Club Band*).

A particular trait of these Arks and similar objects, especially those that we would deem tourist souvenirs, is that they are miniatures of something else. Think of the travel souvenirs you may have collected or may have seen. A miniature Eiffel Tower key chain? A small version of Mount Rushmore in a snow globe? On one level it makes sense that these are miniature. You can't bring Teddy Roosevelt's gigantic stone face home to display in your living room, can you? Yet in an important work, Susan Stewart argued that there is more to the miniature than just the practicality of being able to take it home. Things that are very small come to reflect "interiority"—that is, the interior life of the individual who possesses them. It helps transform something that is intended for public consumption into something that is private and personal. It helps an individual integrate that place (Paris, Mount Rushmore) into their own psyche. The small size of the object elicits this response more powerfully than larger things. Perhaps that is why the large Arks in Shaban's shop do not sell as well as the smaller ones.

Now, some of you may be convinced by this and see uncomfortable parallels in your own lives. Others may be scoffing, thinking that this is just junk that shopkeepers are trying to sell you. Commodification has become an important part of the tourist industry. And while we know that pilgrims often brought back souvenirs from their visits to the Holy Land, the scale of this has transformed immensely with the advent of industrial capitalism. It is part of what you do on your holiday. You buy things. These things were objects, mass produced in factories usually nowhere near the place where you were traveling. They are shipped unceremoniously in large cartons and then unpacked in shops that are part of the destination of the traveler. The tourist feels as though they are engaging directly with the local culture and acquiring objects to concretize that moment. But they are also participating in the same kind of global economics as they do at home.

Now, some might take these commodified forms of the Ark as tacky, as items that take away from the deeply held religious meaning of the "real" Ark (even if these tangible objects are actually more "real" than an Ark that hasn't been seen in thousands of years). The influential art historian Walter Benjamin argued something similar about art, an argument that may be equally applicable to religious items. For him, the commodified and mechanical reproduction of pieces of art took away from their impact. Think about the *Mona Lisa*, a painting that has been endlessly copied and remade into other products—coffee mugs, neckties, lapel pins, and now even facemasks in response to COVID-19. Does this relentless reproduction of the image diminish the power of the original painting? The bored faces of the tourists viewing the *Mona Lisa* suggest that this is the case. What about the Ark? Here it probably depends to some degree on the religious tradition of the purchaser. Some religious traditions use these objects as means of concentrating

146 READERS OF THE LOST ARK

one's faith, on helping the religious message gain that kind of interiority Susan Stewart discusses. For some, such images may be sacrilegious. For secular purchasers, and especially Indiana Jones fans, it may just be something that goes on the shelf of the collection.

Merchandising Indy's Ark

So how did Ark souvenirs become entangled with Indiana Jones merchandising? In the previous chapter I brought up the relationship between *Star Wars* and Indiana Jones, as both are Lucasfilm properties. George Lucas's commercial genius came to the fore when he negotiated with the studio that released *Star Wars* in 1977 that he would keep the merchandising rights for the film he wrote and directed. This was an atypical deal, as usually directors did not retain as much of the intellectual rights to their creations as Lucas did. Before *Star Wars* though, merchandising was only a minor part of the financial returns from a film. *Star Wars* changed that. People wanted toys, posters, comics, and clothing, anything that materially manifests *Star Wars*. Since Indiana Jones was also a Lucasfilm production, the merchandising efforts were similar but did not succeed to nearly the extent that *Star Wars* did. Now, what is perhaps the most common "reception" of the Ark is as it is depicted in one of the theatrical posters for the film originally displayed in theaters (Figure 7.2), and now displayed in basements throughout Europe and North America.

Indiana Jones action figures were made and continue to be made when new films are released, but these are never overly popular, other than in the initial mad scramble of collector purchasing. Various Ark action figures have been produced over the years, but I think that most ended up as collector's fetish items rather than as toys played with in earnest by children (Figure 7.3). The Ark of the Covenant and the Idol of the Chachapoyans (the golden idol Indy loses at the beginning of *Raiders*) are sometimes included as collectible items. These toy Arks are almost always visually faithful to the depiction of the Ark from the film, although the scale in relation to the action figures is inconsistent.

Why do these toys matter? *Star Wars* toys were one of the most important media forms through which the movie was experienced in the 1970s and early 1980s. As numerous media scholars have pointed out, in the long wait between the release of the three original *Star Wars* films, and especially

TOYS AND TEACHING TOOLS 147

Figure 7.2 This well-used VHS copy of *Raiders of the Lost Ark* bears on its cover the US theatrical re-release poster painted by Richard Amsel in 1982, the same image as the poster on my wall and the walls of countless other archaeologists. This is likely the most reproduced image of the Ark in circulation today.

Figure 7.3 Toy Indiana Jones and Ark from the Disney Collectible set, released in 2010

before home video was affordable, toys became one of the key ways through which children experienced the *Star Wars* universe. They were able to play with figurines of the main and peripheral characters, either expanding the adventures of well-articulated characters like Han Solo or figuring out the back story of aliens who appear only in passing in one scene. Jonathan Gray goes so far as to say that children came to be the ones in charge of the narrative. They exercised a kind of control over the toys that children do not feel that they experience in their own lives. Playing with these figurines and vehicles helped build the fantasy for children, facilitating their imaginative explorations. The toys made the *Star Wars* world inhabitable for children. This was a world, that through play, they could actually travel to and become part of.

Unlike *Star Wars* figures, where playing with them was ubiquitous for a generation of North American and European boys, Indiana Jones action figures were never common children's toys. The fact that the original Kenner line of toys produced around the release of *Raiders of the Lost Ark* was so limited has meant that these now fetch very high prices on the collector market.

TOYS AND TEACHING TOOLS 149

Reproductions were released in 2023 so that people like me, who never had them as children, could finally own these figurines. This suggests something interesting is going on with these collecting activities that is different from *Star Wars* collectors. People are not purchasing Indy action figures for a nostalgia that directly reflects childhood activities. Rather, they are participating in a kind of nostalgic purchasing that suggests a wished-for nostalgia, connecting them to a franchise like *Star Wars* collectors do, in a way that they might have connected to *Star Wars* as children. Now, however, they are articulating a relationship with a different franchise that bears different connotations. The collecting of such toys reflects both a reference to childhood but also a kind of engagement that was not part of one's childhood. The toys might still make the Indiana Jones world inhabitable in the same way that the *Star Wars* toys did, but for adults. They also reflect a nostalgic evocation of how *Star Wars* toys made that world accessible to them as children, and these feelings are now transferred to Indiana Jones.

Perhaps the impulse to collect Indiana Jones toys is related to the playacting of Indy by adults. That playacting sometimes manifests as the collecting of souvenir versions of the artifacts that Indy himself sought. That collectors would collect replicas of the things that their hero, a famous collector, collected has a kind of obvious symmetry to it. Fans want to possess what Indy sought. They want to possess it so that they can feel like Indy collecting artifacts. They want to impress other fans with their successes as collectors. And they want to display their fan culture as parts of their identity through these material forms. Within this fandom is a particular subgroup who makes their own artifacts and many homemade Arks of the Covenant are proudly displayed in fan circles. Almost always, these are objects that are meant to look like the Ark in the film and they are judged by other fans based on their fidelity to the film version, not to the biblical description (which is largely irrelevant).

Why do these Indiana Jones fans want these things? The easiest answer is that the collecting of these movie items offers a compelling blend of nostalgia and identity articulation. Lincoln Geraghty, in his studies of film and television souvenir collecting, has argued that these movie souvenirs reflect the possessor's engagement with the particular film, entangling their own life story with these films. Because movies can be watched repeatedly, the experience of a film does not have to be ephemeral. Having these things showcases the collector's relationship to the film and/or the character of Indiana Jones, and fan culture provides a forum to display this relationship and negotiate it

150 READERS OF THE LOST ARK

with others who have a similar relationship. For many of these fan-collectors, including the Indiana Jones fans, the collecting of merchandise becomes of greater interest than the original films. These kinds of movie memorabilia are called paratexts by media scholars, items produced in relation to other media. For many types of cinematic consumption, and *Raiders of the Lost Ark* certainly falls into this category, engagement with paratexts can become more important than watching and rewatching the original movie(s). Relationships between collectors are mediated through the exchange of such souvenirs, and even if these relationships are only temporary, the exclusivity of the collecting venture of a specific film ties these people into a larger community. Engaging with Indiana Jones paratexts is not an activity that only occurs in isolation; for many fans, the communal nature of the engagement is central. It is not just about finding a new Ark toy. It is about sharing with other collectors what has been found. On one fan site on Facebook, there is a steady stream of people posting pictures of their Indiana Jones film Blu-Ray cases. Presumably most people who are active on the site own physical copies of the movies, and so these images do not provide any novel information for collectors. Rather it points to the need for such posting, for mediating the relationship one has to the rest of the fan community through the display of objects.

The collecting of Indiana Jones toys, Indiana Jones cosplay, and other activities as mediated through these paratexts allows fans to expand their engagement with the franchise beyond the films themselves. These other activities allow fans to imagine and create new meanings, expanding the original universe of the films, and not remaining bound to the visions of the original media producers. Engagement like this facilitates the elaboration of a larger world beyond that of the original film. Paratextual engagements can even be places of resistance to the media producer. Indiana Jones fan communities often support and expect quite significant criticism of two of the films, *Indiana Jones and the Temple of Doom* and *Indiana Jones and the Kingdom of the Crystal Skull*. The reactions to *Dial of Destiny* are more mixed. The disdain displayed by avid fans toward these films shows that fandom does not necessarily require one to like the original media form. The level of active resentment fans display toward the original films is striking but in no way unusual for fan culture.

The Ark is a minor component of this fan culture, but, in some ways, this is perhaps now one of the most common receptions of the Ark. Here it is not a biblical reception but a cinematic paratextual reception. Take for example a souvenir coin minted by IconCoins.com called "The Lost Ark of the Covenant." There is no explicit mention of Indiana Jones, but the font, bullwhip, and fedora on one side of the coin make the connection clear. The other side of the coin depicts the Ark from the film, as well as a mixture of other symbols, some referencing *Raiders* and some more biblically oriented. The Ark in collectibles like these does not really reference the Bible though, even when something like the tablets of the Ten Commandments is shown in relation. Rather, the Ark is emblematic of wished-for traits of the Indiana Jones collector, who, just as Indy collects antiquities, now has collected something in imitation of what that heroic figure sought. The Ark becomes a proxy for the collector's wished-for masculinity, adventurousness, and intellectual relationship to the past. Indy fans tend to reject the colonialist implications of Indiana Jones, but these impulses also likely lurk beneath the urge to collect these Arks.

These "fan Arks" neither really reference the Bible nor the more archaeological meanings of other Indiana Jones merchandise. The Ark in these contexts references cinema nostalgia, 1980s popular culture, geek fandom, and any number of possible things completely unimaginable by the biblical writers who originally described the Ark. Whatever it is that motivates collectors at an individual level, there is now a curious overlap of communities interested in Ark of the Covenant replicas. Some Indiana Jones fans will buy little model Arks and pay a premium for officially licensed ones. These increase in value depending on rarity. For example, an officially licensed Ark of the Covenant business card holder, made by Gentle Giant, now goes for over $450 on e-Bay. This kind of interest feels religious, as does the fervor of the collectors who post in Indy fan forums. But there are also more traditional religiously motivated individuals who want miniature Arks of the Covenant and will buy the unlicensed, cheaper versions of these Arks. Perhaps more surprising, but more explicitly religious, are the giant replica Arks that become the focus of spiritual devotion in new Christian movements.

Arks for Religious Devotion

In March 2013, a Filipina woman named Grace Gupana gifted the city of Jerusalem a gigantic Ark of the Covenant. A devoted Christian, Gupana is a businessperson who made her fortune selling homeopathic products. Subsequently, she experienced a revelation, and now goes by the title Sister

152   READERS OF THE LOST ARK

Grace and claims to have her own church in the Philippines. She wanted to give a gift to the state of Israel and to all Christians, Jews, and Muslims. The gift was a physical representation of the Ark, but it was also the message that her Ark brought with it. It was not a message of peace, or unity, or interfaith dialogue that one might expect with a gift dedicated to all the "People of the Book" (the religions that have the Old Testament as their basis). The message was directed toward nonbelievers. For Gupana, it was the sheer size of the Ark that would make atheists, agnostics, and people of other traditions rethink their stance toward God. That, and she hoped that the Ark would make it into the *Guinness Book of Records*, in a highly specialized category of largest replica of historical religious object. Size does seem to matter to her, as she holds the record for largest flag (a giant Israeli flag unraveled at Masada that is the size of two football fields). She also claims to have made the longest drawing of the beasts of the book of Revelation, and a number of the largest screenings of people for blood type and various medical conditions (diabetes, blood pressure, and cholesterol).

In opposition to the impact of miniatures I discussed earlier, gigantic things have their own kind of charisma, drawing people to them as spectacles that stand outside of normative life. Why would I pull over to the side of the road to look at the world's largest nickel in Sudbury, Ontario, in northern Ontario? I don't really know why. It was something to do to break up a really long drive, but it also carries with it a kind of charisma that is otherwise lacking in Sudbury. Now Jerusalem is not lacking in charisma or in spectacles to be visited, but the same impulses may have been at work in the creation of this Ark. Clearly Gupana is enraptured by scale and size, and there are likely personal psychological motivations that could be unpacked here. More generally though, her argument that the size of the Ark will convince nonbelievers is not as bizarre as it may seem. Now, is it likely that a dedicated atheist seeing such a large Ark will suddenly embrace religion? Likely the opposite will happen; it's hard to imagine that such rhetoric would work for someone who is not a member of the faith community. But for believers, the situation is different. Seeing that an object associated with God's miracles can actually be built, become a "thing," solidifies beliefs that events mentioned in the Bible could have happened. Add to that the spectacle of the object, in this case its size, and the giant Ark can seem to reflect the reality of God's miracles on earth. We have talked about this in the previous chapter, the "false syllogism" that the ability to replicate something can stand as proof of its historicity. Like seeing miracles on film, seeing giant

TOYS AND TEACHING TOOLS 153

versions of ancient things can convince some that the events of the Bible were historical.

Gupana's Jerusalem Ark was massive—almost 800 kg in weight and 3 m tall, 5 m long, and 1.6 m wide. It was mostly wood with the long poles made of iron and cherubim made of stone, all painted in gold. It is not only the size which differed from the description of the Ark in Exodus 25. Running along the side of the Ark, just below the mercy seat, the artists inscribed the words of the Shema, one of the main prayers in Judaism ("Hear, O Israel, YHWH is our God, YHWH is one"). Two "stone tablets" are attached to the side. One is labeled "Yahweh's Covenant The Ten Commandments" and then lists the commandments below. The other is more unusual, labeled "Yahwehs (sic) Ordained Festivals Honor and Keep." What follows are a list of Old Testament and Jewish holidays, sometimes bearing a scriptural reference to where they are mentioned in the Bible. Gupana's artistic vision inspired these design choices, but it took twelve artists to manufacture this.

Mirroring, likely purposefully, the story in Samuel, Gupana's Ark resided in a tent at first, made of large white sheets of fabric. One room was devoted just to the Ark. Another had benches surrounding a chest that said "Kingdom of Jerusalem." Then, in a modernized version of David's procession, on Jerusalem Day in May 2013 (the holiday celebrating the reunification of Jerusalem after the Six-Day War), she conveyed the Ark by truck to the front of the Israeli Supreme Court. The site reflects David's procession of the Ark to the seat of governance in Jerusalem but also reflects her message of the Decalogue standing as a foundational legal guideline. It was then moved to IDF Square/Kikar Tzahal (formerly Allenby Square), near the Old City. It was there that the Ark met its demise. In May 2017, early one Shabbat morning, vandals destroyed the Ark. Reports held that police watched the vandalism but did not stop it. However, they did arrest one individual, a Haredi-Jew. The vandalism was not atypical of the responses of some Haredi community members to perceived sacrilegious behavior. Gupana responded as one might expect, with sadness over the vandalism, commenting that "the punishment of those who destroyed the model of the Ark of the Covenant will come from God." That the vandals were Jewish led her to state: "My pain and sorrow are very great today, and the Jewish people, on the day of the giving of the Torah, must respect the believers of all religions."

The Jerusalem Ark was not the only such Ark given by Gupana, just the largest. She claims to have made seven, one for each continent, spending millions of dollars. While the size of the Ark is part of her message, each

154   READERS OF THE LOST ARK

context also provides different readings. Her gift to the Apostles of Jesus Shrine in Karen, Kenya, was not quite so large and not as explicitly aimed at nonbelievers. As she consecrated the Ark at a ceremony in Kenya, Gupana stated: "today, the Jubilee land was receiving the Horn of the Ram. . . . Any accusations and any words of killing are now gone because we will restore your land." Here the Ark is to function as a kind of protective device and as we shall see in the next chapter, this is not uncommon in African traditions of the Ark.

A smaller Ark is located within her so- called Ten Commandments Building in Baguio City in her home country of the Philippines. The building itself, Gupana claims, holds the world record for the largest replica of the Ten Commandments, a plausible claim since two sides of the A-shaped building are flanked by 12- m- high, vaguely tablet- shaped walls, inscribed with the commandments, five on each side. Within this unusual building is an altar, a replica of the Ark, various international flags, and a banner bearing much of the information found on the sides of her replica arks elsewhere.

Gupana's Arks are not the only Arks that serve as devotional pieces for contemporary Christians. In October 2019, the Universal Church of the Kingdom of God (UCKG) announced a "Day of Victory," when the Ark of the Covenant was brought to Toronto, Canada. There is no mention that this is a replica, or a metaphor. Rather, the website proclaimed that the Church "is pleased to receive the Ark of the Covenant straight from the Temple of Solomon." This Temple of Solomon is not located in Jerusalem, however; it is in São Paolo, Brazil. It was built as a replica of the Temple of Solomon, but unlike the Iron Age temple, worshippers on a massive scale (at least 10,000) are welcomed into the precinct. The interior of Solomon's Temple was re- stricted to only a priestly elite. The Brazilian complex is enormous, with hel- icopter landing pads and residences for church officials, certainly on a scale much larger than the Jerusalem Temple. Despite the Evangelical Christian orientation of the church, the Temple of Solomon is decorated with Jewish motifs. The Holy of Holies, however, is not where the replica Ark is kept but rather the location where the conveyer belts transport offerings directly from congregants and visitors. Those interested in the more historical Temple of Solomon can visit the attached museum.

Sadly, I missed the arrival of the Ark of the Covenant in Toronto. The ar- rival of the Ark was, however, recorded and preserved on YouTube. It is a fairly typical Evangelical event service, presided over by Bishop Joshua, who has a very large following on social media. The Ark is first mentioned when

Bishop Joshua brings new attendees up on stage. One of these new attendees is from a "Hindu family," and the man wears a track suit and bears a bindi on his forehead, a sign of his "otherness" for the congregation (even though he is clearly already a believer as becomes obvious as the service unfolds). As Bishop Joshua explains, the miracles about to be performed are universal, not limited to Christians. He explains: "The Ark of the Covenant is God Himself and God is not a religion. God is not a church. . . . He brought Himself here to reveal Himself to you. . . . The Ark of the Covenant is the presence of God." Bishop Joshua explains that there is only one way for him to prove this to the attendees: "if they receive a miracle."

As the time nears that the Ark will be brought out, Bishop Joshua makes it more clear how the blessings of the Ark will work. He explains that it will bring: "the blessing of God to your finances, to your family, to your health, to your career, to your love life, to your salvation." He asks the congregants: "Do you believe in it?" The crowd responds in the affirmative. Bishop Joshua asks those who believe to stand and then explains that they are about to welcome the Ark. He prays to God, asking Him to go in front of and behind the Ark, to give blessings to all the participants (as already described). And then he says: "In the name of Jesus, let us welcome the Ark of the Covenant." Then the Ark is brought in. It is carried by four priests in white vestments, bearing it with the staves as described in the Bible (Figure 7.4). Unlike the biblical accounts, armored security walk behind the Ark, dressed in generic security uniforms. One man walks in front, dressed in ritual clothing meant to imitate the High Priest of Jerusalem that looks much like the outfit Belloq wears in *Raiders of the Lost Ark*. Trumpets sound as the Ark enters the performance space. The Ark itself seems much like that described in the Bible, with similar proportions and features. The cherubim are human-shaped figures with wings pointing toward the center. Other details are consistent with typical academic takes on the Ark, except perhaps what may be tiny stars of David all along the upper edges. It looks bright and new, shiny and gold.

My initial reaction is that these congregants are not Old Testament readers, since those near the Ark stretch out their hands to touch it, clearly unafraid to meet the fate that Uzzah did. Bishop Joshua proclaims that they should: "spread out your hands to the Ark—all your hands please." To be fair, no one actually touches the Ark. It is brought on stage and set on a table covered with a cloth, ready for the service. As it is placed, Bishop Joshua points to the audience and proclaims blessings upon them. All of the priests follow, facing the audience and thrusting their arms out toward them, forcing the

Figure 7.4 The priests in linen bring in the Ark. Note the priest in Levitical attire in the background. Digital enlargement from video uploaded to YouTube (https://www.youtube.com/watch?v=ORU5QtUDXGI)

power of the Ark onto those who have gathered there. In typical faith healer fashion, Bishop Joshua tells the audience to close their eyes and put their hands on their site of bodily illness, where that "infirmity will disappear in the name of the Lord Jesus Christ." He then starts a "call and response" moment, where the audience calls for healings and blessings. He then asks the audience who was healed simply by the arrival of the Ark, and while we can only see a small segment of the audience on the video, presumably many raised their hands.

The service goes on much as is typical of these kinds of traveling faith healing shows, with music, testimonials, scriptural exegesis, video presentations mixing travel footage with biblical reenactment, and inspirational sermons. The Ark, which was what brought the audience, plays a part in the conclusion of the events as Bishop Joshua explains that it will next travel to the United States, and from there, "another country and another country." Referencing Exodus 13:20–22, Bishop Joshua describes this Ark as a pillar of cloud by day and a pillar of fire by night, through which God leads the way for each community that experiences it. This pillar of fire led the Israelites before the Ark was built, but that does not matter here. Bishop Joshua ends the service with his arms raised above the Ark, offering a blessing to the crowd and stating that "the Lord is the Ark." Then, for the video presentation, as inspirational music plays, his image fades out and is replaced by "before and after" pictures of people who have been healed by the Ark.

Toronto was not the only city to welcome a visit from Bishop Joshua and the Ark. Indeed, videos like this can be seen for many locations, with different versions tailored to different communities. The recording of the Ark's visit to Texas features an historical discussion of Solomon's Temple, using the São Paolo Temple as a visual referent. It shows the priests transporting the Ark on what looks like a fire truck with flashing lights above and an escort of black cars following behind. The Ark is covered with the expected blanket, and the priests pray above it before the convoy begins its transit. Unlike Toronto, when the Ark lands in Houston, it gets a full entourage to parade it from the airport to the church. Toronto traffic makes for difficult parades, but this kind of spectacle seems more suitable for Texans than Ontarians.

Such services are not unusual in twenty- first- century Evangelical Christianity. The Ark could be substituted for any number of holy items or relics as a focus of devotion. It works in these contexts because it is recognizable by community members who will associate it with a divine power. Evangelical theologies emphasize both an individual experience of the divine and the importance of missionary works in relation to those experiences, both emphasized in these Ark encounters. The powers of the Ark as described in scripture are vague enough for individuals to have personal experiences that are different from the experiences of others, without this contradicting scripture. The Ark provides a focus of devotion that is distinct from the charisma of the church leader. The Ark is safe as an object of veneration from a Protestant perspective that would normally look scornfully upon such object interactions as being Catholic or idolatrous.

More nondenominational physical recreations of the Ark can be found in biblically oriented museums and amusement centers created for different reasons. The BibleWalk wax museum and dinner theater in Mansfield, Ohio, features what their website describes as "our award-winning, custom-made replica of the Ark of the Covenant." Located in its "Miracles of the Old Testament" display, the replica is found among different wax scenes from the Old Testament. Located on the grounds of a Methodist church, the Diamond Hill Cathedral, the wax museum was created after the pastor and his wife visited a more secular wax museum in Atlanta. It was not completely secular though, since it culminated in a scene of the Last Supper. The Old Testament

158   READERS OF THE LOST ARK

walk is just one of the options for visitors; others include scenes from the New Testament, the Reformation, the history of martyrdom, and one that explains how the visitor can gain access to the kingdom of God. There is also a collection of four hundred woodcarvings, some of which are biblical, but others are of pets and wildlife. There is also a dinner theater, featuring a show named "Dining with Grace."

The Ark is marketed as one of the highlights and is the climax of the Old Testament walk. The scene is relatively simple. The Ark sits in a burgundy curtained space, with only the Jewish High Priest (wearing what looks like a chef's hat) posed beside it. The Ark itself is different from many of these object renderings already discussed. It is simpler, with little detail in its ornamentation, and very short poles with which the Ark would be carried. What is most striking is the depiction of the cherubim, here capturing all the literal details given in the Bible but completely aniconic, neither referencing sphinxes nor angels. The booming narrator's voice reads out the passages from Exodus 25 and 28, but once it gets to Hebrews 9, the curtain behind the Ark opens, revealing a crucified Jesus. Thus, the Ark is used to show how all of these important moments from the Old Testament culminate in Jesus.

The BibleWalk Museum is less unique than it might first appear to those unfamiliar with religious-based theme parks and museums. There are many such exhibits found throughout North America, running from minor, amateurish displays usually pushing Creationist agendas, to the massive Museum of the Bible located in Washington, DC, funded by the owners of HobbyLobby and raising the ire of archaeologists for its penchant for purchasing illegally looted antiquities. The relative frequency of these exhibits points to the importance of object-oriented teaching in North American Protestantism, a type of teaching that emphasizes a physical experience of the Bible much as North American Protestant theology often emphasizes a personal experience of God. An Anabaptist version of the Ark can be visited at the Mennonite Life Visitors Center in Lancaster, Pennsylvania, at the Biblical Tabernacle Experience. In Collinsville Mississippi, tourists can follow Pastor Bill Freeman, dressed in replica Israelite priestly garb, on the "Promised Land Journey," where a facsimile Tabernacle, Ark, and other items can be viewed in a building behind the aptly named Covenant Life Church.

So why have such experiences of the Ark and its associated buildings continued to appeal to North Americans for the past two hundred years or so? Such visits help people build their own personal relationships to the past. Through the physical experience of these biblical objects that they have

TOYS AND TEACHING TOOLS 159

heard about in church all of their lives, and the viewing of reconstructions of such objects, believers can have moving religious experiences. While none of these visitors will confuse these Arks for the real one, encountering a replica offers a comforting affirmation that such objects could have existed, and the illogic of a false syllogism goes unnoticed. And while these visitors are normally not going because they are experiencing a crisis in faith, a tangible experience of the Bible can be spiritually rewarding for members of these communities.

Reconstructions of the Ark, Solomon's Temple, and the Tabernacle all reflect hyperreal approaches to the past. Hyperreality is a concept that was coined by Jean Baudrillard but reflects thinking of scholars like Marshall McLuhan who investigate the relationships among media, consumerism, and perceptions of the world. Hyperreality is a situation where the representation of something becomes confused for the real thing. What is "fictional" or "replica" becomes confused with what is "factual" or "original." The participant in a hyperreal spectacle loses track of what is real and what isn't real. Sometimes that is part of the fun, like for visitors to Disneyland who can lose themselves in a fantasy form of community rooted in animation and Walt Disney's retrofuturism and American utopianism. Sometimes it is troubling, as we shall see in Chapter 9 in our exploration of pseudoarchaeology. Hyperreal presentations of the ancient world reflect efforts to create convincing embodied experiences of antiquity for modern consumers, not through the interaction with actual artifacts but through the engagement with convincing replicas. A physical, biblical Ark becomes a hyperreal spectacle, an exhibition through which the replica comes to stand in convincingly for the real and functions as evidence that the original was real.

Arguably the most politically provocative of these Ark reconstructions is one located in the Old City in Jerusalem. It is part of the display put on by the Temple Institute (*Machon HaMikdash*), which is an organization that aims to educate people about the Temple, with the long-term goal of regaining access to the Temple Mount and building a Third Jerusalem Temple. The organization was founded in 1987 by Rabbi Yisrael Ariel, who the organization's website proudly proclaims "served in the paratrooper brigade which liberated the Temple Mount in the Six Day War of 1967, and was one of the first soldiers to reach the Mount." Members of the Institute believe that Jews should not sit idly by, awaiting the arrival of the Messiah. Rather, they believe that they should pursue the return of the Temple to the Jews in order to actively participate in this important moment, and that God wishes them

160 READERS OF THE LOST ARK

to act. Now the institute hosts a visitor's center where tourists can see a scale model of the Second Temple and reconstructions of the various vessels used in both temples. The Ark of the Covenant replica sits behind a red curtain (*parochet*), decorated with golden Greek-style sphinxes, where the body is a bird and the heads are female with Hellenic hairstyles, one with long flowing hair and the other with hair tied up. The wings of the sphinxes curve over their heads, and the two face each other. The curtain retracts dramatically to reveal a golden Ark, with similar sphinx-style cherubim and simple geometric designs in different parts of the Ark. The staves, however, are set along the short sides of the Ark, facing out toward the viewer, with a length that has been shortened from that described in the Bible. It is impossible to imagine how this Ark could be carried, but the deviations from expectations make sense, given the space confines of a visitor's center in Jerusalem's Old City. A depiction of this Ark stands as the logo for the organization. Here the replica Ark, and the other replicas of Temple materials, are invoked to encourage the state of Israel to retake the Temple Mount. The Institute makes no effort to hide these overt intentions, although they do acknowledge that this may not happen for generations.

For most of these museums, however, the Ark makes for a good material representation of ancient Israel. These contemporary reconstructions of the Ark reflect very specific pan-regional movements in modern Christianity (especially American Protestantism) and Judaism. I feel like most of these Arks do not resemble the Ark that Indiana Jones chases, and while I cannot prove it, I think that it may be somewhat of a conscious choice by these artisans. They want an Ark that will be recognizable as such by the audience, but they do not want one that will evoke the film. They reflect a distinctly different tradition of the Ark. The souvenir Arks available in the Old City of Jerusalem try to evoke both the film and this more religious reception of the object. Yet there is another Christian tradition in which the Ark plays a central role, one utterly uninfluenced by Indiana Jones. The Ark is very important in the Christianity that has been practiced in Ethiopia for centuries. Not only do Ethiopian Christians believe that the Ark of the Covenant resides in their country, replicas of the Ark play a central role in every church in the nation. These Ethiopian Arks are the subject of the next chapter.

8

The Romance of Solomon and Sheba

Ethiopian Ark Traditions

I grew up reading Victorian and Edwardian adventure fiction, the kinds of books that were the precursors to Indiana Jones, filled with what we now see as imperialist propaganda, uncomfortable depictions of white saviors inserting themselves in the affairs of others depicted in a derogatory light. Stories by H. Rider Haggard and John Buchan filled my imagination with ideas of lost African kingdoms, bursting with treasure and magic. Haggard, through novels about his hero Alan Quatermain, channeled nineteenth-century ideas that the Phoenicians, Egyptians, and other Bible adjacent groups migrated deep into the heart of Africa, establishing colonies that explorers had yet to find. Rhodesian archaeologists used these theories to justify colonial rule in southern Africa; Haggard used these ideas to imagine ancient Near Eastern cultures still surviving into the present. Buchan relied on older, medieval traditions, of a powerful Christian kingdom in Africa, established by Prester John, a descendent of one of the magi who visited Jesus in the manger in Bethlehem. While the scholarship Haggard drew on has no historical justification (but rather reflects a legacy of European colonialism), Buchan's kingdom of Prester John is often thought to be based on European conceptions of medieval Ethiopia and the Christian kingdom centered there. That Christian kingdom, according to Ethiopian tradition, has its origins in biblical Israel, with its first emperor being a lost son of Solomon who brought the Ark from Jerusalem to Africa.

Many, if not most Ethiopians, believe that they know the current location of the Ark of the Covenant, and they know this with certainty. In Ethiopia, the Ark is not considered to be lost. It is, according to very old traditions, held in the Church of Our Lady Mary of Zion, in the city of Aksum in Tigray province. The church and complex have been destroyed, rebuilt, renovated, and reconstructed, and buildings have been added and removed for centuries. Tradition holds that while the Ark has occasionally been taken away into hiding in some periods of conflict, it has mostly remained in Tigray since

Readers of the Lost Ark. Kevin M. McGeough, Oxford University Press. © Oxford University Press 2025.
DOI: 10.1093/9780197653913.003.0009

162 READERS OF THE LOST ARK

ancient times, held in the same complex. The Church of Our Lady Mary of Zion that stands in this complex today dates from the sixteenth century. A chapel built in the 1950s held what Ethiopians believe is the Ark until 2014; now a newer chapel is its supposed home. The whole church complex stands on a massive, very ancient platform, suggestive that there was once a monumental structure on the site, certainly a building much larger than the current one.

The Ark is the central concern of this religious complex. As with the church at Kiryat Yearim, the Church of Our Lady Mary of Zion is dedicated to Mary as she (or her womb) represents the new Ark. Like the Ark carried the laws of the Old Testament, Mary carried Jesus, the Christian replacement for Mosaic law. Always near to the Ark in Aksum is a guardian, a male who is assigned this responsibility for life, although he is expected to choose a successor when he becomes too aged. A story goes that one person assigned to take care of the Ark fled to the hills when he found out, not wanting to be stuck in the church for the rest of his days. His colleagues tracked him down and forcibly made him take on his responsibilities. I have no idea whether this story is true, but it strikes me as a reasonable reaction to being assigned such a task.

Aksum is an important political site, and that importance predates the belief that the Ark resides there. Since the late Middle Ages, it has been where the emperors of Ethiopia are crowned. Located here is the "Throne of David," the stone seat where the emperor sits for his coronation, for this location and the Ark of the Covenant have been, as shall be explained, central to the legitimation of Ethiopian leadership. The current condition of the church is uncertain since 2020 when the civil war in the region intensified. There have been reports of massacres at the church, and at the time that I write this, the situation remains unstable.

Legend of the Queen of Sheba

So why would people think that the Ark of the Covenant would turn up in Ethiopia of all places, after going missing for about twenty- five hundred years? The reason is that the people of Ethiopia are heirs to a very old and charismatic tradition about the Ark. As we shall see in this chapter, the Christianity practiced in this part of Africa (through the Ethiopian Orthodox Tewahedo Church) is centered on the Ark of the Covenant. The Ark cannot

THE ROMANCE OF SOLOMON AND SHEBA 163

be separated from Ethiopian national history, the country's church architecture, religious objects, and festivals. Most academics do not believe that the original Ark of the Covenant is here, but Ethiopians and Rastafarians do, as do fans of the pseudoarchaeology writer Graham Hancock (discussed in Chapter 9), who has convinced his readership of this.

The most important written account that explains how the Ark came to be in Ethiopia is the *Kebra Nagast* ("The Glory of Kings"), an eight-hundred-year-old text. It is written in a Semitic language related to Hebrew and Arabic, known as Ge'ez. The *Kebra Nagast* explains how the Ark of the Covenant came to be in Ethiopia, a story that begins with the Queen of Sheba. While the Old Testament does not tell us who she was, most scholars assume that she was from somewhere in Arabia, but there are divided views on her historicity. Some suggest that she may have been from Africa, which is not so far-fetched as it may sound, since parts of Africa are very close to Israel, and in the Iron Age, numerous trade routes, including ones through Arabia, connected the two continents.

According to the *Kebra Nagast*, the biblical Queen of Sheba was Queen Makedo of Ethiopia. As recounted in the Old Testament, the Queen of Sheba visited King Solomon in Jerusalem. Unlike the Old Testament, however, the story told in the *Kebra Nagast* is of the king and queen's romantic relationship through which Queen Makeda becomes pregnant with King Solomon's child. Before Queen Makeda leaves to return to her home country, the king gives her a ring, which she is to give to their child as proof that he is in fact the son of Solomon. Twenty-two years later, the son of this union, Menelik, travels to Jerusalem to meet his father, King Solomon. Upon seeing the ring, Solomon tries to convince Menelik to become his heir and take the throne of Israel, since Menelik is, chronologically, Solomon's first-born son. Menelik refuses, wanting to return to Ethiopia. Solomon, then, dispatches a group of men from his kingdom to accompany Menelik on his return to Africa. These men are unhappy about this and unbeknownst to Menelik, steal the Ark as they are forced to leave their country. Both Menelik and Solomon discover the theft while the group is heading home. Before Solomon can capture them, however, Menelik, the Ark, and the young men are magically transported in safety back to Ethiopia.

When Menelik returns, Queen Makeda cedes her throne to her son, and he becomes king of Ethiopia. His authority comes to be rooted in his relationship to the Ark and in his descent from the Davidic line. The Ark appears to be a powerful weapon just as is in the book of Joshua in the Old Testament.

164 READERS OF THE LOST ARK

Menelik uses it to vanquish his enemies just as Israel did. There is much more to the story but rather than summarize the whole thing here, you can just read it instead (and you can find my recommendations for editions in the Bibliographic Essay at the end of this book).

That a group of young men were so easily able to steal one of the holiest objects in Israel points to how we are to interpret what happened. The theology of the story presumes that there was some level of divine intervention. God approved of these events, and even perhaps facilitated them, just as was the case when the Philistines captured the Ark. God wanted the Ethiopians to take the Ark, and an angel of the Lord expresses that view in the story. Indeed, the *Kebra Nagast* offers a justification for the Ark being taken from Jerusalem by explaining how Solomon became idolatrous after its disappearance. Divine favor has abandoned Israel. The new royal line favored by God was still Davidic but now Ethiopian, not Israelite.

The larger argument of the *Kebra Nagast* is that the kings of Ethiopia have been divinely chosen. The book is very concerned with dynastic genealogies, showing how all the kings of Ethiopia are of Menelik's line, and thus of Solomon's line. This was not the earliest Ethiopian tradition linking historical kings to legendary figures. There is an even older tradition that the king was the descendent of the god Mahrem, a god worshipped before Ethiopia became Christian. The relationship between the two traditions is not well understood, but it may be that the *Kebra Nagast* was an adaptation or transformation of the earlier one, changes that made the idea of divine kingship more palatable in a monotheistic society. Rather than a deity, the king is claimed to be the descendent of a king chosen by God who possesses the instrument (the Ark) through which God becomes manifest on earth.

The argument that the Ethiopian dynastic line descended from Solomon was still being made well into the 1950s. Emperor Haile Selassie I, in the 1955 Revised Constitution, declared himself the descendent of Menelik, son of King Solomon and the Queen of Sheba. This is enshrined in the instructions for the succession of the throne, reading: "The Imperial dignity shall remain perpetually attached to the line of Haile Selassie I which descends without interruption from the dynasty of Menelik I, son of the Queen of Sheba and King Solomon of Jerusalem." The revised Ethiopian constitution was overturned with the 1974 coup in which Haile Selassie was deposed. Traditions related to the Ark, however, have remained important. While these arguments may seem far-fetched and their propagandistic elements too overt to be convincing, Ethiopia is not the only country to claim descent

THE ROMANCE OF SOLOMON AND SHEBA   165

from a fictive ancient Near Eastern ancestor. There is a Scottish dynastic lineage that situates the origins of the rule of that land back to Queen Scotia, the daughter of an Egyptian king who fled the Nile Valley. Some Scottish traditions claim that she met Moses in Egypt, before the Exodus. In any case, the Ethiopians are not alone in claims of biblical or ancient Near Eastern connections for the leaders.

So who wrote the *Kebra Nagast* and why? No one is quite certain. Some editions of the text have a colophon, which is a statement of who wrote the manuscript and/or who copied it. The colophon that survives claims that the version we have was written down in about 1225 CE, first in Coptic, then translated into Arabic, and then into Ge'ez. No earlier versions of the text in another language are preserved, however. The *Kebra Nagast* is a remarkable amalgam of biblical storytelling reinterpreted through methods expected of premodern Christian and Jewish interpreters of the time (see Chapters 3 and 4), blended with Ethiopian traditions. Experts on the text attempt to date some sections to different periods of Ethiopian history and to different Ethiopian political situations, much as source critics attempt to do for the Old Testament. Whatever the case may be, the *Kebra Nagast* was written long after Israel's Iron II period, when King Solomon would have lived and when the earliest events in the manuscript were said to have occurred.

It is within a period of shifting power and unstable dynasties that the *Kebra Nagast* seems to have been written. In 1314, Amda Seyon I came to power as the next king or first emperor (depending on one's perspective) of Ethiopia. Accounts of Amda Seyon's military exploits are well preserved, and he is most associated with what has sometimes been called a "Solomonic Restoration" given the claims made regarding Solomonic descent. After a period of warfare led to the splintering of the state, this "Solomonic" dynasty ended up in charge, replacing the previous dynasty (the Zagwean Dynasty), which itself claimed descent from Moses. The *Kebra Nagast* provided a unifying narrative for the fractious groups of local leaders who Amda Seyon I was trying to lead. This story was very successful and intensified in Ethiopia as a kind of Christian nationalism. In particular, the new Solomonic Dynasty used this story to justify various military actions against internal and external Muslim groups. It is perhaps in the reigns of the kings who followed Amda Seyon I that the stories of the Ark emerge. The Ark comes to be a potent symbol in this rise of Christian nationalism that superseded local-regional claims to leadership. The Ark reflects a hybridization of Jewish and Christian practices through the guise of Solomonic dynastic claims. As the conflicts with Islam

166 READERS OF THE LOST ARK

in the region continued, the Christian nationalism justified by the *Kebra Nagast* became more important. Monastic communities came to play an important role in Ethiopian culture, and it is perhaps from this community that theologies surrounding the Ark come to prominence in mainstream Ethiopian religion.

The *Kebra Nagast* has had a powerful influence outside of Ethiopia as well, perhaps most notably as an inspirational text in the emergence of Rastafari (better known as Rastafarianism) in Jamaica. As Gerald Hausman has described it, the *Kebra Nagast* offers an entry point for thinking about "Blackness in biblical lore." In other words, the book articulates a vision of biblical times rooted in African experiences that can inform African religiosity today. For Jamaicans in the 1930s, Emperor Haile Selassie of Ethiopia came to be seen as Jah (God) incarnate, or at least as a prophet, after Reverend Leonard Howell and others articulated a role for the emperor in biblical prophecy. Incorporating these beliefs with the Pan-Africanism of figures like Marcus Garvey, Rastafari emerged as a loose religion that provided inspiration for Black Jamaicans in the context of British imperialism. While not read widely in the Rastafari movement, the stories of the *Kebra Nagast* and the Ark were transmitted orally and accepted with the same authority as the Old and New Testaments.

Aksum and Christianity

The *Kebra Nagast* tells one account of how Jews and Christians came to be in Ethiopia. Scholars reconstruct this history differently, although there is considerable uncertainty about some of the issues. Many would begin the story with the kingdom of Aksum, which was in what is now Ethiopia, Eritrea, and extending across the Red Sea into south Arabia. Aksum refers to both a major city (perhaps a capital city if such anachronistic terminology can be used) and a territorial state that emerged in the aftermath of warfare between competing smaller states. When, exactly, it came to dominate the area is unclear. Its strategic position between Arabia, sub-Saharan Africa, Greco-Roman Egypt, and the larger Roman Empire meant that it could connect these regions and profit from the trade that went in all directions. External historical sources show that the kingdom was the main regional power by 100 CE and flourished until 950 CE. However, more recent archaeological research has suggested that this chronology may not be accurate and that the

THE ROMANCE OF SOLOMON AND SHEBA   167

history of the kingdom of Aksum needs to be revised. Archaeological work in Ethiopia and Aksum has been intermittent. The political instability of the region has meant that despite the excellent preservation of materials and the good potential for archaeological research, the actual ability to conduct field-work has been limited.

The Ark-centered theology of Aksum likely emerged in medieval times, after the Solomonic descent of the emperors had become well-established. The *Kebra Nagast* was written as shifting political tides within Ethiopia changed the balance of power. As the political dominance of the region of Aksum waned, the city itself strove to hold on to some kind of power and succeeded at establishing itself as an ecclesiastical center. For historians, the strongest evidence of this is the book of Aksum (*Liber Axumae*), which likely reflects King Zara Yaqob's (r. 1434–1468) attempts to legitimize his dynasty. The collection of documents, which began to be collected during his reign, serve both to legitimize Aksum as an ecclesiastical center and his relationship to Solomon as laid out in the *Kebra Nagast*. Zara Yaqob had himself installed as emperor at Aksum, seeking to draw connections between himself and this ancient center of the Ethiopian empire, while simultaneously seeking to draw an end to theological fights between different Christian factions. The king also expanded funding to Christian institutions throughout the country, working to further instill a Christian nationalism over the country's feudal organizations. European nations, seeing in Ethiopia a Christian ally against the Muslim world on the other side of Africa, increased their ties to the kingdom. Thus, this Christian African empire came to be centered in Aksum, and the Ark, the symbol of this kingdom, came to be associated with the region.

The *Liber Axumae* provides ambiguous evidence on when the Ark traditions were established. It dates to a period where scholars of Ethiopian history are somewhat divided in terms of whether they see continuity with the past or disruption. For those who see something new emerging at this time, the churches and theology of this period seem more tied into the Christian trends of the larger European medieval world. Those who see con-tinuity would likely emphasize the processes through which local theologies developed in tandem with local dynastic politics and other trends in Africa. Life is complex, and probably both sets of scholars are right. There are signs of local Ethiopian religion practices (like rock-hewn churches) and practices that are connected to other events going on in north and east Africa at the time. But there are also signs that Ethiopian Christianity was participating

168   READERS OF THE LOST ARK

in the wider European interest in relics—the tangible, material artifacts associated with saints and biblical events. And this is the context in which the Ark comes to be of importance in Ethiopian political life. What greater Old Testament relic could there be but the Ark of the Covenant, especially given the Ark's prominence in the *Kebra Nagast*? As we have already discussed in Chapter 4, the Ark was a powerful relic for Saint John Lateran's Basilica during the medieval era.

Jewish and Christian Cultures in Ethiopia

Christian Ethiopians are not the only people who play a role in the story of the Ark in Tigray. Ethiopian Jews, who until recently lived in the area, contributed to the theologies of the Ark as well. Numerous Jewish communities have played a role in Ethiopian history, from the Falasha or Beta Israel (which some take as less derogatory than Falasha but remains a lesser-known name), who mostly migrated to Israel at the end of the twentieth century to the Qemant, who preserved the animal sacrifice traditions of Iron Age Judaism, non-Christian minorities have contributed to Ethiopian receptions of the Ark. The Ark is the kind of symbol that would appeal to the diverse religious populations of Ethiopia and provide a central point of religious focus that could bring a national unity to very different groups of people.

The focus on the Ark unifies the churches of Ethiopia and is symbolized by the reverence of objects called *tabot* (*tabotat* plural) in Ge'ez. These are small but religiously powerful representations of the Ark found in every church. Ge'ez and Hebrew are both Semitic languages, and there should be no surprise that the two languages share seemingly similar vocabulary. *Tabot* is very similar to the Hebrew word for Ark (*taboh*). Only this is the wrong Ark, for, as we discussed in Chapter 1, the word used for the Ark of the Covenant in Hebrew is *aron*. The Ge'ez word is cognate with the Hebrew word for Noah's Ark, and this suggests that the term was brought into use by a community who was reading Bibles where the word for both Arks was the same.

For Ethiopian Christians, the religious objects known as *tabot* symbolize one of the tablets of the Ten Commandments, the Ark of the Covenant itself (in whole or in part), or both simultaneously. The distinction is not necessarily clear, although particular individuals or churches may believe very strongly that it is one or the other (more often the Ark than the tablets of the

THE ROMANCE OF SOLOMON AND SHEBA   169

commandments). Edward Ullendorff, the influential scholar of Ethiopian Christianity, explains that whether the *tabotat* are supposed to look like the Ark, or the tablets of the covenant (the most important contents of the Ark), it amounts to the same thing. The *tabotat* are the Ark represented *pars pro toto*, meaning one element of the Ark is used to stand in for the whole. However individual worshippers understand them (and we should expect that that varies), they generally reference the Ark of the Covenant and the Ark believed to be in Aksum. This means that the Ark is central to Ethiopian Christianity for it is the *tabot* that is consecrated in an Ethiopian church not the church itself. The *tabot* is what gives every church its sacral power. Each is kept in the Holy of the Holies of the church, an architectural feature that is integral to every Ethiopian church.

The Holy of Holies was one of the distinctive features of Solomon's Temple in Jerusalem, as discussed in Chapters 4 and 5. Contemporary Ethiopian churches are modeled explicitly on the Temple of Jerusalem, in obvious keeping with the tradition of the relationship among Ethiopia, the Queen of Sheba, and Solomon himself. Church interior layouts emulate the Solomonic Temple's tripartite structure, at least in terms of division of space if not actual function and shape. The outside areas of Ethiopian churches vary. Some are rectangular like the description of the Jerusalem Temple, but some are octagonal. There is an inner chamber where congregants are allowed, and where they receive communion. The innermost area, where the *tabot* are kept, is restricted to the priests. Architecturally there may be similarities to the Temple of Solomon, but in terms of the use of the space, Ethiopian churches function like other Christian churches. These are not the locations of animal sacrifice and royal authority like Solomon's Jerusalem Temple was. The churches are the locations of liturgical events where community members are expected to congregate, even if they cannot enter the presence of the *tabotat*.

Tabotat function in Ethiopian tradition like the Ark of the Covenant. They are where God can make Himself present on earth. Unlike the Ark of the Covenant, there can be multiple *tabot* and multiple appearances of God on earth simultaneously. The *tabotat* are not to be viewed by the laity. Only specific priests can view them at any given time. When they are brought out of the Holy of Holies, they are covered with a blanket, just as the Ark was. And just as the Ark was covered, this is done to protect the people from its power, not to protect the *tabot*.

The *tabotat* are brought out once a year for the celebration of Timqat, the Ethiopian version of Epiphany, and the most important religious celebration

170   READERS OF THE LOST ARK

for Ethiopian Christians. Timqat, which happens on January 19 or 20 every year, blends Old and New Testament traditions together. It is the celebration of Epiphany, of Jesus's baptism in the Jordan River by John the Baptist. This is the tradition of Eastern Orthodox churches; western churches celebrate Epiphany in association with Christmas and the recognition of the Christ child as a divine being. The *tabot,* which normally represents the Ark of the Covenant now stands in as a representation of Jesus. Here the Ark is treated just as it was in medieval Christian thought, as something that both prefigures and stands in for Jesus. The name "Timqat" is a Ge'ez word meaning "to reveal," which makes sense for Epiphany, because when Jesus was baptized, tradition holds, Jesus's divinity was revealed.

The festival lasts for three days. On the first, the *tabotat* are brought down to a river in a celebratory procession. If no river is nearby, celebrants construct their own dams to prepare a location for the baptism. The *tabotat* are covered with their multicolored and elaborate robes, with umbrellas often held above them. Priests, dancers, and musicians process around the priests bearing the *tabotat.* Here the processions are explicitly imitating David's procession of the Ark into Jerusalem, and the events are simultaneously solemn and joyful, with singing and dancing part of the revelry. While the priests and those who bear the *tabotat* wear very colorful robes, the laity mostly dresses in clean, white garb. Ethiopian Christians focus their worship directly at the *tabotat,* seeing in them the physical presence of God. Ululation is common among female participants. On the second day of festivities, water is sprinkled upon the *tabotat,* which have remained by the river overnight, while some worshippers immerse themselves or even dive into the water in commemoration of their own baptisms. Afterward, the *tabotat* are processed through the streets again and returned to their home churches. Similar celebrations accompany the procession home. Only one *tabot* is not returned on the second day—the *tabot* from St. Michael's Church (not the church where the Ark is said to be stored).

Just as with the Ark, the *tabotat* are brought out when the community is experiencing distress, and such processions may be used to bring an end to community problems, like famine or plague. Tradition holds that they are used in warfare, carried in front of the army just as the Ark was. Perhaps the most prominent of these traditions today surrounds the celebration of the Battle of Adwa, an 1896 battle in which the Ethiopian army vanquished an invading Italian force. Emperor Menelik II was said to have brought a *tabot* with him and some suggest that this was the reason for his success that day.

THE ROMANCE OF SOLOMON AND SHEBA   171

The victory at Adwa meant that Ethiopia did not come under European authority like much of the rest of Africa, at least until the Italians invaded again in 1935, under Mussolini.

Yet *tabotat* were also involved in a decisive Ethiopian military loss to Europe. In 1867, a delegation of British citizens was taken prisoner by Ethiopia, the result of increasingly strained diplomatic relations. Emperor Tewodros II had imprisoned two British missionaries, members of the London Society for the Promotion of Christianity Amongst the Jews, after feeling that they had insulted him. He later took the British consul captive as well when the consul tried to arrange the release of the missionaries. The imprisonment of the consul, however, was less likely due to the missionaries and more likely related to the emperor's unanswered demands that Queen Victoria supply him with weapons. While she ignored his requests, Tewodros was losing power along the coast of his kingdom. Negotiations for the release of prisoners broke down, and he had captured more hostages in the interim. The British, after delivering an ultimatum that the prisoners be released or military action would be taken went unanswered, sent an invasion force led by Robert Napier. In December 1867, nearly twelve thousand British troops landed in Ethiopia. These forces made their way to Magdala (now known as Amba Mariam), the mountain village which Tewodros had established as his power base after taking it by force from the Wollo Oromo people.

Magdala had become the seat of Tewodros's power, and there he had gathered to himself treasures from around Ethiopia, intending this to be the central location of culture and learning in his kingdom. But with the advance of the British army, and their overwhelming force powered by mechanized weaponry, it was clear that Tewodros was going to lose and so he killed himself. The British took the city in the Battle of Magdala on April 13, 1868 (Easter Monday). Napier let his troops burn and pillage the village, and many of the treasures that Tewodros had gathered over the course of his own campaigns were looted by the British at this time. The scale of looting was striking, even for nineteenth-century standards. Once, however, the initial frenzy settled down, in British fashion, the looting was regularized so that all soldiers could receive a "fair" share of the plunder relative to their rank and standing in the military. The treasures were hauled out of the city, which was burned and destroyed, and auctioned off a few days later so that the proceeds of the looting could be distributed in cash rather than in goods. The accompanying archaeologist, Richard Holmes, oversaw some of

172   READERS OF THE LOST ARK

the distribution of materials that would later come to reside in the British Museum and the Victoria and Albert Museum.

Among those looted treasures are several *tabotat*, and a campaign in Ethiopia called Afromet (Association for the Return of the Maqdala Ethiopian Treasures) works to have these and other looted objects returned to Africa. The organization, one of whose founders was Richard Pankhurst, son of the suffragette Sylvia Pankhurst, saw the looting of Magdala as one of the major cultural tragedies of Ethiopian history. Afromet's success in getting items returned has been piecemeal but frequent. In 2003, for example, one *tabot* came up for auction in London and was purchased by an Irish doctor who, recognizing what it was, wanted it returned to Ethiopia.

One of the stumbling blocks faced in repatriation is that institutions, like the British Museum, have policies in place against repatriation, and those policies are, in Britain's case at least, enshrined in law. Afromet argues that there has already been a precedent set for the British government's return of the looted treasures. Emperor Yohannes IV, the successor of Tewodros, wrote to Queen Victoria asking for the return of two items. While one item, an icon, was not returned, the British did send back a copy of the *Kebra Nagast*, since they already had one. For Afromet, this constitutes the legal precedent to justify the return of the Magdala Treasures from the British Museum and the Victoria and Albert Museum.

The British Museum has eleven *tabot* in its collection. These were all accessioned from the Magdala auction, collected by Richard Holmes in 1867. They have never been on display as far as I know, and even the museum keepers claim not to work with them. The British Museum provides information about the objects but not images, respecting the belief that they are not to be viewed by people other than the priests responsible for them. A delegation of the government of Ethiopia has requested that they be returned. At the time I am writing this, it seems unlikely that such repatriation should occur, even as European and North American museums are inundated for requests from different countries for the return of antiquities. The most famous of these cases is that of the Elgin Marbles, also known as the Parthenon Sculptures, which were taken from Greece and some of which were acquired by the British Museum. One solution that has been offered for many of these cases, including for the *tabotat*, is to loan them to the country of origin for an unspecified length of time. While that may seem like an easy solution, where the country of origin effectively regains access to its missing artifacts, it is not so simple. A loan agreement necessitates a legal acknowledgment of

THE ROMANCE OF SOLOMON AND SHEBA   173

ownership and would formally undermine a country's claim that the artifacts belonged to them. It is not just an issue of semantics. Repatriation is one of the most complex issues facing museums today.

Despite wanting to, I cannot fully ignore the question of whether the Solomonic Ark of the Covenant is in Ethiopia, in the Church Zion. You have probably already guessed that I do not believe it is there. I believe that the Ark that is the focus of Ethiopian worship dates to medieval times and reflects the culture of relics that was so prominent then. For an archaeologist like myself, the claim that the artifact is there but cannot ever be looked at by anyone is suspiciously convenient. As we shall explore in the next chapter, this is a common theme of pseudoarchaeology. Arguments are made that are not based on evidence but an explicit lack of evidence. The fact that no one can ever verify the presence of the Ark is not compelling evidence for my academically conditioned instincts. I have no doubt that there is *an* Ark in Saint Mary of Zion. I just do not believe that it was taken from Solomon's Temple, nor do I think that it is the same physical Ark described in the Old Testament.

Yet while it is mostly forbidden from viewing, there are some notable figures who have claimed to have seen the Ethiopian Ark and described it. Now, as already discussed, anyone who has participated in the Timqat ceremonies in Tigray may have seen what they thought was the Ark, covered by textiles. Some take this as the real Ark, while other participants say that it is a replica that is brought out for the event. Only the guardian of the Ark could know for sure.

There are some, however, who claim to have seen it unadorned by its covering. The earliest recorded instance, excluding the accounts in the *Kebra Nagast*, is that of the Arab geographer Abu Salih, who lived in the thirteenth century. He visited many Ethiopian churches and claims to have seen the Ark. His description is not evocative of Exodus 25. The Ark he claims to have seen was much smaller and did not have a mercy seat or cherubim. Rather the top was adorned with a cross and precious stones, all flourishes that may have been expected of a medieval-era piece of holy equipment but not an Iron Age one.

The most recent observer who seems credible is Edward Ullendorff (1920–2011), who writes about Abu Salih's observations in his own book *Ethiopia and the Bible*. Ullendorff was a prominent Semiticist and was one of the world experts on Ethiopian religion, from the perspective of academics, of course, not practitioners of the faith. When interviewed by the *LA Times* in 1992, in response to Graham Hancock's book *The Sign and the*

174   READERS OF THE LOST ARK

Seal (discussed in the next chapter), Ullendorff admitted to having seen the Ark himself in 1941 while in the British army and stationed in Aksum. He described it as an empty wooden box, clearly of "middle to late medieval construction," a description that lines up well with the historical circumstances of the emergence of the church and *Kebra Nagast* as well as the description by Abu Salih. He says that in 1941 there was no problem gaining entrance to see it, but now, people are kept away "to maintain the idea that it is a venerated object." He chose never to publish a description of what he saw himself so as not to cause harm to the Ethiopian believers with whom he worked or to hinder his research activities in the country.

Did any of these people see the object that Ethiopians claim is the Ark? That is impossible to say. Perhaps it does not matter whether it is the biblical Ark, because it is an Ark that is very real for the faith of many Ethiopians. The concentration of faith on that object offers a theological truth for that community that supersedes the kinds of historical or scientific questions asked of scholars. While I have never seen the celebration of Timqat in person, the connection that it brings to the community is readily apparent even in film, photographs, and written descriptions.

Yet not all such claims about the Ark should be afforded the label of theological truths. As we shall explore in the next chapter, one of the most prominent proponents of the idea that the biblical Ark is in Ethiopia is Graham Hancock. He is what I and most others in the professional fields of archaeology, history, and biblical studies would call a pseudoscholar or pseudoarchaeologist. While his book on the Ark is not his most outlandish book, it bears many of the hallmarks of this kind of approach to history. In the next chapter, we shall explore his work and the works of others who make unreasonable claims about the Ark. We will explore what those claims are, why they are problematic, why people make them, and why audiences believe them.

9

Aliens, Radios, and Conspiracies

The Many Arks of Pseudoarchaeology

Every time I teach my first-year archaeology class, students get excited when we start discussing pseudoarchaeology, archaeology that isn't really archaeology, but the body of thinking generated by people operating on the fringes of the discipline. Pseudoarchaeologists make outlandish assertions that no real archaeologist would make. These are the people who claim to have found Noah's Ark, that technology from the lost city of Atlantis was used to build the pyramids, or that the Nazca lines in Peru are landing pads for alien spacecraft. My first-year class usually has about two hundred students in it. Most have encountered these kinds of arguments and immediately start laughing about them. More than a few are relieved to take a break from the more technical elements of the course, discussing how radiocarbon dating works, or the statistical methods we use to interpret the thousands of animal bones found in an excavation. For many of the students, however, these discussions of the boundaries between what is scholarship and what is nonsense are more meaningful. Some, after class, come and talk to me about how one parent or another relative is obsessed with ancient aliens theories and how frustrating arguments around the dinner table have become. Our University of Lethbridge neuroscience students often want to talk to me about one particular pseudoscholar who our university embarrassingly gave an honorary degree at the behest of the psychology department decades ago. A few sometimes want to argue with me, often over a few beers, that aliens really did build the pyramids. And while the beer is tempting, those discussions never are because they are always the same. They have been the same for the past twenty years that I have been teaching. And if I'm lucky enough to teach for another twenty years, I imagine they won't change in the future either.

Scholars use the term "pseudoarchaeology" to refer to approaches to thinking about the past that do not follow the norms expected of the profession. Pseudoarchaeologists are amateurs who have not been trained in the discipline. They are not the amateurs or avocational archaeologists

Readers of the Lost Ark. Kevin M. McGeough, Oxford University Press. © Oxford University Press 2025.
DOI: 10.1093/9780197653913.003.0010

176   READERS OF THE LOST ARK

who often make legitimate contributions to the discipline, but who have day jobs in other fields. Pseudoarchaeologists are a more specific group. They usually make their living as writers, journalists, or media producers. Sometimes they operate from a faith perspective, most often rooted in either Evangelical Christianity or the New Age movement. Sometimes they are con artists, purposefully engaging in fraud (be especially wary if someone shows up at your church or synagogue claiming to have found Noah's Ark and needing money). Pseudoarchaeologists may claim that they are just making arguments that professional scholars are too scared to make or that "mainstream" archaeologists cannot imagine because they are too entrenched in professional conventions (we aren't). What makes their claims pseudoarchaeological is that their arguments are not based on evidence. Their arguments are based on the absence of evidence and are reliant on the logic that it is very difficult to prove that something is *not* true. They argue that there *could* be evidence, but it is unavailable to them for some reason or another. Perhaps, like stories of Atlantis, the civilization has completely disappeared, with no traces remaining, other than confused allusions in ancient literature or art. Sometimes, we are told, a Middle Eastern government forbids access to the area and so the pseudoscholar's expeditions are prevented. They will try to assure readers or viewers that if only they were granted permission to excavate the area, they would find the evidence. It must be, they imply, that someone doesn't want them revealing hidden truths. They never admit that it is because a government regulator doesn't want an inexperienced group vandalizing a site. Their arguments are often structured on irrational or antirational principles, favoring revelation and speculation over scientific reasoning. These are the kinds of presentations of the Ark that will be treated here, and, despite the fact that they are mostly based on a lack of evidence, they are shockingly similar.

After reading this chapter, I hope that you will be able to identify pseudoarchaeological treatments of the Ark and the ancient world easily. This can be more difficult with biblical archaeology than with other fields of ancient studies. The Bible complicates things. The different faith communities from which scholars operate complicate things. The use of the Bible for political arguments relating to the Middle East complicates things. Within the field of biblical archaeology, practitioners debate the boundaries of legitimate research, with many since the 1970s rejecting the name "biblical archaeology" as problematically privileging the Bible beyond how scholars should treat an historical document. As we saw in Chapter 2, archaeology is useful for providing some types of information about the Bible and biblical times but not useful for other types of information. Understanding the differences between biblical and archaeological evidence is one of the important elements of distinction between legitimate biblical archaeology and pseudoarchaeology. We no longer dig with the Bible in one hand and a trowel in another, and if a scholar claims to be doing so, you should be suspicious of their claims. As we saw in Chapter 2, scholars do not agree on how historical the Bible is, and so there is a lot of room for argument. When you are evaluating an archaeological claim about the Bible, make sure to ask yourself what kind of evidence that claim is based upon.

The Sign and the Seal

The previous chapter was probably not the first place that you encountered the claim that the Ark of the Covenant is in Ethiopia. For some of you, it may just have been a kind of factoid, lurking in the corners of your mind, that the Ark was probably there, hidden away in some church. But why would you know about this? Not from Saturday or Sunday school, nor from your freshman world history class in college. You have probably seen some kind of late-night documentary on the Discovery or History channel about this. Or perhaps you heard it from someone who had heard it from someone who had read Graham Hancock's *The Sign and the Seal*, which was likely the source that one of those documentaries cribbed from. Published in 1992, this book has become lodged in public consciousness about the Ark and is consistently one of the top-selling books on archaeology, much to the chagrin (and possibly envy) of those of us who are trained in the field and write on actual archaeological matters. It is not nearly as big of a seller as his 1995 follow-up work, *Fingerprints of the Gods*, in which Hancock retells Ignatius Donnelly's 1882 theory that Atlantis was the progenitor civilization for *all* earlier civilizations. Because of *Fingerprints*, Hancock fans, a substantial number of which seem to be people who work in the entertainment industry, believe that there was some ancient, white civilization that existed 10,000 years ago that professional archaeologists don't want you to know about. These claims are why Hancock is famous now, but the subject I want to discuss here is how he has framed thinking about the Ark. Despite that his first book, *The Sign and the Seal*, is not as outlandish as *Fingerprints of the Gods*, it has many of the hallmarks of what we call pseudoarchaeology.

178   READERS OF THE LOST ARK

The Sign and the Seal is a captivating read. It is a typical journalistic approach to popular archaeological writing, describing the author's visits with numerous scholars, and showing how those encounters led him to better understand the Ark. The search for the Ark functions as a kind of scaffolding for Hancock to discuss different historical circumstances related to the Ark, somewhat like this book, but I don't claim that I am going to find the Ark. Hancock adds a kind of detective element to his story. It is interspersed with the occasional moments of danger as he travels to different parts of the world in, coincidentally (?) times of extreme unrest, like the start of the First Iraq War or the 1990 Temple Mount Massacre in Jerusalem. The writing about the Ark is clear and lucid, and very enjoyable. It comes across, to a professional academic like myself, as the work of an amateur historian, more than the extreme pseudoscholarship that we will discuss later in this chapter, and to which Hancock's later writings bear more of a similarity. What is not clear to me is whether Hancock really believes some of the more outlandish claims he makes in *The Sign and the Seal.* Indeed, the book ends ambiguously with Hancock asserting that he has never seen the Ark, that he is not worthy of seeing it, but hinting that it may reside in Ethiopia. Hancock never actually comes out (in the book) and says that it is in Aksum. In later interviews, he explains that some of his theories are speculative but that he is on solid ground in arguing that the Ark is now in Ethiopia. Whether he truly believes what he has written, Hancock concludes that during the time of King Manasseh, the Ark was taken from the Temple. It was smuggled out of Israel and was taken to Ethiopia, but not in line with the traditions described in the *Kebra Nagast.* Rather, it was first kept at the Jewish settlement in Elephantine, Egypt. For good measure, Hancock also throws in references to the Knights Templars, arguing that they also searched for the Ark and offering the possibility, but not necessarily saying that he is convinced of this, that they were involved in some construction projects in Ethiopia.

What is key to Hancock's logic in all the options that he offers is that his claims about the Ark are *possible*, and there is no evidence that they did *not* happen. As with much pseudoarchaeology, this is the logical loophole on which the arguments must rest. For most scholars will agree that it is very difficult to prove that something did *not* happen. Most professional archaeologists and historians work from what has happened and what there is evidence for having happened. We work with what we would call positive evidence, such as an inscription that states that an Assyrian king conquered a city or an assemblage of material culture that shows that a new people moved to a region. In the case of Hancock's arguments, there is often no evidence to suggest that things happened as he claims. What he suggests is not impossible, but if historians worked on that logic, we would be reading books with many spurious claims.

Hancock builds his claims on other logical fallacies. One of the most egregious is a kind of logical flaw that historians (and most academics, especially hard scientists) are usually trained in graduate school to watch out for, a logical flaw in which correlation is mistaken for causation. For historians, the correlation versus causation fallacy is a bit different than for chemists, physicists, and biologists who set up experiments and control different variables. Historians want to understand the relationship among various historical events, attitudes, beliefs, and so on. They study documents and material culture from the past and try to understand if there is a causal relationship among different elements that they observe. Did one set of beliefs cause an event to occur? Or were those beliefs held at the time of the event but did not lead to that event? Can we identify patterns that are meaningful? Or are what look like patterns just coincidences? These issues are complex, and working through these problems is part of the work of a professional historian.

Hancock and other amateurs or pseudoarchaeologists, however, ignore the problem that correlation does not necessarily equate to causation, and even willfully manipulate it. They rely on the importance of coincidence and use coincidence to convince their readers. In his later work, *Fingerprints of the Gods*, for example, Hancock shows similarities in architecture among cultures found on different continents as evidence that there must have been some kind of progenitor culture. These are the "fingerprints" to which the title of his book refers. So, for example, one observes that there are pyramids in Africa and Mesoamerica. He does not see this as a logical correlation of engineering, that it makes sense for the largest part of a monumental building to be on the ground and the smallest part to be on the top, and hence a pyramid shape could be invented by many people in many places independently. Hancock's logic argues that there was a causal element to this coincidence of style, that some missing civilization taught people on both continents how to build this architectural form. We don't make this claim about the ubiquity of bridges because we use bridges in our own architecture and so see them as normative. As pyramids are not typical in European and North American architecture, they now strike us as unusual. But when one goes searching for these kinds of coincidence, it is easy to fall into a trap that we

180   READERS OF THE LOST ARK

call "confirmation bias," where one finds what one is looking for and ignores evidence to the contrary.

This is the same logic that we find in *The Sign and the Seal*; it is just not as extreme. One example will suffice to draw this out, involving "secret maps" that Hancock claims to have discovered that offer clues to the Ark's whereabouts. He sees hints about the Ark in Wolfram von Eschenbach's thirteenth-century German poem *Parzival*, about the quest for the Holy Grail. One might ask what this poem has to do with the Ark, and the correct answer to that question is "nothing." Hancock, however, sees in the poem a cypher for the location of the Ark of the Covenant. The evidence for this requires one to accept various significant leaps of logic and then take the volume of those "coincidences" as evidence that the poem is a kind of literary map. None of the evidence is even remotely convincing. For example, Hancock notes that a character in *Parzival* named "Feirefiz" has a strange name. He argues that this could be interpreted as the French term "vrai fils," meaning "true son," even though the poem is written in German. Then he notes that Menelik, the supposed son of Solomon according to the *Kebra Nagast*, is called "true son" in one passage (in translation). This proves, to him, that *Parzival* explicitly references the *Kebra Nagast*. Now, if you are wondering how this can be convincing, you haven't missed anything. It isn't, and you have understood the weakness of such an argument. It is by adding up a series of spurious correlations like this that Hancock concludes that the location of the Ark has been secretly embedded in the Middle High German poem. And if you aren't reading his book closely, not paying attention to the series of convoluted and dry discussions of translation issues, you may just trust the author. Popular culture convinces us that such "maps" do exist. As I discussed in Chapter 6, the decipherment of maps and cyphers drives much archaeological adventure fiction. Whether watching Indiana Jones or reading Dan Brown books, even though we know they are fiction, the cumulative effect of these stories is to make it plausible that such cyphers may have existed.

Hancock's logic is typical of pseudoarchaeology and bad amateur history. He throws Atlantis into the mix (usually a sign of pseudoscholarship), which seems to be a way of setting up his next book more than to explore issues surrounding the Ark. Just as typical of pseudoscholarship is his referencing of the "Hermetic tradition." This is a school of thinking that has been present in European intellectual circles since ancient Greek times, in which it is believed that Egypt was the seat of ancient knowledge. This knowledge was personified by the Egyptian god Thoth, who in Greek times was associated with the god Hermes (and hence the term "Hermetic"). In more recent times, various people and groups have been seen as the bearers of Hermetic knowledge, including the Knights Templars and Freemasons, both of whom are mentioned by Hancock. By situating his work in this intellectual heritage, he may be trying to convince readers of the legitimacy of his approach. But the logic is bad. It is like a chemist situating their work within the context of alchemy. True, chemistry does have intellectual roots in alchemy, but the fundamental assumptions of the two approaches to the world are very different.

Hancock connects the Ark to the Hermetic tradition through Moses, who was often credited with bringing this supposed line of ancient Egyptian knowledge out of North Africa. Especially since the Renaissance, there have been treatments of Moses where his vision at the Burning Bush, his experiences of God at Sinai, his supposed magical powers, and his having been raised in an Egyptian court have been taken as evidence that he was trained in this secret Egyptian knowledge (as discussed in Chapter 2). Even Sigmund Freud, in his last work before his death, *Moses and Monotheism*, argued that this is how Moses should be understood. Hancock uses a variation of these interpretations and calls Moses a "civilizing hero." He further explores this in *Fingerprints of the Gods*, where he claims that these civilizing heroes spread technological knowledge from Atlantis, although Moses is not mentioned in that book. Freudian civilizing heroes are not developed this fully in *The Sign and the Seal*, however.

Hancock connects the idea of the civilizing hero to the Ark by playing with some problems of biblical chronology, especially how forty years seem to elapse between events in the life of Moses without mention in the book of Exodus. Between leaving Pharaoh's court and his encounter with the Burning Bush, the Bible tells us little of what Moses was up to. Based on literally no evidence (and to be fair, he admits this), Hancock reconstructs this period of Moses's life as one where he visits Serabit el-Khadem (a real archaeological site in the Sinai) and there learns to fashion new technologies, procuring meteoric materials. This gives him both the technological skills and materials to construct a "portable miracle machine" and "manmade weapon." The reason for such a weapon is clear: to help the Hebrews conquer the Promised Land. And this is why the Hebrews must wander in the wilderness for forty years, not as punishment for worshipping the Golden Calf, but so that Moses can provide them with the military training they will need to defeat the Canaanites. The Ark will help them with that but also helps Moses enforce discipline, for whenever someone doubts his

182 READERS OF THE LOST ARK

authority, he can use the technology of the Ark to make a miracle to convince the Hebrews to support him. Hancock admits that this is a "highly speculative thesis." But he also describes it as "a rational explanation" for those who want to read the Bible literally. It offers a technological explanation for the miracles of the Bible rather than having to accept that there were divine miracles. Such explanations are appealing to people who want to harmonize biblical literalism with more mechanistic worldviews. This theory explains why the Bible describes Moses's face as glowing after engaging with the Ark; the glow was caused by some kind of radiation from meteors. None of this makes any sense nor is the reconstruction of Moses's life based on any evidence whatsoever. Hancock relies on a sympathetic reader who is willing to accept that something like this could stand as an explanation because there is nothing to say that the Ark was *not* built this way. The Ark could have been some kind of ancient technology, but the author does not have the technical knowledge to understand it. The reader doesn't expect Hancock to understand the intricacies of radioactive technologies, however, and so this omission doesn't undermine his argument. This is another rhetorical stance of pseudoarchaeology. These technologies don't need to be fully explained, just suggested.

Secret Treasure Hunts

Hancock's book shows how a mix of fact and speculation can be blended in a convincing fashion. This is what much pseudoarchaeology does. It blurs the lines between historical evidence, scholarly reasoning, rampant speculation, and fabricated data. For the nonspecialist readers at whom these works are aimed, it is not necessarily clear when these authors are veering into pseudoscholarship. This is partly related to the distinct style of presentation, which is purposefully unpolished and has all the hallmarks of amateur writing. The authors position themselves as outsiders, as nonacademics, as nongovernment officials, who just have important stories that need to be told. Their works are not expected to have the kind of polish one expects of other types of publications. The photographs should be grainy, typos are to be expected, and the author isn't expected to get all the facts exactly right, because they are not part of the establishment who controls the facts.

The Sign and the Seal is the kind of treasure hunt book that has come to be common in pseudoarchaeology. And it is far from the only one that uses the Ark as the central object of its quest. Jonathan Gray's *Ark of the Covenant* (1997) is an extreme example of this kind of book; it blends reporting of an actual search for the Ark with pseudoscholarly readings of the past, conspiracy theories, and Christian apocalypticism. The logic is rarely clear, and the connections with the Ark are often tenuous. There is a tone of urgency within the book, and it is filled with warnings that you must read every word of some chapters but that you should skip others if you aren't ready for the truths that he is about to reveal.

These "truths" begin with the opening chapter that situates the book within the context of the assassination of Israeli Prime Minister Yitzhak Rabin, an assassination that Gray will later try to show was a mistake. Gray perpetuates an Israeli right-wing conspiracy theory that Rabin wanted to fake an assassination attempt to gain sympathy in an upcoming election, but the assassin accidentally used real bullets instead of blanks. By opening the book this way, the reader is left to presume that the Ark has something to do with these conspiracies in Israeli politics, but how exactly is never made clear.

After these introductory matters are dealt with, Gray offers a history of the Ark. However, it is the history of fringe scholars, involving not just biblical references, but some of the standard arguments of pseudoarchaeology. He writes about the Phoenicians traveling to North America, suggests that the crucifixion was not quite as reported in the Gospels, and ties these ideas in to different prophecies about the end times. After this difficult-to-follow historical overview, Gray offers a discussion of Ron Wyatt's quest for the Ark, the same Ron Wyatt that I mention in Chapter 5. The difference between the two discussions, however, is that Gray presents Wyatt's excavations as triumphant and asserts that he did, indeed, find the Ark. In an interesting twist of logic, Gray explains that God had promised Wyatt that he would find the Ark, not that he could retrieve it, and this is precisely what has happened. Gray and Wyatt know where the Ark is; they just cannot get to it. The book then explores the importance that the Ark will play in the coming days of Judgment and offers advice on how to accept Jesus into your heart in preparation for the end times. Gray repeats some common themes in contemporary Protestant apocalypticism, describing how the New World Order and the One World Economy, all led by the Antichrist, are developing.

Gray's book is extreme in that it combines so much different fringe thinking about the Ark in one volume. Yet it really shows how malleable this pseudoarchaeology can be for many communities. Here he has taken the story of an amateur archaeologist who was under the delusion that he knew

184 READERS OF THE LOST ARK

where the Ark was located and transformed it into a story that well matches the expectations of a specific subculture of American Protestantism, the same subculture that made the *Left Behind* series of books so popular. Ark stories are easily transformed into what the author wishes them to be. And since the powers of the Ark are so nebulous, the object can easily be situated at the center of any of these cultures. Tales of amateur treasure hunters looking for the Ark are readily adapted for whatever community is the target audience for the story.

The Ark as an Ancient Technology

What is perhaps captivating about the Ark for these fringe groups is that it can be thought of as having many of the hallmarks of an ancient technology. Its appearance is well known and like many technologies today has a box-like shape that could contain some type of device. Yet the "functions" of individual elements of the Ark are ambiguous. It offers the possibility to imagine that it was a kind of equipment that worked as an energy source, communication device, or both. That it is related, in the Bible, to God's contact with humans and His presence on earth only furthers the possibility that the Ark was an ancient technology. Like Belloq says in *Raiders of the Lost Ark*, "It's a transmitter, a radio for speaking to God." Through these pseudoarchaeological fabrications, the memory of the Ark becomes a memory related to future technologies, not ancient traditions.

For UFOlogists, that the ancients believed that the Ark was a means of communicating with the divine is exciting. While some who study UFOs associate them with religious experiences, others treat religious experiences as confusions for alien encounters. The appearance of Catholic saints or Ezekiel's biblical vision of a floating wheel are taken as early sightings of UFOs. The Ark does not have to be read in a Christian or Jewish light, but reports of its miracles can be taken literally. These accounts preserve that something was witnessed and written about in the Bible, was known in ancient times, but what was witnessed was not understood. Perhaps, for fringe interpreters, the Ark was a device for communicating with otherworldly creatures. The desire for those who study UFOs to have direct contact with alien beings is alluring. The Ark, then, can be imagined in this hopeful manner as evidence that extraterrestrial contacts can be mediated through technology. Perhaps studying the Ark can lead to the development of new technologies that can be marshaled toward the same goal. Depending on the author or, more importantly, the target audience, extraterrestrial and God become interchangeable as the voice on the other end of the Ark telephone.

The Ark has been easily incorporated into the technology-oriented mythological thinking that has been particularly apparent in North American and European popular culture. In the nineteenth century, the development of the telegraph was partially responsible for the rise of spiritualism, the practice in which the living attempted to make contact with the dead. The ability to speak to voices that were bodily distant lent itself to the idea that the chasm between the living and dead could similarly be crossed. Such technologically inspired fantasies were given a more extraterrestrial bent in the 1940s and 1950s with the development of radio. The potential for communicating with alien planets seemed plausible with this new technology. The rational-technological potential of these new communicative devices was merged with esoteric or antirational imaginings about unseen worlds. Understanding the Ark through these lenses was not such a stretch then, given the tradition history of it being the location where humans communicated with God. Rather than thinking of the Ark as a throne on which God made His presence felt, the Ark was transformed into a telephone or radio, a device through which God could talk to humans from afar.

The father of pseudoarchaeology and the grand doyen of ancient astronaut theorizing must be Erich Von Däniken. In 1968, the Swiss author published *Chariots of the Gods?*, a book that would go on to become one of the most influential works in fringe theorizing about the past, and the bane of archaeologists and historians for the decades to come. Von Däniken offers inconsistent accounts of alien encounters, but there are some standard ideas. Ancient mythology tells stories of ancient aliens who visited the earth. The gods, with their seeming supernatural powers, were aliens who had access to technologies that seemed magical to the ancient peoples who could not comprehend science. These aliens are sometimes credited with key moments in human progress; this is the driving idea behind the film and book *2001: A Space Odyssey* (1968), but ancient aliens theorists don't treat this idea as fiction. Von Däniken pulls together much spurious evidence to prove his point and connects mystical-seeming ancient sites from around the world to argue that alien visitation was a global phenomenon. The book spawned many sequels, numerous imitators, a theme park, and endless documentaries on the subject. The fact that Von Däniken was convicted of fraud and wrote one of his books from prison seems only to have increased his credentials among

186   READERS OF THE LOST ARK

fringe theorists who believe the establishment actively seeks to mute voices like his.

There is only brief mention of the Ark in *Chariots of the Gods?* It is worth quoting at length, not because of the quality of the ideas, but because the basic argument is repeated over and over in the pseudoscholarly literature. Von Däniken starts by explaining how Moses received very specific instructions on how to build the Ark, implying that some being with highly advanced technical skills was the instructor. This instructor taught someone how to use the properties of various kinds of metals to produce an electrical machine. But the people who built the Ark had little scientific knowledge in which to contextualize it and so they made mistakes. Von Däniken uses the example of Uzzah, reaching out to grab the Ark and being killed for doing so as proof that the Ark was electrical. Uzzah was not killed because of divine anger at polluting the Ark with unclean hands. He died because he touched an electrically charged machine. Von Däniken writes:

> Undoubtedly the Ark was electrically charged! If we reconstruct it today according to the instructions handed down by Moses, a voltage of several hundred volts is produced. The condenser is formed by the gold plates, one of which is positively, the other negatively, charged. If, in addition, one of the two cherubim on the mercy seat acted as a magnet, the loudspeaker— perhaps even a kind of set for communication between Moses and the spaceship was perfect. The details of the construction of the Ark of the Covenant can be read in the Bible in their entirety. Without actually consulting Exodus, I seem to remember that the Ark was often surrounded by flashing sparks and that Moses made use of this "transmitter" whenever he needed help and advice.

The leaps in logic here are many. There are blanket assertions that are not true. There is no way that following the actual instructions for constructing the Ark that are preserved in the Bible will create a condenser. This is just not true. Then there is the "if" statement regarding the cherubim. Beyond the fact that the sentence is grammatically nonsensical, here he just throws in two ideas, magnets and loudspeakers, that have no foundation in the text or in science. He then admits to not having needed to consult the Bible, because the evidence is so clear. These kinds of leaps of logic are found throughout the book. Yet what is so striking is how the rhetorical style hides the fallacies. This single paragraph has driven much Ark interpretation in

ALIENS, RADIOS, AND CONSPIRACIES   187

the decades since, attesting to just how convincing this rhetorical strategy can be.

Yet it was likely not reading these words in the book *Chariots of the Gods?* that spread this vision of the Ark so widely. Perhaps many more people heard the words spoken in the 1970 documentary of the same name that truly popularized Von Däniken's theories. The narrator explains that the danger that the Ark brought was not because of the presence of God. Rather, the machine itself was dangerous, and God's prescriptions to stay away from the Ark were ancient equivalents of modern safety manuals. The narrator explains:

> Moses was even to provide special shoes and clothing to protect his workmen. Shoes and clothing that would insulate them properly. If we were to build a replica of the Ark today according to Moses's instructions, we would have a condenser charged with several hundred volts. One side of the plates carrying a negative charge, the other, a positive one. The Bible says the Ark bristled with sparks and bright flashes, as in these old paintings.

This is very similar to what was written in the book, but here spoken by a narrator with a scientific-seeming mid-Atlantic accent while the camera pans over historical biblical paintings. The use of historical paintings suggests that people used to know that the Ark sparked and flashed. What is brought out more in this documentary is the safety element, and viewers would have easily been able to imagine this vision of the Ark in relation to industrial or electrical safety instructions they would have encountered at work or at home. The narration creates an obvious linkage between the ancient and the modern worlds through such concern for safety issues.

One of the functions of the Ark, the documentary continues, was as an audio amplifier. The narrator asks: "Could the gold sheath [the plating on the Ark] have been a form of loudspeaker reproducing the Lord's voice from afar?" The answer everyone should give to this is "no." But this is a typical rhetorical strategy of pseudoscholarship. Framing an ungrounded assertion in a "could it be possible" style question makes the unreasonable seem to be something that should be considered. This sets a foundation for the idea that God was an alien speaking to Moses, that all the ancient gods were aliens.

One striking divergence between the book and the documentary is the documentary's report on a supposed experiment in which an Ark was constructed in a scientific lab according to the instructions in the Bible. Here the documentary takes the book's "if we were to build" idea and claims

188   READERS OF THE LOST ARK

that this was actually done. It is again worth quoting what the documentary claims at length because the "facts" of this experiment are repeated in the literature. Reports of the experiment are provided while the camera pans over what is an obvious replica Ark, where the metallic qualities are exaggerated, followed by some kind of ambiguous industrial-research illustration. The narrator asserts: "In 1961 a group of Minnesota college students took this seriously enough to construct an Ark according to His directions. Their instructor, however, had to have the model destroyed because of the dangerously high electrical charge it developed." This is simply not true. The documentary has simply reframed a speculative possibility that Von Däniken wrote about as an experiment that happened. No specific college is mentioned, let alone an instructor. No suggestion of what course this could be is offered. I have never been in a Bible class where the students have wanted to make electrical conductors (although Shawn's experimental archaeology classes could venture down such a road, I guess). Conveniently, as is always the case in pseudoscience, the results are not available to be tested for some reason. Here, the machine had to be destroyed for safety reasons. Of course, the implication is that the viewer could replicate the experiment should they choose to do so. This supposed experiment is reported again and again as evidence of the electrical powers of the Ark.

A 1978 book called *The Manna Machine*, written by George Sassoon and Rodney Dale, built on this idea that the Ark was some kind of mechanical device. Sassoon was an engineer with a literary pedigree, the only child of the poet Siegfried Sassoon (best known for his ruminations on World War I). George Sassoon was also an avid UFOlogist and spent his life investigating and writing on this phenomenon. Rodney Dale was a professional nonfiction writer, and it is unclear how seriously he took UFOs or the ideas espoused in *The Manna Machine* (as he was an avid investigator and debunker of urban legends). The authors claim to have retranslated the sections of the *Zohar* that discuss the Ark (publishing the translations in a later book) and concluded that the Ark was a nuclear reactor. It was used to power another machine, a machine that transformed algae into food for the Israelites when they were wandering in the wilderness. This food is what was called manna in the Old Testament, the mysterious food source that allowed the Hebrews to survive in the desert. The machine ran for six days but had to be powered off every seventh day for maintenance. It was this mechanical schedule that led to the requirements for a sabbath day, a day of rest. The rest was initially intended for the Ark, not for humans!

The Manna Machine clearly inspired Erich Von Däniken, and he returned to the subject of the Ark in his 1979 *Signs of the Gods?* There he uses Sassoon's and Dale's theory as his stepping-off point, but mixes in readings of biblical, apocryphal, rabbinic writings, and the *Kebra Nagast* to expand it, arguing that the Ark and manna machine were gifts to the Israelites from alien visitors. Von Däniken claims not to have all the answers to the mysteries that surrounded this ancient gift, but he can at least say that Moses knew that the aliens were from another planet, and they used their advanced technology to impress the Israelites. For Von Däniken, it was clear that the extraterrestrials wanted to isolate a group of humans for two generations as some kind of experiment, but the nature of that experiment remains unknown. He also argued that the aliens must not have had access to a space fleet at the time that could accommodate such large numbers of people.

What happens to the Ark next is unclear to Von Däniken. He believes that after it was no longer necessary to produce manna, the Israelites forgot how to work the machine. The Ark still remained dangerous, and the occasional radioactive accident made people leery of it, David so much so that he would not allow it into his palace, and Solomon so much so that he constructed a separate building to store it. From this point forward, Von Däniken offers two theories about the Ark's fate and a possible means of harmonizing both ideas. The first is that, as Jerusalem was about to be destroyed by the Babylonians, the aliens did not want the Ark to fall into King Nebuchadnezzar's hands, so they helped the prophet Jeremiah hide the Ark. For some reason the aliens could not take it themselves. Von Däniken also offers another possibility. He suggests that Jeremiah hid a false Ark, an Ark that was just a replica. Von Däniken recounts the story from the *Kebra Nagast* (the story of how the Ark got to Ethiopia, discussed in Chapter 8) and supplements it by suggesting that aliens gave Solomon's son a flying vehicle to transport the Ark to Ethiopia. Solomon, wanting to hide the fact that the Ark was stolen right from under him, built a replica and so no one beyond a small circle knew that the Ark was no longer in the Temple. That must have included one group of aliens, the ones who helped Jeremiah, who did not know or remember that another group of aliens had helped Solomon's son take the Ark away. He concludes by stating that no one knows where the Ark is now but offers the suggestion that perhaps the Vatican has it, playing on a particular brand of anti-Catholic conspiracy theory, suggesting that Mussolini's fascists took the Ark when they invaded Abyssinia and gave it to the Vatican as some kind "act of homage."

190   READERS OF THE LOST ARK

The blending and harmonizing of all sorts of different ancient accounts is part of what makes Von Däniken's and others' arguments convincing to a subset of people. He references actual ancient documents, documents that people are unlikely to have read, that offer a level of authenticity to his claims. The interaction with the biblical account also helps, as he can show that not much needs to be changed in the Bible to make his version of the story make sense. Von Däniken also builds on his audience's tendency, as nonconformists, to want to see the Bible as somehow having misled people for all these years. The logic he uses is to take advantage of the gaps in the biblical stories, filling in what the Bible itself does not explain.

Since the idea that the Ark was some kind of ancient machine has been established within these circles, similar ideas have been repeated and recycled in different formats in all sorts of spurious works. David Medina's 2014 book *The Ark of the Covenant and Other Secret Weapons of the Ancients* is one example. There he suggests that the Ark had nuclear powers (provided by aliens) or paranormal powers (given by supernatural beings). Which is the case is not so clear, but some unpacking of his arguments illustrates the particular blend of technocratic fantasies which Medina perpetuates. The Ark in Medina's book is an Ark that reflects an ancient technology, lost to the present. The gold plating of the Ark, the cherubim, and other physical features are reinterpreted as functional elements of what could be electrical, magnetic, or nuclear devices. These claims are all variations on Von Däniken's themes.

Medina follows Von Däniken's claims that the Bible contains very specific details about its construction, and yet, unlike Von Däniken, acknowledges that there seems to be nothing even remotely electrical in any biblical passage. Bezalel does not seem to have been an electrician. Yet Medina has an answer for this. What should be descriptions of electrical equipment have been replaced by descriptions of "harmless ornamental borders." The Levites, he continues, "wisely re-described some of the components to obscure the obvious truth yet left enough evidence for the diligent enquirers to reconstruct the original meaning at a future date when the time was right for it to be known." In other words, the Bible has been written in code, and he is one of the diligent enquirers who has cracked it. Medina participates in a long tradition, though, of believing that the Bible bears purposefully obscured knowledge. As we've seen periodically over the course of this book, people living as long ago as Roman times (such as the early rabbis) and maybe even as long ago as Old Testament times, such as the prophets who wrote of apocalyptic

ALIENS, RADIOS, AND CONSPIRACIES   191

visions, have thought the Bible contains information that has been purposefully hidden in codes.

There is no consistency to Medina's attribution of powers to the Ark. For example, in his discussion of the use of the Ark in Joshua's battle at Jericho, he explains: "A popular belief is that the high-pitched frequency of the trumpets caused the wall to disintegrate. Although this is probably true, the laser beams directed at it during the thirteen circuits made by the ark would have weakened the wall considerably." Medina clearly wants to appease readers who want to take the traditions about Jericho seriously, but with the Ark functioning as a technologically advanced weapon, not a source of divine power. Elsewhere he postulates that the tablets Moses placed in the Ark were plutonium and uranium, that the cherubim formed a parabola, that the Ark produced radiation and electricity when in the Tabernacle, but only radiation when outside of the Tabernacle, and that the Ark was an electrical cell.

When the Ark is invoked in this literature, each author seems to be trying to add some new twist to the claims that the Ark is some kind of electrical power box with radio-transmitting powers. Take David Hatcher Childress, one of the many authors profiting from the current ancient aliens craze. In his *Ark of God*, he asserts that the Egyptians were well-versed in electrical engineering and explains how various Egyptian art depicts electrical devices. All of this is nonsense. His addition to pseudoarchaeological fantasies about the Ark is that he imagines it used Egyptian electrical technology, and he even suggests that the Ark would have been part of an electrical system within the Great Pyramid at Giza. By framing his claim within a discussion that presumes that it is a well-known fact that the Egyptians used electricity like we do (which is not true at all), it makes it seem that Moses could have been an electrician. Childress offers explanations rooted in contemporary science, such that the Ark used Tesla coils or was a Van de Graaf generator. Since these are "real" technologies, reference to these technologies may convince some readers that the Ark *could* have been electrical. And, since "Tesla" carries so many ambiguous connotations surrounding early electricity and modernity, just using that name may be evocative enough. The reader of Childress's book has been inundated with many of these claims, a rhetorical strategy referred to as *copia*. All that matters is that the reader now believes ancient electricity was possible; it doesn't matter which specific technology the Ark was powered with.

These various books reach a limited audience. It is really television that now perpetuates these fantastic Ark stories. The History Channel's

192 READERS OF THE LOST ARK

most-watched show is *Ancient Aliens*, the inspiration for seemingly endless memes that my students print out and tape to my office door to torment me. It, of course, featured an episode on the various possible extraterrestrial functions of the Ark. Episode 10 from season 6, "Aliens and the Lost Ark," does not add much that is new to the various alien theories. There are segments on Ethiopia, on the Ark being a "manna machine" (like Sassoon and Dale's theory), and on the Ark being a nuclear device, with the concomitant suggestion that the priestly garb was like the protective gear one wears during an X-ray. The episode also suggests that there may be more than one Ark, or that the Knights Templars took it.

Perhaps the most novel discussion in the program is the segment treating the Ark as an electrical device, fulfilling the promise of the fake experiment first mentioned in the *Chariots of the Gods?* documentary decades ago. While the ideas in the segment are not new, they are delivered by Michael Dennin, a professor of physics and astronomy from UC Irvine, who adds some seemingly scientific legitimacy. He explains how the Ark could work as an electrical capacitor, by illustrating which parts of the Ark, on his life-size model set up in his laboratory, functioned to conduct positive and negative charges. After explaining how the device works, Dennin discusses biblical descriptions of people seeing God on the mercy seat. He argues that these descriptions are consistent with what people would have seen if they were witnessing electrical currents arcing between the cherubim. Dennin's discussion of science and religion is typical of his approaches to public outreach, where he tries to convince the public that science and religion are not antithetical. The type of argument he makes about the Ark is very representative of this movement, which tries to harmonize biblical miracles with scientific explanation. Elsewhere in the *Ancient Aliens* episode, we hear that a sonic boom could have knocked down the walls of Jericho. Dennin's message is usually aimed at convincing conservative Christians not to see science as oppositional to faith, and his best-known publications are aimed at that audience. Recontextualized on *Ancient Aliens*, Dennin's message merges thinking about antiquity with the new technocratic mythologies that have been discussed in this chapter.

Generally, I feel that pseudoarchaeologists usually seek to anchor their arguments in some kind of reality; it is just that they are imagining a reality that is different from that presented in mainstream scholarship. By embracing these arguments, audiences can enjoy thinking about mysterious things, and they can receive a satisfactorily enigmatic solution to the mystery

ALIENS, RADIOS, AND CONSPIRACIES   193

presented, one that seems to have a foundation in technological realities but still facilitates a belief in the fantastic. Shifting the mysteries of the Ark from the realm of religion to the realm of science fiction, ancient aliens fantasies reflect a disillusionment with mainstream religion. At the same time, they satisfy the urge for new forms of technocratically oriented religion.

These imagined realities may be more interesting, more romantic, or more comforting for people than historical facts. Even conspiracies are comforting, because that means that there is a reason why things have happened. In *The X- Files* fashion, conspiracies simultaneously offer fear and solace. Psychological studies of conspiracy theorists emphasize the seemingly ironic comfort that the paranoid gain from believing such things. Whether rooted in anti- Semitism, anti- Catholicism, or anti- left- wing politics, beliefs that the Jews, the pope, or the Clintons are secretly running the world, concerns and reassures the paranoid simultaneously. The possibility that life events are random can be more frightening than the possibility that an evil elite controls everything.

How does the Ark play into these conspiracies? The repeated claims that the Ark was some kind of alien weapon, alien transmitter, or other type of alien technology are part of the background fringe history that has built the foundation for these kinds of extreme views. Like Noah's Ark, Atlantis, the Nazca Lines, Stonehenge, or the supposed secret library beneath the Sphinx, these objects of pseudoarchaeological speculation that are the repeated subjects of books and documentaries have created a modern mythos of the ancient mysterious. The authorities (whoever they are) want to keep these "truths" obscured (for whatever reason).

Confusing Fact and Fantasy

What might be striking to you by this point in the book is how many similarities there are between these fringe accounts of the Ark and *Raiders of the Lost Ark*. For Indiana Jones, the Ark was discoverable through secret codes left by the ancients (the staff of Ra and the Map Room of Tanis, for example). The Ark was a weapon, powerful enough that it could have allowed Hitler to win the war and was worth devoting significant funds to find. The Ark was a conductor of electricity, or something akin to electricity, as displayed by the energy that is released by the Ark to kill the Nazis at the end of the film. The pseudoarchaeological treatment of the Ark is further exaggerated in *Indiana*

194   READERS OF THE LOST ARK

Jones and the Kingdom of the Crystal Skull. There we find out which warehouse the Ark has been stored in by the US government—Area 51. Area 51 is, according to conspiracy theorists and pseudoscientists who believe that the government is hiding knowledge about aliens, the location where a UFO that supposedly crashed in Roswell is now stored. While the fourth Indiana Jones film was clearly playing on that kind of pseudoscience, the films may destabilize audience understandings of what is fact and fantasy.

Reading the Ark in the context of fringe science points to much more serious concerns about how the boundaries of science, history, and fantasy are purposefully obscured through contemporary media outlets. These new media forms really began to emerge in the 1970s and then exploded in the 2000s as the media landscape became significantly more diverse as television expanded beyond the main three American network channels. This has become even more extreme with the advent of streaming. As these channels chase ratings, legitimate educational programs like *Nova* on PBS are overshadowed by infotainment programs on channels like History and Discovery and streamed through other services.

When ancient aliens programming is repeatedly interspersed with documentaries on World War II and the American Civil War, audiences start to become conditioned to accept that all of what appears on the channel can be considered "real." The effect is so powerful, and so unapparent, that viewers cannot fight it because they do not realize that they are being manipulated. Numerous psychological studies on the effectiveness of film for propaganda have demonstrated that it has particular impacts on the brain related to memory creation that are ripe for confusing trustworthy and untrustworthy recollection. People use the same parts of their brain to create memories of their lived lives as they do for creating memories of watching films. This makes sense because watching films is an activity that people do in their lives and can remember doing. If films mirror real life, then the memories that are formed can confuse lived experiences with cinematic images. Strangely though, there is a really important difference in these kinds of memories. Studies have shown that while individual memories of actual experiences get weaker over time, the impacts of targeted propaganda increase in the individual over time, a phenomenon called "the sleeper effect" by media scholars.

During World War II, the American government had the brilliant film director Frank Capra produce explicit propaganda films, recognizing that movies were more effectively convincing over the long term than statements made by politicians. Politicians and other authorities tend to illicit suspicion on behalf of their audiences. Statements made by these sources are treated with a critical stance, often even by those who support the views being espoused, and these suspicions are incorporated into the memories that are formed. Audiences interact with film in a different way. While watching films, an individual may react in a critical fashion. Yet after time has elapsed, and the source of the memories has been forgotten, the memories themselves are still vivid in the mind of the individual, but a critical stance has not been incorporated into the formation of the memory. Without being able to remember the source, that same capacity for critical thinking has been eroded.

Pseudoarchaeological presentations about the past are not necessarily conscious propaganda efforts of these media outlets. Many of the techniques that are used are the same, but for commercial gain, to hook viewers into repeated viewings, not for any kind of explicit brainwashing. The lack of intention does not mean that the impacts are not the same. Pseudoarchaeological presentations on television follow documentary forms, and we have been conditioned, as viewers, to think of documentaries as presenting "facts" as opposed to fictional filmed accounts. Documentaries use various conventions to convince us of their factualness and because we have become so conditioned to accept them, they are more convincing than explicit claims to truth. Now, when viewers watch a documentary that describes the Ark as some kind of battery built by aliens, they may respond critically in the moment. The problem is that those critical feelings about the documentary do not last. They are replaced with memories of the presentation, and perhaps memories of some kind of expert explaining the situation. But viewers often cannot remember the source or the lack of credibility of the expert who has been filmed in the same fashion as any "talking head" on a news program. And when such messages are repeated, the ability to discriminate between good and bad sources is eroded.

Now, of course, this does not mean that all viewers will uncritically accept that the Ark was brought to Earth by aliens because of such documentaries. Most will not. On an individual level, everyone will respond differently. Cumulatively, however, the saturation of the media landscape with such messages, and the confusion of genre conventions between legitimate news accounts and ratings- chasing nonsense documentaries, disrupts the distinction between journalism or scholarship from fantasy, propaganda, or pseudoscience. Furthermore, studies have shown that even if viewers are watching something explicitly fictional, religious elements of that fiction are sometimes processed as nonfiction, especially among viewers who have tendencies to want to believe in such phenomena. So documentaries about the mystical, supernatural, or alien powers of the Ark may be especially convincing for some viewers.

How do archaeologists combat this? Studies have shown that the most effective way to assist the development of critical stances toward cinematic presentations is to call into the question their legitimacy at the moment that viewers see them. Of course, it is impossible to intervene with all pseudoarchaeological presentations, given their prominence in our media landscape, so only the most prominent of such presentations can be expected to generate this kind of response from the profession. But this is important work.

Take, for example, Graham Hancock's 2022 Netflix documentary series *Ancient Apocalypse*. Organizations like the Society for American Archaeology (SAA) immediately issued a public statement criticizing the documentary and Netflix. Some in the field complained that this just gave Hancock's documentary more press, and that is true. However, the psychological impacts of propaganda described above mean that the approach of calling out the documentary's illegitimacy was more important than the potential such statements had of attracting new viewers. The obvious response from Hancock, that such a statement by the SAA proved that archaeologists were threatened by his ideas, plays into his larger narrative, and likely convinced many of his followers that archaeologists have something to hide. We are threatened, but we do not have anything to hide. As professionals, many of us paid by taxpayers, we have an ethical obligation to take a stance against the presentation of archaeology that is used illegitimately and harmfully. Trust me. None of us would want to hide some elaborate discovery of aliens or lost Ice Age tribes; we would use it to get promotions and funding at our own institutions. But because of the psychological impacts described above, we need to point out these problems when viewers are watching such programs or else the effectiveness of the critique is minimized. The critique must be built in as part of the memory of the viewer right from the formation of that memory.

The relationship between media memories and the Ark is more complex than simply whether one thinks the Ark looked like the version that Indy chased in *Raiders of the Lost Ark*. As I have argued quite a bit through this book, for many, that has become the default vision of what the Ark looked like. Outside of faith-based receptions, these pseudoarchaeological documentary visions of the Ark are likely the next most influential. Here the readings of the Ark are not focused on what it looked like, but rather what it was and what it did. In my anecdotal experiences of discussing the Ark with nonarchaeologists over many years, I have seen how these memory processes have played out, where the legitimacy of the source of information about the Ark, and the specifics of that information, have become confused, while certain beliefs about the Ark have become cemented. The most common comment I hear about the Ark is that it is probably in Ethiopia. This comes not from knowledge of Ethiopian traditions but through Graham Hancock's account, whether directly from having read the book, or now more likely, through watching documentaries inspired by his book that elide the complexities of its reception history in Africa.

Returning to the issue of why professional scholars get so upset by pseudoarchaeology, it may not be apparent why these fantastic receptions of the Ark should be so problematic. You may have noticed that I have tried to be agnostic about the other reception traditions discussed in this book, and that I generally take an agnostic stance about whether there ever was a real Ark (I think it is more likely than not that it did exist in some form). The answer of why the receptions described in this chapter bother me is straightforward. I think they perpetuate racism. For me, archaeological and historical studies are fundamentally about understanding other people, people in a different time and place. And I believe that attempting to genuinely understand others is a powerful means of combatting racism. So why are these receptions racist? They are problematic in several ways. The overarching problem is that they are predicated on the idea that ancient people lacked the intelligence or sophistication to achieve what they did. Now, it is not like the Ark is one of these achievements that seemingly need explanation in the way that these documentaries present monumental architecture as mysterious. Rather, the Ark is used as evidence for lost ancient or alien technology that "proves" the idea that science inconceivable to us now was known to the ancients. Because of the ambiguities in the reception history of the Ark, it can be deployed as evidence for ancient aliens or other spurious viewpoints. Since it is plausible to people that the Ark had some kind of dangerous power, it is easy to incorporate it as evidence in these kinds of pseudoarchaeological arguments.

Treatments of the Ark specifically, however, feed a very particular form of anti-Semitism as well. Now, I am not accusing any of the authors I have discussed in this chapter as anti-Semitic, or at least as purposefully putting

198   READERS OF THE LOST ARK

forward anti-Semitic ideas. However, these ideas feed into a type of anti-Semitism that emerged in the scholarship of the ancient Near East at the end of the nineteenth century. For biblical scholars and Assyriologists, we refer to the origins of this kind of anti-Semitism as the *Bibel und Babel* controversy, referencing the German academic discussions from which this emerged. As Mesopotamian writings were translated at the end of the nineteenth century, the fact that there was a shared Mesopotamian and biblical culture became apparent, given some of the similarities that were identified. So some scholars began to postulate that the Old Testament was really a corruption of better, Mesopotamian ideas. The Old Testament origins of Christianity were seen as corrupt and somehow deficient, but the New Testament did not have to be discarded because of this. The Old Testament was just taken as an insufficient record about pre-Christian traditions. This became another way that Christians could justify anti-Semitism. Scholarly discussions like these led to other efforts to contextualize the New Testament and the early Church in European thinking rather than Old Testament thinking, and scholars looked for non-Jewish origins for Christian practices, like celebrations surrounding Christmas and Easter. Watch for it. Every year around Easter, memes circulate around the Internet describing the relationship between Easter and the Mesopotamian goddess Ishtar, when in fact, there is no connection other than that the two words sound vaguely similar. These kinds of intellectual apparatuses, based on bad scholarship, informed the anti-Semitism of the twentieth century, most notably that of Nazi Germany but other manifestations as well. So, to my mind, seeking an alien origin for the Ark, or arguing that it was given to the Israelites by some technologically masterful race now long lost, does the same thing. These perspectives take a Jewish tradition and provide a way for people to imagine it as separate from Jewish culture. And if the Ark doesn't have to be Jewish, then many other elements of biblical culture don't have to be as well. Thus, the foremost religious object of ancient Israel is made into something that is not Jewish.

The point of this chapter has not been to convince pseudoarchaeologists that they are wrong. As I have hopefully illustrated, the rhetorical strategies that they employ make it almost impossible to convince them that their interpretations are unfounded. I hope it has illustrated how interpretive strategies are enacted in pseudoarchaeology, what kind of reasoning (especially fallacious reasoning) is typical, and to hint at some of the harms that can come from reading the Ark in this light. I think that a particularly dangerous stance that we can fall into when engaging with pseudoarchaeology is that we should keep an open mind. That is the wedge that is used to slip in a lot of bad reasoning. Rather, I think we need to approach any argument that is claimed to be rooted in archaeology in terms of the evidence. If there is evidence, the claim is worth considering. If there isn't, why would we bother?

Conclusion

I have two distinct relationships to the Ark that, in theory, I am able to keep separate from one another. Yet, in practice, I think that they might bleed together. The first is my professional, academic relationship to the Ark. As a specialist in ancient Near Eastern religion and someone who practices an historical-critical approach to biblical studies, the Ark is a curious component of Iron Age Israelite religion, because of how much it matches other kinds of religious equipment but also in how it seems adapted to the idiosyncrasies of the worship of Yahweh. It is entangled with one of the most substantive debates in biblical studies, a controversy that polarizes scholars that nothing else in the field does right now. It is a debate that emerged when I was an undergraduate student and has remained unresolved throughout my entire career. This is the argument over the historicity of the United Monarchy, of the kingdom of Saul, David, and Solomon, and has profound implications for the Ark. It leads to the question of whether it ever existed as an historical object, or if it was just the imaginings of people from a later time. While I feel that it is more likely that it did exist than it didn't, that the stories about it don't make as much sense if one doesn't reconstruct an historical object behind them, this uncertainty means that there are many contextual questions that must remain unresolved. How innovative was the Ark as a means of adapting traditional cultic objects for a new monotheistic and aniconic context? Did it take the traditional statue of a god for a temple context and remake it into a throne for the deity instead? How much of a role did it play in the justification of royal authority? Or the authority of the Jerusalem Temple and/or the Levite priests who were the ones allowed to engage with it? How did the miraculous stories of the Ark reify existing power structures or help create new ones? We can answer some of these questions from a narrative perspective. That is to say, when we treat the Bible as literature, we can understand the different roles that the Ark plays from the standpoint of the final editor of the text. The stories about the Ark are flexible enough that they can be just as meaningful no matter which historical context one reconstructs for their origins. These are the

Readers of the Lost Ark. Kevin M. McGeough, Oxford University Press. © Oxford University Press 2025.
DOI: 10.1093/9780197653913.003.0011

CONCLUSION 201

kinds of engagement with the Ark that my academic archaeological and biblical training have prepared me for.

And yet there is also my second relationship to the Ark, one that is much older than my professional training, my relationship to it that was inspired by popular culture. My experiences as an Indiana Jones "fanboy" compel different kinds of thinking about the Ark. I imagine the Ark in the form that I first encountered it, as Indiana Jones and Sallah lifted it out of its resting place in the Well of the Souls. I cannot help but think of it as something that should not be opened, even though there is no historical or biblical precedent for this, only cinematic precedent. Why is this such an important mode of thinking about the Ark for me? I'm not sure. For other fans, it is the sense of community that the Ark and Indy's other treasures help mediate. I don't really like being part of a fan culture, but I also can't help it. In any case, this is really the Ark that I imagine when I'm thinking about it.

I do not think I am alone in this. In the first half of the twenty-first century, the reception of the Ark cannot be disentangled from *Raiders of the Lost Ark*, even if its wider reception has settled into three dominant modes: as mediated through Judaism and Christianity, as mediated through *Raiders of the Lost Ark*, and as mediated through pseudoarchaeology (which blends both other modes together). That is not to say that older forms of reception no longer influence our interpretations of the Ark of the Covenant. People still treat it metaphorically, as was the case in rabbinic Judaism and medieval Christianity. People still read the biblical accounts seriously and try, through close reading and intertextual analysis, to learn as much about an historic Ark as possible. People still look to Egypt and Mesopotamia for similar kinds of objects. Despite this, it is very hard to imagine an Ark distinct from Indy's. Whether one is thinking about the Ark as an object of faith, as a radio to talk to aliens, or as a souvenir from a favorite movie, the power of the visual representation in the film drives our imagination. It is a religious artifact, it is a movie prop, and it is an object of mysteries. All of these receptions are held simultaneously.

These reception tensions can be seen in a Christian metalcore band named Ark of the Covenant. Hailing from Connecticut, according to an interview on the HxC (Hardcore Church) YouTube channel, Ark of the Covenant plays music that is intended to send a message that it is all right to be frustrated with the church. You can dislike church authority but still be a good Christian. This kind of anti-institutional, but still religious, messaging makes sense within the context of Christian metal. Their songs address issues of

202 READERS OF THE LOST ARK

faith and moral issues surrounding those who claim to be Christian but don't act like Christians. Such frustration makes sense for the genre of metalcore, which blends heavy metal and punk styles, with very aggressive vocals. As for the name, on the Sounds Heavy podcast, the bassist Daniel Graves explains that he joined after the band formed but that no one ever talks about why they called themselves Ark of the Covenant. The interviewers laughingly suggest that it is an obvious name for a Christian metalcore band. Heavy metal often references the ancient world, especially Egyptian and Norse antiquity. In Christian metal the references are biblical, and the word *covenant* is often invoked in the circles of people to whom this music is aimed. On the same podcast, the bassist laughs about how the band is often trolled by Indiana Jones fans, reflecting the truly dual sets of audiences interested in the Ark in the twenty-first century. It is hard to imagine that the band would have called themselves Ark of the Covenant had Lucas and Spielberg chosen another artifact for Indy to seek.

The tension between the Ark as a religious object and as a popular culture artifact may not be as extreme as it seems. Fans, religious believers, and ancient aliens theorists treat the object somewhat similarly. The actual views of the Ark held by individuals in any of these communities, or who self-identify across communities, however, likely vary quite considerably. Still, they are mostly visualizing the same Ark. It is a golden box with anthropomorphic figures on top that was built in biblical times, and it has subsequently gone missing.

A more complex tension that is still present and that has been apparent since biblical times is between treating the Ark as an historical object and treating the Ark as metaphor. People can do both simultaneously, just as ancient and medieval interpreters did. Still, the way the Ark is invoked is different. As a metaphor, the Ark's meanings are perhaps more restricted. In Judaism it continues to stand as a symbol of pre-rabbinic Judaism, as a Judaism centered in the land of Israel with a capital city of Jerusalem. Yet as a Torah Ark, it also stands for the replicability of the Temple for Jews living outside of the land and symbolizes shared space for Jews living in the diaspora. For Christians, its metaphorical meanings have perhaps become less overt than they were for medieval Christians. It still seems to represent God's laws and wisdom. But perhaps for many, like the members of the rock band that took its name, it really just represents a "cool" approach to biblical things. For others, like Bishop Joshua who brought the Ark to Toronto, it is a means for concentrating and directing the faith of worshippers, a means of

CONCLUSION   203

harnessing that faith to gain access to the healing powers of God. For both Jews and Christians, objects that stand in for it now still assist people in gaining a closer experience of God.

Medieval approaches to thinking about the Ark do persist. The Ark continues to be viewed metaphorically, as an object whose contemplation can help explain theological truths. That the Ark of the Covenant could be an instrument of atonement was suggested by John Diodati in the seventeenth century, and that idea continues into popular culture in the present. Nick Cave's song "The Mercy Seat" tells the story of a death row inmate dying in the electric chair and eventually admitting to the crime of which he is accused. The title makes obvious reference to the Ark, one which may be missed by many listeners. But the Ark's invocation cannot be missed in the lyrics. Midway through the song, the inmate sings about the Ark, describing it as made of gold in heaven but constructed of wood and wire on earth. He explains that while his body lights on fire, God is nearby. In a song replete with biblical allusions, "an eye for an eye, a tooth for a tooth," the mercy seat is not the cover of the Ark of the Covenant but the electric chair. The electric chair here is the instrument of judgment, through which the execution of the prisoner may bring about his redemption. As Johnny Cash covers it, that sense of redemption seems clear by the end, and the singer on death row seems to have made his peace before dying. Yet in the original performed by Nick Cave and the Bad Seeds, the song ends with more of a sense of defiance, as we hear the inmate argue that there "was no proof" and that he "is not afraid to die." Jesus was also executed, the singer reminds us, as he complains about all things being labeled "good or ungood." He sings "And I've got nothing left to lose / But I'm not afraid to die," the listener ponders the relationship between law and redemption, and about the morality of punishment as the inmate describes his experiences in the electric chair in increasingly more graphic detail.

There are other similarities between contemporary Christian and Jewish thinking about the Ark, especially on the margins of both of those communities. For contemporary Christians concerned with the end times, the Ark remains a potent symbol of the Second Coming of Christ that will be inaugurated when the Temple is rebuilt in Israel. Self- proclaimed "end times expert" Michael Snyder claims that authorities know exactly where the Temple is located, that it is not lost at all. His view is not unusual among this particular subgroup of twenty- first- century Christian apocalypticists. In a curious twist of reception history, Snyder and other "end time experts"

204 READERS OF THE LOST ARK

discuss the location of the Ark in a recent article in *Charisma* (a magazine representing the charismatic movement in Christianity). Their discussion is similar to that found in ancient literature, arguing about whether it was Josiah or Jeremiah who hid the Ark, citing the same traditions discussed in Chapter 3. Ancient arguments about the Ark are picked up centuries later, but they are now used in an entirely different context. Contemporary Christian apocalypticists hold a curious relationship with ultra-conservative Zionist organizations, as both are interested in the reconstruction of the Temple in Jerusalem. In that same article in *Charisma*, the Christian end time experts defer to the knowledge of an organization called the Temple Institute, the organization discussed in Chapter 7, which is dedicated to rebuilding the Temple on the Temple Mount in Jerusalem. Here the goals of these different religious movements coalesce in their desire for a new Jerusalem Temple, and the Ark stands as a potent symbol for both. The Ark of the Covenant stands simultaneously for a biblical past and a messianic future.

Christians and Jews interested in restoring the Temple Mount to Israeli control are audiences that twenty-first-century Ark explorers cultivate as supporters for their quests. Here, religious faith and pseudoarchaeology bleed into one another. In the early twentieth century, Parker and others could target mainstream donors, people with a general interest in archae-ology. Now though, these explorers target more specific audiences, in this case Christians and Jews who are not happy with the status quo agreement over the Temple Mount. Those two audiences gathered in December 2018, for an explicitly interfaith conference, intending to garner support for Israeli control over the Temple Mount, and one such Ark explorer made an ap-pearance. His presentation is hyperlinked in this same article of *Charisma* just mentioned, showing just how interconnected these kinds of theologies are. The conference was held at the Menachem Begin Center in Jerusalem, a location chosen because four years prior, an activist for Israeli control of the Temple Mount had been shot there by a Palestinian (the activist was not killed but went on to a career in Israeli politics).

The treasure hunter at this conference was James Barfield, the director of the "Copper Scroll Project." The Copper Scroll is one of the Dead Sea Scrolls, but it is an unusual one. Unlike the other scrolls found at Qumran, this one was literally made of copper. That is not all that is strange about it. The Copper Scroll is a list of sixty-four locations where treasure was supposedly hidden. No one knows if the treasure listed ever really existed, and there are competing theories that are equally plausible. Generally, the theorists can

CONCLUSION 205

be divided into two camps: those who believe that the treasure was real and those who believe it was legendary. Within each of these camps are a variety of different historical contexts to explain the creation of the text, the hiding of the treasure, or the imagining of such wealth. Perhaps it was metaphorical, or the text has some other meaning that we do not understand. Perhaps the treasure was found by the Romans. In any case, its riddle-like descriptions of what could be vast amounts of silver and gold have been inspirational to the pseudoarchaeological community.

Barfield is one such pseudoarchaeologist who believes that he has deciphered the Copper Scroll. Describing himself as a retired criminal investigator (he was an arson investigator), he states that he doesn't know why scholars couldn't identify the locations of the hidden treasure. But he claims to have done so. He explains that his methodology is rooted in his professional experiences as an investigator, looking at evidence and figuring out who committed crimes. The implication here is that his detective-like procedures are a better avenue for understanding the scroll than those more typically used by Hebraists. In his presentation at the Temple Mount conference, he reads sections of the scroll and then points out the exact places at the site of Qumran to which the scroll alludes. He reads the Copper Scroll just like a cinematic treasure hunter reads a set of clues about where the ancient loot has been hidden. He takes the clues as descriptions to places on the site and then looks for the locations in Qumran that best match those descriptions.

Then he brings in the scientific instruments that can almost confirm his findings, instruments that were used to scan some of the locations where he believes that the gold was buried. Barfield shows images of, and describes the capabilities of, a sophisticated seeming technology—a Lorenz Z1. Now, archaeologists use all sorts of tools to engage in remote sensing, to measure the properties of the soil of an area to know what might be located beneath the surface. Sometimes this is done before excavating to make sure that you are digging in the right place. Other times it is done so that you don't have to excavate, so that you can leave the archaeological remains undisturbed and still get a sense of what is there. The Lorenz Z1 is a metal detector and is the type of metal detector used by gold prospectors, less so by archaeologists. Barfield shows the results of his scans and images of a team using a Lorenz Z1 at another site. The results indicate the possibility that vast amounts of non-ferrous metal (metal without iron in it like gold and silver) are buried exactly where he believes the Copper Scroll says. But as anyone who uses remote sensing technology will argue, Barfield explains that the only way to know for sure what is there is to dig it up. Archaeologists call this ground truthing, but Barfield is not an archaeologist. He is an amateur treasure hunter, and this is a device that is marketed for people like him, people who loot sites looking for buried gold.

Why does Barfield think that there is gold hidden at Qumran? He has been influenced by another pseudoarchaeologist, Vendyl Jones, who searched for the Ark at Qumran, quasi-legally. Barfield was clearly influenced by Jones's reading of the Copper Scroll in relation to apocryphal literature that describes Jeremiah having hidden the Temple treasures. Based on this, Barfield argues that there are literally billions of dollars of gold (in one hidden area at least 900 talents of gold), much silver, and treasures from the Temple, which, elsewhere he posits may include the Ark of the Covenant. In his presentation he compares a map of Jerusalem to a map of Qumran and then reorients the Qumran map 180 degrees. In doing so, Barfield claims that there are striking similarities between the two sites and that Qumran was created as an "inverted version of Jerusalem at time of Jeremiah." Following this logic is difficult because the two map overlays do not look much like one another and so the similarities aren't readily apparent. More problematically, however, is that he is comparing two modern maps, which are themselves abstractions of sites, abstractions that do not reflect how ancient people would have conceptualized space. Playing with image overlays until one finds a "match" may make for a good visual presentation, but one can manipulate any series of images in this fashion to come to the conclusions one wants.

While in his presentation Barfield claims that the Israel Antiquities Authority takes his claims seriously, he has not been granted permission to dig, nor is he likely to. And he reminds the audience that illicit excavations are illegal. How much he cares about or believes that the Ark and other Temple treasures are there is unclear. Perhaps he is saying this to excite the religious audience to whom he is pitching his argument. It is the treasure that he is after; it is the gold that seems to excite him. It is not clear what he wants, however. Does he want the treasure for himself? Barfield seems to recognize that in Israel, he will not be allowed to keep what he finds (unlike in the United Kingdom, where metal detectorists are paid handsomely for their finds). In Shelly Neese's book about the Copper Scroll Project, however, Barfield does explain what he wants. He wants to give this gold to the state of Israel. By publicizing his "findings," he is trying to sway public opinion to pressure the Israel Antiquities Authority to allow him to excavate.

CONCLUSION 207

There is no reason to be convinced of Barfield's understanding of the Copper Scroll. Barfield's claims bear all of the classic hallmarks of pseudoarchaeology. He is an amateur that has discovered something that professional scholars could not or have not admitted to. He has cracked the code of an ancient cypher. The cracking of the code has *almost* been confirmed by advanced scientific instruments. But the authorities have prevented him from finishing the work, for unspecified reasons. Finally, his goals are not to better understand the ancient world, but to find a vast amount of hidden treasure. It is easy for me to immediately discount his claims, and you can read Robert Cargill's more thorough step-by-step refutation of his claims, listed in the Bibliographic Essay at the end of this volume. Yet Barfield's YouTube channel has more than three thousand subscribers. His story is more captivating than the mundane reality and is something enjoyable (and free) to watch that can be justified as educational. It fulfills many of the media tropes that make pseudoarchaeology so popular. It is more fun to believe that he is correct, or that at least he could be correct.

But why are Ark hunters so problematic? Why should we care if someone makes claims like Barfield's? The problem is in how the Ark continues to lie on the fault line of many social, political, and religious issues. When these fault lines intersect with the political tensions of Jerusalem, the results can literally be life and death. People are willing to engage in violent actions because of their stance on who should have access to the Temple Mount. Amateur Ark hunters that stumble into this conflict, like Lt. Montague Parker did (as discussed in Chapter 5), can cause troubles that go far beyond the destruction of archaeological heritage. And what is particularly concerning about apocalyptic believers is that some don't believe that violent responses are necessarily bad. The onset of a major world war is expected in many end times theologies. Believers are not concerned about the consequences of their actions causing violence. In fact, such violence may be seen as hastening the arrival or return of the Messiah.

Despite the odds against anyone actually succeeding, I think people will keep looking for the Ark. But what are people really searching for when they are searching for the lost Ark? Are they looking for fortune and glory like the members of the Parker Expedition, colonialists who needed a way to make names for themselves in the declining days of empire? Are they looking for some kind of self-justification, like British Israelists wanting to prove that they are descendants of a lost tribe of Israel? Are they looking to prove that their church is the central church of Christendom like St. John Lateran's

208 READERS OF THE LOST ARK

Church in Rome? Or to restore the Temple of Jerusalem like Rabbi Getz? Or to bring about the Second Coming like those crawling through the caves of Mount Nebo, looking for the Ark that Jeremiah hid that won't be revealed until the end times? The Ark's gravitas and its ambiguous meanings make it a powerful potential symbol for any number of movements or any number of ambitions. What the real raiders of the lost Ark are actually raiding is different for everyone.

The Ark's ambiguity allows it to be reimagined continually and given new meanings in new contexts. It is a tangible thing, and that tangibility makes it easy to imagine. The object Indy chased is close enough to that described in the Bible that we can all instantly conjure up a mental image that looks roughly the same. This cannot be said for other famous biblical objects. Ask any two people to describe Noah's Ark, and despite the physical description(s) in Genesis, you aren't likely to find agreement. The physicality of the Ark of the Covenant has remained stable in imaginations for at least two thousand years, and there is no hint that that is abating. That we can all picture it and picture it in the same way gives it a "realness" that is convincing for religious believers and nonbelievers alike.

Yet while we all agree on what the Ark of the Covenant looked like, and do not agree on what Noah's Ark looked like, the opposite could be said of these two Arks in terms of public understanding of their functions. Noah's Ark may look different to everyone who imagines it, but most will agree on its function as a boat to keep Noah's family and the animals of the earth alive during the flood. No such agreement can be discerned in popular imaginings of the Ark of the Covenant. Even scholars who have devoted their lives to the study of Israelite religion and material culture cannot agree on what it was supposed to have done. Scholars ponder whether it was a receptacle for holding the Ten Commandments, some kind of furniture for God, a means for transporting the deity, a representation of the deity Himself, or all of these things simultaneously. As we have seen, nonacademic suggestions for what the Ark was used for are even more diverse. Pseudoarchaeologists suggest that it could be a radio transmitter, a nuclear power source, or some kind of alien technology that was confused for magic. That such diversity of functions can be ascribed to the Ark also gives it an interpretive power, for people can imagine it to have done whatever they want it to have done. The Bible's ambiguity gives interpretation a level of flexibility, with only a few constraints. It has to have been a powerful object or at least an object that ancient Israelites might have believed was powerful.

CONCLUSION   209

In the Introduction, I discussed how Malcolm Quinn's study of the swastika was influential in my approach to the Ark here. I described both the Ark and swastika as metasymbols, symbols that can have many meanings and can be easily manipulated to bear different messages. Both the swastika and the Ark have stable visual appearances that only change in minor ways over time. Yet both are hollow signifiers to some extent—that is, we agree on the physical appearance of both, but the ancient meanings are somewhat ambiguous. Both act as powerful symbols in the modern world because of their presumed antiquity. That antiquity lends them a certain authority even if the nature of that authority is ambiguous.

Yet how the Ark and the swastika have been deployed as symbols is quite different. The swastika was used by the Nazis because of its seeming wide geographic attestation in antiquity. It was deemed powerful because it was found in so many places originally, places that the Nazis associated with the Aryan race. The case is the opposite with the Ark, which begins its story as a unique object, and replicas of the Ark are understood to be replicas. Most traditions hold that there is only one original Ark. The swastika was purposefully employed as a symbol by the Nazis as a symbol of identity, as a tool in the fashioning of a new self-identity. The Ark, even though most understand it as having originated within Judaism, has not come to stand as a symbol for any one particular group. In the twenty-first century, the swastika can only have one meaning, and even when one is found in its original ancient context, its presence is jarring and instantly evocative of Nazism. The Ark, however, continues to have multiple meanings for multiple groups. No one has successfully co-opted it. The swastika cannot be interpreted apart from Nazism anymore.

One of the distinctions between the Ark and the swastika is that there is a richer origin story of the Ark from antiquity. It is not just a mute design that moderns have filled with interpretation. The Ark has a well-established, though complicated ancient story, but a story that can be understood and related to. Its antiquity gives the Ark a kind of charisma that many people find alluring. It is an object that is remote in time and space. Even for those who live in the Middle East today, the Ark is still distant, for it comes from an imagined biblical space, a place that has been continuously reinterpreted through the lens of imagination for two thousand years. As those temporal and spatial distances increase, so, too, does the charismatic attraction of the Ark. This is evident in how Gregory Peck's David in the film *David and Bathsheba* ponders the Ark as a mute receptacle of the memory of his famed

210 READERS OF THE LOST ARK

ancestors. The Ark's persistence as an imagined but seemingly real thing allows the moderns who reinterpret it an entry point to something very old and distant. Receptions of the Ark seemingly lessen that distance.

For some of us, thinking about the Ark is a kind of escapism. While watching a cinematic reception of the Ark like an Indiana Jones film may be explicitly understood as entertainment, the engagement with antiquity offers a more specific escapism, where people imagine an ancient world very different from their own. That the imagining is rooted in historical reality affords it more seriousness and perhaps the ability for that entertainment to be justified as educational. It is a kind of escapism nonetheless. The Ark adds further levels to this, however. For those collecting Indiana Jones toys, it is a diversion into childhood nostalgia, or a means of experiencing childhood play in a way that reminds one of the kinds of play that were so rewarding.

Contemplating the Ark can also be comforting. That the object is part of a centuries-old religious tradition adds to its gravitas. For Jewish and Christian believers, the ability to physically imagine the Ark brings a kind of comfort in how it can seemingly confirm one's faith. I have already discussed that this is a logical fallacy—that just because something can be imagined physically does not mean it existed. Still, even though the reasoning is fallacious does not mean that it is not powerful. For many believers, the reception of the Ark in different physical forms, whether those be paintings or souvenir models, offers an almost scientific confirmation of their faith, that their faith can be harmonized with the physical world experienced in the believer's day-to-day life. Pseudoarchaeological treatments of the Ark build on its religious attributes. By taking an object of faith-based power and reimagining it as an object of scientific power (even if that science is construed as lost ancient or alien knowledge), the religious context of the Ark is transformed. These are technocratic appropriations of elements of religious culture, where an object of Jewish or Christian faith is transformed into an object of scientific (but really pseudoscientific) ascendency.

For me, perhaps the comfort in contemplating the Ark is more in line with the response that Gregory Peck's King David had. Peck was in awe of how the legendary ancestors of Israel had been in the presence of the Ark, and how it now being in his presence connected him to them. For me, thinking about the Ark connects me to the centuries of others who have done the same. From some of the greatest philosophical minds in human history, to some of the most rabid crackpots of the present day, we all share a connection. We have found these biblical references to this object so captivating that we have been

CONCLUSION 211

compelled to write more about the Ark. A poem that helps me make sense of my own view of the Ark is Walt Whitman's "Song of Myself, 51." If you don't remember it from high school English class, it reads as follows:

The past and present wilt—I have fill'd them, emptied them.
And proceed to fill my next fold of the future.

Listener up there! what have you to confide to me?
Look in my face while I snuff the sidle of evening,
(Talk honestly, no one else hears you, and I stay only a minute longer.)

Do I contradict myself?
Very well then I contradict myself,
(I am large, I contain multitudes.)

I concentrate toward them that are nigh, I wait on the door-slab.

Who has done his day's work? who will soonest be through with his
   supper?
Who wishes to walk with me?

Will you speak before I am gone? will you prove already too late?

Substituting the Ark for the self in this poem, the vision that the past and present have wilted, both filling the Ark and then being emptied from it, captures how this object has been imagined and reimagined. That it is filled with contradictions, and that it is filled with multitudes, allows for the varieties of contested meanings and visions of the Ark that have allowed it to remain such a potent object of interest. Whitman's poem applied to the Ark invites further conversations and expects that there should be multiple views, influenced by the past but shaped in new ways in the future. Ending the book with a reflection on this poem helps me draw it to a close, with the hope that readers will continue the conversation with me, even as my book comes to an end.

In the final scenes of *Raiders of the Lost Ark*, the Ark is secreted away into a government warehouse, lost again as it was before Indy found it. The government agents who first called on Indy to search for the Ark stop any further conversation about it, refusing to tell the archaeologist where the

212 READERS OF THE LOST ARK

government has taken it or allowing it to be studied further. In real life, the film has done the opposite. It has, if anything, given a more concrete form to the popular perception of the Ark of the Covenant, while not undermining any of the reception traditions that have surrounded it for the past two thousand years. The Ark won't fall out of the public imagination anytime soon. We will still imagine an Ark, lost in biblical times that still might, someday, reveal answers to its mysteries. Perhaps you, the reader who made it this far, feels as lost as the Ark though, still not really knowing what it is, what it did, where it might be now, or if it even existed. These are questions that defy definitive answers, but perhaps those kinds of questions don't matter so much as what the Ark of the Covenant can be.

Bibliographic Essay

Hopefully this book has raised more questions for you than answers. Hopefully it has inspired you to do your own research on the Ark of the Covenant or on the ways that other ancient things and ideas continue to have meanings in new contexts. Rather than bog down the main text of the book with footnotes and citations, I have chosen to supplement the book with a list of sources organized by chapter.

Introduction

Most of the Introduction is autobiographical, reflecting an academic approach called "autoethnography." As may be apparent from my introductions to most of the chapters, which front my own experiences in relation to the topics, I have used autoethnography in a somewhat informal fashion. On the one hand, it helps make clear my perspective as a secular Canadian trained in archaeology and history. On the other hand, it shows how my own thinking has been entangled in experiences beyond the library.

In the Introduction, I familiarize readers with the field of study known as "reception history." While people have been working on reception history for centuries, the origins of the current academic approach can be found in the writings of Hans-Georg Gadamer ([1960] 1989). A good place to start exploring biblical reception history, beyond this book, is the Oxford Handbook (Lieb et al. 2011). For a more academic discussion of my own approach and the works that have inspired my attempts at reception history, see McGeough (2015a). Quinn (1994) has greatly influenced my own work on reception history, as he offers an approach that mirrors the study of symbols and visual culture with that of more traditional historical and archaeological analysis.

214   BIBLIOGRAPHIC ESSAY

Chapter 1

If you just want short introductions to the Ark in the Bible, I recommend Seow's (1992) and George et al.'s (2009) encyclopedia entries. There are many larger studies of the Ark in the Bible as well. Eichler's (2021) book-length treatment of the Ark is highly recommended. The same author compiled an extensive bibliography on the Ark of the Covenant in relation to biblical studies for Oxford's Online Bibliography series (Eichler 2017). Another technical, and extremely thorough treatment of the Ark in the Hebrew Bible, is Fisher (2018).

A very in-depth discussion of the practices surrounding the Temple in Jerusalem according to the biblical account can be found in Haran (1985). German-language readers will find Schmitt's (1972) work provides an excellent entry point into German scholarship (as well as other scholarship) on the Ark and Tabernacle up until his time. Levine (1969) offers another introduction to the Tabernacle that is useful for Ark research.

There are also many studies of specialized topics related to the Ark's appearance in the Bible. Many of these are attempts to figure out exactly what the Ark was. Scholars who believe that the Ark was furniture include Gunkel (1906), Haran (1985) (and other articles cited there), Metzger (1985), de Vaux (1967), and von Rad (1966). Those who treat it as a portable shrine or container include Morgenstern (1945) and Sevensma (1908). Metzler (2016) and Wilson (2005) offer alternate views. At one time, it was also common to consider the Ark as a miniature version of a temple, rather than as temple furnishings, for example as in Arnold (1917) and May (1936).

The idea of a distinct "Ark Narrative" located within the books of Samuel was first suggested by Leonhard Rost (1926). Since then, the thesis has been almost taken for granted, with more scholarship devoted to refining the thesis than refuting it. Different interactions with Rost's thesis can be found in Ahlström (1984), Bodner (2006), Campbell (1975), Eynikel (2000), Miller and Roberts (1977), Sommer (2009), and Van Seters (2009).

Readers interested in the use of the Ark in the book of Joshua and its function in the narratives about the conquest of Canaan can look to Coats (1985). Hillers (1968) provides a fairly in-depth discussion of the Ark in Psalm 132. For studies of the Ark as portrayed in Chronicles, see Begg (2003), Eskenazi (1995), Porzig (2014) and Rezetko (2007).

One important type of secondary source for those interested in the biblical study of the Ark is Bible commentaries. There are a few that I have made

BIBLIOGRAPHIC ESSAY   215

extensive use of that I would like to highlight: Cassuto (1967), Childs (1974), Hyatt (1971), Japhet (1993), McCarter (1980, 1984), Noth (1962), Propp (2006), and Tigay (1996).

Chapter 2

Sources on Israelite religion include Albertz and Schmitt (2012), Hess (2007), Haran (1985), Nakhai (2001), and Zevit (2001). The best resource to begin the study of the iconography of ancient Israel is Keel and Uehlinger (1998), although the Ark is not a subject of this work itself. McClellan (2022) has a good chapter on the Ark, considering its physical form in relation to shifting Israelite attitudes toward divine representations.

The stone table found at Beth Shemesh has not yet been published. For discussion of its possible relationship to the Ark of the Covenant, see Bunimovitz's and Liederman's comments in Staff (2019). A good introduction to the recent excavations at Beth Shemesh can be found in Bunimovitz et al. (2009). There are many articles on the Tel Aviv University–Collège de France joint excavations at Kiryat Yearim (Finkelstein et al. 2018; Finkelstein, Nicolle, and Römer 2020; Finkelstein and Römer 2020).

This chapter touches on nineteenth- century European explorations of the Holy Land. For more on that bibliography, see the discussion for Chapter 5 and also McGeough (2015a). Claude Conder's and Lord Kitchener's original comments on their evaluation of Kiryat Yearim can be found on page 18 in their monumental *Survey of Western Palestine* (Conder and Kitchener 1883).

Scholars have long looked to ancient Egypt to better understand the Ark. There are a number of excellent studies on older European traditions about Moses's time in Egypt and the relationship between Egyptian mysticism and the origins of Israelite religion: Assmann (1997), Hornung (2001), and Ucko and Champion (2003). The most thorough overview of the Ark's parallels in ancient Egyptian material culture and religious practices is Falk (2020).

Outdated treatments of Egyptian Ark parallels can be found in Gressmann (1920) and Hartmann (1918), who both took the Ark as a kind of coffin for Yahweh. Other scholars who consider the Ark in relation to Egypt (and offer different readings than those offered in this book) include Homan (2002), Noegel (2015), and Zwickel (1999). For more on Egyptian processional equipment specifically, see Brand (2001) and Thomas (1956).

216   BIBLIOGRAPHIC ESSAY

For more in-depth discussions of the *cherubim*, I recommend starting with Eichler (2021) and going from there. The overview of the scholarly opinions on this and the related bibliography are exhaustive. Mettinger (1999) and Meyers (1992) are dictionary entries on the topic. Keel and Uehlinger (1998) discuss *cherubim* in the context of other imagery from Iron Age Israel. The word *cherubim* is likely related to the Akkadian word *karābu* or its related *kāribu*. To learn more about these Akkadian words, start with the entries in the *Chicago Assyrian Dictionary* (Gelb et al. 1956–2010a, 1956–2010b).

Chapter 3

The study of ancient synagogues is a subfield of its own, and excavations in Israel continue to reveal more information. Hachlili (2013) provides a good overview, and more specialized studies can be found in Hachlili (1977, 1997, 2000, 2002). Other studies of the archaeology of synagogues include Catto (2007), Levine (1982, 1987), and Shanks (1979). Goodenough's (1953–1954) series *Jewish Symbols in the Greco-Roman Period* offers a detailed discussion of archaeological discoveries and associated iconography related to ancient Judaism, including three volumes on Dura- Europas. Articles on specific topics related to ancient synagogues and early Judaism used in the writing of this book include Fraade (2019), Harland (2013), Meyers and Meyers (1981), Ollson and Zetterholm (2003), and Ryan (2023).

Introductions to the Ark's appearance in postbiblical Jewish literature can be found in Cline (2007) and George et al. (2009). Introductions to that literature can be found in many of Jacob Neusner's works (1970, 1987, 1988a, 1988b, 1994). Other introductory sources include Bowker (1969), Holtz (1984), Kugel and Greer (1986), Stern (2004), and Strack ([1931]1969).

For those wanting to read the ancient texts discussed in this chapter, a number of resources can be recommended. A dependable translation of Philo that is readily available is that published as part of the Loeb Classical Library. The discussion of the Ark described in Chapter 4 refers to text translated in the version called *Philo Supplement II: Questions and Answers on Exodus*. This is an old translation (from 1953) by Ralph Marcus. The discussion of Philo's treatment of the Ark in *Questions and Answers on Exodus* centers on Book II:53– 56, and Book II:68. Book II:53 is the section I discuss which deals with the incorruptible materials of the Ark. Book II:54 is where one can find Philo's ruminations on the Ark's gold plating. Book II:68

BIBLIOGRAPHIC ESSAY 217

discusses Exodus 25:11. Begg (1998) was consulted on the treatment of the Ark in Josephus. My quotations of Josephus come from William Whiston's translation, originally published in 1737 and still used despite its flaws (Whiston 1981). Josephus's description of the Ark can be found in *Antiquities of the Jews* Book III, chapter 6.5. The description of the Ark that is quoted can be found in Whiston (1981: 73). The story of the Samaritan comes from *Antiquities of the Jews* Book XVIII. Chapter IV, and the translation cited can be found in Whiston (1981: 380).

There are multiple versions of the *Mishnah* available. The two English translations used here are Danby (1933) and Neusner (1988b). For those wishing to follow up with some of the references to the Talmud, the website *Sefaria* offers free access to these texts with multiple translations. My references best harmonize with the William-Davidson English translation of the *Talmud* (which can be found in print as Steinsaltz 2013).

An extensive resource on the literature of early Judaism is Louis Ginzberg's multivolume work, *The Legends of the Jews* (1909). The story of the Ark flying on its own during the Israelite sojourn is retold in Ginzberg III, p. 243 (see also notes in VI, p. 85, notes 456–457). The Midrash on Joshua is retold in Ginzberg IV, p. 6 (notes given are in VI, p. 172 [note 15]). The rabbinic take on Uzzah's death is retold in Ginzberg III, p. 395. David's negligence is also discussed in Ginzberg III, p. 194. The story of how Solomon uses the Ark to identify who is circumcised is retold in Ginzberg IV, p. 146, with his discussion of sources in VI, p. 290, notes 42–44. Discussion of how the Ark will be revealed again in Messianic times is retold in Ginzberg III, p. 161. The tradition that Elijah will restore the Ark and Temple vessels is retold in Ginzberg III, p. 48 (VI, p. 19, note 112). That its discovery will bring the Messiah can be found in IV, p. 234. Discussion of the Ark in the location where creation began can be found in Ginzberg I, p. 12, with notes in V, p. 15.

This chapter includes some discussion of where ancient writers thought that the Ark was taken after the destruction of Jerusalem. Sources consulted include Cline (2007), Day (2005), Milikowsky (2015), and Price (2005).

Chapter 4

A good starting source on medieval Christian thinking about the Ark is George et al. (2009). Sources on replacement theology, what is also known

218   BIBLIOGRAPHIC ESSAY

as supersessionism, especially related to Pauline theology, include Griffith-Jones (2004), Harris (2009), Sanders (2015), and Ziesler (1990).

There are also numerous works on specific topics related to this chapter that may be of relevance to thinking about treatments of the Ark from the period. A good introduction to medieval angelology is Keck (1998). For issues of Christian site identification and pilgrimage, see Davidson (1993), Frend (1996), Maraval (2002), and MacDonald (2010). French-language readers will find Revel-Neher's (1984) survey of the Ark in Christian art to be an excellent introduction to the topic.

The commentaries I consulted for the book of Hebrews are Attridge (1989) and Buchanan (1972). The commentary on Revelation that I used is Ford (1975). There are many editions of Saint Thomas Aquinas's *Summa Theologica*. An easily accessible version that is now entirely online (http://www.newadvent.org/summa) is the translation by the Fathers of the English Dominican Province (1920). A more authoritative version that includes the Latin (in sixty-one volumes!) is known as the Blackfriars edition (Aquinas 1964–1980). For a good translation of Bede's *On the Tabernacle*, see Holder (1994). The quoted translation of Bede's discussion of the allegory of the Ark is taken from Holder (1994: 12). The translations of his commentary on Exodus 25 reproduced in Chapter 4 come from Holder (1994: 13, 18, and 20), respectively. The anonymous text *The Cloud of Unknowing* can be further explored in Underhill (1922). A translation of the major works of Richard of St Victor can be found in Zinn (1979).

Chapter 5

There are many good studies of European exploration of the Holy Land, and most of these will have a chapter or two on the exploration of Jerusalem: Bar-Yosef (2005), McGeough (2015a, 2015c), Shepherd (1987), and Silberman (1982). Wilson and Warren (1871) is one of the many reports produced by nineteenth-century explorers, and it gives readers a good sense of what their explorations were like. Early French publications of excavations in Jerusalem (including some by Father Vincent) are translated into English in Shanks (2004). Other treatments of explorations of Jerusalem were consulted: Gonen (2003), Hassner (2009), Kenyon (1974), Kletter (2020), Lawler (2021), Mazar (2002), Price (2008), Ritmeyer (2006), and Ritmeyer and Ritmeyer (1988). General treatments

BIBLIOGRAPHIC ESSAY 219

of Jerusalem that were consulted include Avigad (1980), Bahat (1994), and Ben-Dov (2002).

Accounts of the Parker Expedition can be found in Addison (2021), Foley (1935), Melander (1916), and Silberman (1982). Juvelius 1916 (*The White Camel*) offers fictionalized accounts of the events in a series of short stories, but you'll have to be able to read Finnish to understand it. If you find an English translation, please let me know! Le Queux (1910) is a contemporary fictionalized account based on the author's interactions with some of the Parker team. The archive of the Parker family related to the expedition can be found in Jerusalem, at the Ben Zvi Institute.

Father Louis-Hugues Vincent was allowed to chronicle the archaeological discoveries of the Parker Expedition, whose members had no interest in doing so themselves. Those records can be found in Vincent (1911), Warren (1912), Vincent and Warren (1912), and reprinted in Shanks (2004). For a quick overview of the life of Rabbi Yehuda Getz, see Shragai (2018). The quotations of Rabbi Getz reproduced in this chapter are taken from Shragai (2018).

Mount Nebo has had fewer "Ark explorers" than Jerusalem, but those that it has had have been influential in pseudoscholarly contexts. For more on Tom Crotser, see N.A. (1983). Futterer's 1950 guidebook, *Palestine Speaks*, offers his most extended discussion of the Ark. No longer being published but still available in various libraries is Futterer's *Eye-Ographic Bible Course* (Futterer 1992), which was reprinted in the 1990s by the Holyland Bible Knowledge Society. There is little about the Ark in this volume, but it is an interesting historical document for those interested in different approaches to Bible education in the twentieth century. More germane to the issue of the Ark is the small pamphlet produced in 1982 by the Holyland Bible Knowledge Society that offers revised and excerpted accounts from Futterer's older works. Also edited by Alyda Overgaard, his long-time secretary and later successor to his institutes, "Adventures of the Golden Ark Explorer" was produced in response to the success of *Raiders of the Lost Ark*. Only about thirty pages in length, the pamphlet offers a shortened form of the stories told about Futterer at the Silver Springs museum. Futterer's comments about looking for rich donors to finance his expeditions come from Futterer (1950: 555).

An in-depth treatment of both British-Israelism and the search for the Ark can be found in Carew (2003). Those who desire to read the writings of the British-Israelists directly can peruse old copies of their periodical *Covenant People*, the name of the periodical at the time of the Tara excavations, and

220 BIBLIOGRAPHIC ESSAY

now named *Thy Kingdom Come Magazine*. Another useful, though older, source on British- Israelism is Wilson (1960). Woodman (1995) offers a good discussion of the political implications of Irish archaeology (despite the title it is not a history of excavations at Tara). There are few English language resources available for the study of Japanese-Israelism. Oyabe (1929) is only available in Japanese as far as I am aware. A summary of that work is presented in an issue of the Jewish Daily Bulletin (N.A. 1929). Most useful, however, will be Cho (2007). While Cho does not summarize Oyabe's arguments, he builds off of them for his own arguments about the replica Ark and its current resting place in the Grand Ise Shrine. For a thorough study of the myth of the lost tribes of Israel, see Tobolowsky (2022). A summary of his arguments (Tobolowsky 2023) appears in the e-newsletter of the American Society of Overseas Research's (ASOR) ANEToday.

Chapter 6

I have written much about the Bible and archaeology in film (McGeough 2006, 2018a, 2018b, 2020, 2022). Some of the most influential sources for me here and in other works are Babington and Evans (1993), Birchard (2004), Burnett- Bletsch (2014), Elley (1984), Holtorf (2007), Reinhartz (2013), Shepherd (2013), Solomon (2001), and Walsh (2003).

This chapter addressed some important concepts in film theory. The famous discussion between Alfred Hitchcock and François Truffaut in which Hitchcock coins the term "MacGuffin" is in Truffaut and Scott (1984). Those wanting to learn more about Paul Schraeder's understanding of "false syllogisms" can read Schraeder (2018). Philip Dunne's comments on DeMille can be found in his autobiography (Dunne 1992). For more on the work of the Victorian painter Edward Poynter, and how his art, and other art like his, influenced the visual presentation of the Bible, see Conner (1985), Harvey (2013), Huckvale (2012), and McGeough (2015c).

The most authoritative treatment of the production of the Indiana Jones films is Rinzler (2008). The early concept art for the Ark can be found in Rinzler (2008: 29). Luceno (2008) is a good source on the films and the paratexts. For more on the music of Indiana Jones, see Audissino (2021).

Despite the sheer volume of documentaries on the subject, the idea that the Nazis searched for occult or magical ancient items is not as straightforward as it would seem from the Indiana Jones movies. This idea seems to have been popularized by Louis Pauwels and Jacques Bergier's (1960) European bestseller *The Morning of the Magicians: Introduction to Fantastic Realism.* Incredibly influential in Europe, the book is mostly pseudoscholarship, but it made widespread the idea that the Nazis were obsessed with the occult, and it continues to inspire conspiracy theorists to this day. More legitimate sources on this topic are Kurlander (2017) and Trigger (2006). For more on the collection and looting of ancient artifacts by the Nazis, see Romano (2023) and the other articles in the special issue of *RIHA Journal* that this article introduces.

For more on archaeological adventure stories, see McGeough (2015a, 2015c). Giovanni Belzoni's ([1820] 2007) account of his adventures in Egypt still makes for interesting reading today and was foundational for how archaeological work is described in narrative (both fiction and nonfiction). Holtorf (2007) describes some of the major features of archaeological fiction. There are too many other studies of archaeological and adventure fiction to do justice to them here, but some of that have influenced my thinking include Brantlinger (1988), Huckvale (2012), Kabbani (1986), Kestner (2010), and Luckhurst (2012).

Chapter 7

Theoretical works on material culture studies that have been foundational for this chapter are Baudrillard (1983, 1996), Benjamin ([1935] 2008), Brown (2001), Meskell (2004), Miller (2010), Park (2010), and Stewart (1984). Another theoretical approach used here is best described as "object biography," exemplified by Appadurai (1996) and Kopytoff (1986). I've already mentioned Quinn (1994) in the Introduction.

One important component of material culture studies is understanding the nature of collecting. There is much scholarly literature available on the study of collectors and their activities. Pearce (2013) is a classic for people working in museum studies. There she articulates why "real" things are so captivating, much more so than copies. Collecting in fan culture is also a subject of this chapter. Gray (2010) explains how media created in relation to film and television is used within fan culture and extends the meanings of the original texts. He adapts the term "paratexts" from literary analysis and deploys it for the study of film, a use I follow in this book. Gray's book also offers an entry point into the vast bibliography available for the study of

222 BIBLIOGRAPHIC ESSAY

fan culture. His comments that children take charge of narratives through toys is found in Gray (2010: 181), and that *Star Wars* toys made the world habitable for children is in Gray (2010: 21). Geraghty (2014) discusses various elements of popular culture collecting, with his chapter on toys being especially illuminating for thinking about how the Ark can be understood in this fashion. Anthropology of "play" is a related topic. I, like most others who study play historically, have been greatly influenced by Johan Huizinga's (1938) masterpiece *Homo Ludens*, in which he argues that play is a constitutive element of any culture. My thinking on play and exhibition culture has been influenced by Bar-Yosef (2005), Long (2003), and Rowan (2004). My friend and colleague James Linville, who convinced me to write this book, is an expert on Christian Bible museums, and his research has informed my own on this topic. Many of the main themes he identifies are found in Linville (2016), and perhaps by the time you are reading this book, his monograph on the subject will be out. Another long-time friend has written an excellent examination of how objects have been used in faith-based teaching and missionary work that can help better understand the types of interactions with the Ark discussed in this chapter (Hasinoff 2011).

Many of the sources for this chapter are journalistic stories, websites, and YouTube uploads. Sources on Grace Gupana that I consulted include Layug (2019), N.A. (2013), and N.A. (2017). The quotation of Gupana's regarding the destruction of the Ark reproduced in this chapter is from Arutz Sheva Staff (2017). Her comments on the Ark in Kenya were taken from Goin (2015). Information about the Ark of the Covenant made by the Universal Church of the Kingdom of God (UCKG) comes from their website, and the quotation reprinted in the text was found at this URL: https://uckg.ca/the-ark-of-the-covenant-in-canada/. The arrival of the Ark of the Covenant in Toronto is preserved on YouTube: https://www.yout ube.com/watch?v=ORU5QtUDXGI. Curiously, the day I discovered this recording, I had just got back from an unrelated "King Tut Immersive Experience" held in the same location (1 Front Street). I was completely unaware of the connection until I started watching the video. The procession of the same Ark to Texas was uploaded to https://www.yout ube.com/watch?v=zo4fBifQWcM. The BibleWalk wax museum has a Facebook page, which I consulted and quoted from: https://www.faceb ook.com/BibleW alk1987/videos/the-ark-of-the-covenant-exodus-2528-hebrews-9/297244124600298/. The "Carpetbagger" also recorded a walk-through of the museum, in which you can see the major

BIBLIOGRAPHIC ESSAY   223

exhibits without having to go to Ohio: https://www.youtube.com/watch?v=VhU1vLyrcVU.

Chapter 8

For further sources on Ethiopian history and archaeology, see Finneran (2007), Henze (2000), Marcus (2002), Munro-Hay et al. (1989), and Tegegne and Belcher (2023). The full text of Ethiopia's revised constitution under Haile Selassie I can be found in N.A. (1956). Some of the sources used for research on Ethiopian religion are Finneran (2002), Fitzgerald and Marsden (2017), Tobolowsky (2022), and Ullendorff (1956). Ullendorff (1968) is an account of the relationship between Ethiopian and Old Testament traditions. Here he provides a good discussion of the Ark and an overview of the Ethiopian traditions surrounding it. Edward Ullendorff never actually wrote about his own experiences seeing the Ethiopian Ark. In 1992, he described what he saw to a reporter for the *LA Times* (Hiltzik 1992a, 1992b), not thinking those remarks would be published. The quotations reproduced in Chapter 8 are from Hiltzik (1992a). After Ullendorff's death, his colleague Tudor Parfitt confirmed the story in an article for *Live Science* (Jarus 2018). For Abu Salih's account of his experiences in Ethiopia, including his viewing of the Ethiopian Ark, see Evetts (1895). The translation is old but still useful and available freely online.

There are fewer translations of the *Kebra Nagast* than one would imagine, given the importance of this document in world history. The best-known translation is that of Budge (1932), which is available cheaply but is severely outdated. Budge's reputation as a translator is not good. Bezold's (1905) German translation is more useful for scholars, as it deals with the sources in much greater detail. A more recent scholarly version is Brooks (1996). Hubbard's (1957) dissertation provides an authoritative treatment of the different sources for the *Kebra Nagast* and, despite being over sixty years old, has not been superseded to my knowledge. For more on the *Kebra Nagast* and its relationship to the Old Testament, see Pankhurst (1986, 1987). Belcher (2009) offers perhaps the most accessible introduction to the *Kebra Nagast*, its composition, its publication history, and its meanings in different contexts. She also compares it to other early traditions about the Queen of Sheba in Judaism and Islam. If my book's "reception history" approach has appealed to you, I'd recommend Belcher (2010), as she takes a

224 BIBLIOGRAPHIC ESSAY

similar approach to the *Kebra Nagast* in American literature from the eighteenth century onward. Hausman (2020) provides a Rastafari treatment of the *Kebra Nagast*. The quotation of his that I reproduce in Chapter 8 can be found on page xiii of his book.

Issues of repatriation are perhaps some of the most polarizing ones in contemporary museum studies. Much has been written on repatriation, though not much of that directly discusses Ethiopia. For a study of an analogous situation, the Benin Bronzes taken from what is now known as Nigeria, see Hicks (2020). Other good discussions include Cuno (2009), Green (2017), and Waxman (2010).

Chapter 9

Despite my better judgment, I am obliged to give the bibliographic references for the various pseudoscholarly works discussed in this chapter. Of course, the books of Graham Hancock (1992, 1995) and Erich Von Däniken (1968, 1980) are most influential, as was the documentary adaptation of *Chariots of the Gods?* (Reinl 1970). I reproduce Hancock's quotation first published in Hitzlik (1992a: 6). I also cite Hancock's interpretation of the name *Parzifal* (1992: 77–78), his description of Moses as a civilizing hero (1992: 340), his description of the Ark as a human-made weapon (the first citation is from 1992: 342 and the second is from p. 287), and him admitting that his thesis is speculative (1992: 347, 355). I cite Von Däniken's description of the Ark (1968: loc. 27 e-book), the English language narration of the documentary (Reinl 1970), and his suggestion that Mussolini seized the Ark and gave it to the Vatican (1980: loc. 20 e-book). *The Manna Machine*, written by George Sassoon and Rodney Dale (1978), is hard to find now in paper form, but electronic versions circulate widely. I also discuss David Medina's 2014 *The Ark of the Covenant and Other Secret Weapons of the Ancients*; Jonathan Gray's *Ark of the Covenant* (1997); and David Hatcher Childress's *Ark of God* (2015). Michael Dennin's approach to Bible and science is exemplified by Dennin (2015). Childress's description of the electrical power of djed pillars and the claim that Moses would have known about ancient Egyptian electrical power sources come from Childress (2015: 406–407). His speculation that the Ark was a modified Tesla coil, or a Van de Graaf generator, can be found in Childress (2015: loc. 785).

BIBLIOGRAPHIC ESSAY 225

Much of my treatment of the psychological issues related to memory formation and media viewing are based on Zacks (2014). Pasulka (2016) offers a compelling argument about how viewers process fiction related to religion and how the lines between fiction and nonfiction are readily blurred through cinematic media. Mander (1978) discusses, from the perspective of a former advertising executive, how film creates an indelible impression on viewers.

Discussion of the telegraph, telephone, radio, and television as technologies that facilitated communication with the dead or with alien civilizations can be found in Sconce (2000). Grünschloß (2007) offers a good treatment of how these technocratic myths manifest in ancient aliens discourse. White (2013) provides easily readable rejoinders to some of the main arguments that ancient things had to have been made by aliens. For more on the general issues of the relationship between archaeology and pseudoarchaeology, see Card (2018), Feder (2019), Holtorf (2007), and Williams (1991). For a thorough overview of mainstream archaeological methods, the textbook I have been using to teach my introductory class on archaeology for the past twenty years is Renfrew and Bahn (2019). Their definition of pseudoarchaeology is concise but very accurate.

Finally, there has been much written on the "Bibel und Babel" controversy in which first German scholars and later others have attempted to resituate Christian origins outside of the Old Testament. For an introduction to this, see Larsen (1995). Watch for claims that Christianity is not rooted in ancient Judaism. These kinds of arguments are more common than one might imagine and are often problematic. The anti- Semitic tendencies in pseudoscholarship lead many authors to try to imagine a non- Jewish version of Christian origins. Now, it is not that Mesopotamian culture cannot be studied to better understand that of the Old Testament. Much of my own work has been based on this approach, comparing the shared institutions of these two regions of the world. Rather, it is when scholars try to appropriate biblical culture as explicitly non-Jewish that these kinds of analyses become troubling.

Conclusions

The *Charisma* article in which various strands of apocalyptic and pseudoarchaeological thinking about the Ark is Akers (2023). The Copper

226   BIBLIOGRAPHIC ESSAY

Scroll Project is mentioned there, but much more is available on this. For those interested in seeing Jim Barfield's presentation about his claims regarding the Copper Scroll, the presentation I write about can be found at on his Copper Scroll Project YouTube site at https:// www.yout ube.com/ watch?v=4wLr6rFSj_Y. Shelly Neese's (2019) book is an uncritical account of Barfield's claims, featuring an introduction by the man himself. Instead of reading that or watching the presentation, I'd recommend reading Robert Cargill's (2009) statement on the problems with Barfield's reasoning. Vendyl Jones's (2005) autobiography about his own quest for the Ark and other pseudoarchaeological pursuits may also be of interest, but with the caveat that what is written there is just as bad scholarship as that of Barfield whom he inspired.

For scholarly information about the Copper Scroll, I'd recommend starting with Wolters (2000), which is an encyclopedia article in Oxford's *Encyclopedia of the Dead Sea Scrolls*. This is a good resource for those just starting to work on the Dead Sea Scrolls. Wolters gives a good introductory bibliography there that I won't repeat here. For a standard translation of the Copper Scroll, and the Dead Sea Scrolls in general, I'd recommend Vermes (1995), which has enough introductory comments on each text to orient nonspecialists.

Bibliography

Addison, Graham. 2021. *Raiders of the Hidden Ark: The Story of the Parker Expedition to Jerusalem.* N.p., Scotland: Edgcumbe Press.

Ahlström, Gösta W. 1984. "The Travels of the Ark: A Religio-Political Composition." *Journal of Near Eastern Studies* 43, no. 2: 141–149.

Akers, Shawn. 2023. "The Ark of the Covenant Found? 'This Isn't Raiders of the Lost Ark.'" *Charisma*, March 28. https://charismamag.com/israeljewishroots/standing-with-israel/the-ark-of-the-covenant-found-this-isnt-raiders-of-the-lost-ark/.

Albertz, Rainer, and Rüdiger Schmitt. 2012. *Family and Household Religion in Ancient Israel and the Levant.* Winona Lake, IN: Eisenbrauns.

Appadurai, Arjun. 1996. *Modernity at Large: Cultural Dimensions of Globalization.* Minneapolis: University of Minnesota Press.

Appleby, David. F. 1995 "Rudolf, Abbot Hrabanus and the Ark of the Covenant Reliquary." *The American Benedictine Review* 46, no. 4: 419–443.

Aquinas, Saint Thomas. [1981] 1920. *The Summa Theologiæ of St. Thomas Aquinas.* 2nd, rev. ed. Translated by the Fathers of the English Dominican Province. Westminster, MD: Christian Classics.

Aquinas, Saint Thomas. 1964–1980. *Summa Theologica.* London: Eyre & Spottiswoode.

Arnold, William R. 1917. *Ephod and Ark: A Study in the Records and Religion of the Ancient Hebrews.* Harvard Theological Studies 3. Cambridge, MA: Harvard University Press.

Arutz Sheva Staff. 2017. "Model of Ark of the Covenant Destroyed in Jerusalem." Israel National News (Arutz Sheva). https://www.israelnationalnews.com/news/230427.

Assmann, Jan. 1997. *Moses the Egyptian: The Memory of Egypt in Western Monotheism.* Cambridge, MA: Harvard University Press.

Attridge, Harold W. 1989. *The Epistle to the Hebrews: A Commentary on the Epistle to the Hebrews.* Hermeneia—A Critical and Historical Commentary on the Bible. Philadelphia: Fortress Press.

Audissino, Emilio. 2021. *The Film Music of John Williams: Reviving Hollywood's Classical Style.* Madison: University of Wisconsin Press.

Avigad, Nahman. 1980. *Discovering Jerusalem.* New York: Thomas Nelson.

Babington, Bruce, and Peter William Evans. 1993. *Biblical Epics: Sacred Narrative in the Hollywood Cinema.* Manchester: Manchester University Press.

Bahat, Dan. 1994. *The Atlas of Biblical Jerusalem.* Jerusalem: Carta.

Bar-Yosef, Eitan. 2005. *The Holy Land in English Culture, 1799–1917.* Oxford English Monographs. Oxford: Oxford University Press.

Baudrillard, Jean. 1983. *Simulations.* Translated by Paul Foss, Paul Patton, and Philip Beitchman. Boston: Semiotext[e].

Baudrillard, Jean. 1996. *The System of Objects.* Translated by James Benedict. London: Verso.

Begg, Christopher T. 1998. "The Return of the Ark According to Josephus." *Bulletin for Biblical Research* 8: 15–37.

Begg, Christopher T. 2003. "The Ark in Chronicles." In *The Chronicler as Theologian: Essays in Honor of Ralph W. Klein,* edited by M. Patrick Graham, Steven L. McKenzie, and Gary N. Knoppers, 133–145. Journal for the Study of the Old Testament Supplement Series 371. London: T&T Clark.

Belcher, Wendy. 2009. "African Rewritings of the Jewish and Islamic Solomonic Tradition: The Triumph of the Queen of Sheba in the Ethiopian Fourteenth-Century Text Kbra Nägäst."

228 BIBLIOGRAPHY

In *Sacred Tropes: Tanakh, New Testament, and Qur'an as Literary Works*, edited by Roberta Sabbath, 441–460. Leiden: Brill. DOI:10.1163/EJ.9789004177529.I-536.87.

Belcher, Wendy. 2010. "From Sheba They Come: Medieval Ethiopian Myth, US Newspapers, and a Modern American Narrative." *Callalloo* 33, no. 1 / *Ethiopia: Literature, Art & Culture* (Spring): 239–257.

Belzoni, Giovanni. [1820] 2007. *Travels in Egypt and Nubia.* Vercelli, Italy: White Star.

Ben-Dov, Meir. 2002. *Historical Atlas of Jerusalem.* New York: Continuum.

Benjamin, Walter. 2008. *The Work of Art in the Age of Its Technological Reproducibility, and Other Writings on Media.* Edited by Michael W. Jennings, Brigid Doherty, and Thomas Y. Levin. Cambridge, MA: Harvard University Press.

Besserman, Lawrence. 1992. "Ark of the Covenant." In *The Dictionary of Biblical Tradition in English Literature*, edited by David Lyle Jeffrey, 53–55. Grand Rapids, MI: Eerdmans.

Bezold, C. 1905. *Kebra Nagast. Der Herrlichkeit der Könige.* Munich: Akademie der Wissenschaften.

Birchard, Richard S. 2004. *Cecil B. DeMille's Hollywood.* Lexington: University of Kentucky Press.

Bodner, Keith. 2006. "Ark-Eology: Shifting Emphases in 'Ark Narrative' Scholarship." *Currents in Biblical Research* 4, no. 2 (Feb. 2006): 169–197. https://doi.org/10.1177/1476993X0 6059008.

Bowker, John. 1969. *The Targums & Rabbinic Literature: An Introduction to Jewish Interpretations of Scripture.* Cambridge: Cambridge University Press.

Brand, Peter. 2001. "Sacred Barks." In *The Oxford Encyclopedia of Ancient Egypt*, edited by Donald Redford, Vol. 3, 171–173. Oxford: Oxford University Press.

Brantlinger, Patrick. 1988. *Rule of Darkness: British Literature and Imperialism, 1830–1914.* Ithaca, NY: Cornell University Press.

Brooks, Miguel. 1996. *Kebra Nagast (The Glory of Kings): The True Ark of the Covenant.* Kingston, Jamaica: LMH.

Brown, Bill. 2001. "Thing Theory." *Critical Inquiry* 28, no. 1 (Autumn): 1–22.

Buchanan, George Wesley. 1972. *To the Hebrews: Translation, Comment and Conclusions.* The Anchor Bible. Garden City, NY: Doubleday.

Budge, E. A. Wallis. 1932. *The Kebra Nagast*, 2nd ed. London: Oxford University Press.

Bunimovitz, Shlomo, Zvi Lederman, and Dale W. Manor. 2009. "The Archaeology of Border Communities: Renewed Excavations at Tel Beth-Shemesh, Part 1: The Iron Age." *Near Eastern Archaeology* 72, no. 3: 114–142. http://www.jstor.org/stable/20697231.

Burnett-Bletsch, Rhonda. 2014. "The Bible and Its Cinematic Adaptations: A Consideration of Filmic Exegesis." *Journal of Biblical Reception* 1, no. 1: 129–160.

Campbell, Antony F. 1975. *The Ark Narrative (1 Sam 4–6; 2 Sam 6): A Form-Critical and Traditio-Historical Study.* SBL Dissertation Series, Number 16. Missoula, MT: The Society of Biblical Literature.

Card, Jeb. J. 2018. *Spooky Archaeology: Myth and Science of the Past.* Albuquerque: University of New Mexico Press.

Carew, Mairéad. 2003. *Tara and the Ark of the Covenant: Israelites on the Hill of Tara (1899–1902).* Dublin: Royal Irish Academy.

Cargill, Robert. 2009. "Pseudo-Science and Sensationalist Archaeology: An Exposé of Jimmy Barfield and the Copper Scroll Project." *The Bible and Interpretation.* https://bibleinterp. arizona.edu/articles/cargill2_08261.

Cassuto, Umberto. 1967. *A Commentary on the Book of Exodus.* Translated by Israel Abrahams. Jerusalem: Magnes.

Catto, Stephen K. 2007. *Reconstructing the First-Century Synagogue: A Critical Analysis of Current Research.* London: T & T Clark.

Cho, Gene Jinsiong. 2007. *The Replica of the Ark of the Covenant in Japan: The Mystery of Mi Fune-Shiro.* New York: iUniverse.

BIBLIOGRAPHY 229

Childress, David. 2015. *Ark of God: The Incredible Power of the Ark of the Covenant.* Kempton, IL: Adventures Unlimited Press.

Childs, Brevard S. 1974. *The Book of Exodus: A Critical, Theological Commentary.* The Old Testament Library. Louisville, KY: Westminster Press.

Cline, Eric. 2007. *From Eden to Exile: Unraveling Mysteries of the Bible.* Washington, DC: National Geographic.

Coats, George W. 1985. "The Ark of the Covenant in Joshua: A Probe into the History of a Tradition." *Hebrew Annual Review* 9: 137–157.

Conder, Claude and H. Kitchener. 1883. *The Survey of Western Palestine: Memoirs of the Topography, Orography, Hydrography, and Archaeology.* Vol. III. London: Committee of the Palestine Exploration Fund.

Conner, Patrick. 1985. " 'Wedding Archaeology to Art': Poynter's Israel in Egypt." In *Influences in Victorian Art and Architecture*, edited by Sarah Macready and F. H. Thompson, 112–120. The Society of Antiquaries of London, Occasional Paper, N.S. 7. London: Thames & Hudson.

Cuno, James. 2009. *Whose Culture? The Promise of Museums and the Debate over Antiquities.* Princeton, NJ: Princeton University Press.

Curl, James Stevens. 1991. *The Art & Architecture of Freemasonry.* New York: Overlook.

Danby, Herbert. 1933. *The Mishnah.* Oxford: Oxford University Press.

Davidson, Linda Kay. 1993. *Pilgrimage in the Middle Ages: A Research Guide.* New York: Garland.

Davies, Brian, ed. 2012. *The Oxford Handbook of Aquinas.* Oxford: Oxford University Press.

Day, John. 2005. "Whatever Happened to the Ark of the Covenant?" In *Temple and Worship in Biblical Israel: Proceedings of the Oxford Old Testament Seminar*, edited by John Day, 250–270. London: T&T Clark.

de Vaux, Roland. 1967. "Les chérubins et l'arche d'alliance, les sphinx gardiens, et les trônes divins dans l'ancient orient." In *Bible et Orient*, edited by Roland DeVaux, 231–259. Paris: Cerf.

Dennin, Michael. 2015. *Divine Science: Finding Reason at the Heart of Faith.* Cincinnati, OH: Franciscan Media.

Dunne, Philip. 1992. *Take Two: A Life in Movies and Politics.* New York: Limelight Editions.

Eichler, Raanan. 2017. "Ark of the Covenant." In *obo* in Biblical Studies. https://www.oxfordbib liographies.com/view/document/obo-9780195393361/obo-9780195393361-0245.xml.

Eichler, Raanan. 2021. *The Ark and the Cherubim.* Forschungen zum Alten Testament 146. Tübingen: Mohr Siebeck.

Elley, Derek. 1984. *The Epic Film: Myth and History.* London: Routledge & Kegan Paul.

Eskenazi, Tamara C. 1995. "A Literary Approach to Chronicles' Ark Narrative in 1 Chronicles 13–16." In *Fortunate the Eyes That See: Essays in Honor of David Noel Freedman in Celebration of His Seventieth Birthday*, edited by Astrid B. Beck, Andrew H. Bartelt, Paul R. Raabe, and Chris A. Franke, 258–274. Grand Rapids, MI: Eerdmans.

Evetts, B. T. A., trans. 1895. *The Churches and Monasteries of Egypt and Some Neighboring Countries, Attributed to Abû Sâlih, the Armenian.* Oxford: Clarendon Press.

Eynikel, Erik. 2000. "The Relation between the Eli Narratives (1 Sam. 1–4) and the Ark Narrative (1 Sam. 1–6; 2 Sam. 6:1–19)." In *Past, Present, Future: The Deuteronomistic History and the Prophets*, edited by Johannes C. de Moor and Harry F. van Rooy, 88–106. Oudtestamentische Studiën 44. Leiden, The Netherlands: Brill.

Falk, David A. 2020. *The Ark of the Covenant in Its Egyptian Context: An Illustrated Journey.* Peabody, MA: Hendrickson Academic.

Feder, Kenneth. 2019. *Frauds, Myths, and Mysteries: Science and Pseudoscience in Archaeology.* 10th ed. Oxford: Oxford University Press.

Finkelstein, Israel, Christophe Nicolle, and Thomas Römer. 2020. "Archaeological Excavations at Kiriath-jearim and the Ark Narrative in the Books of Samuel." In *The Mega Project at Motza (Moẓa): The Neolithic and Later Occupations Up to the 20th Century*, edited by

230 BIBLIOGRAPHY

Hamoudi Khalaily, 313–331. New Studies in the Archaeology of Jerusalem and its Region. Tel Aviv: Israel Antiquities Authority.

Finkelstein, Israel, and Thomas Römer. 2020. "The Historical and Archaeological Background Behind the Old Israelite Ark Narrative." *Biblica* 101, no. 2: 161–185.

Finkelstein, Israel, Thomas Römer, Christophe Nicolle, Zachary C. Dunseth, Assaf Kleiman, Juliette Mas, and Naomi Porat. 2018. "Excavations at Kiriath-Jearim Near Jerusalem, 2017: Preliminary Report." *Semitica* 6: 31–83.

Finneran, Niall. 2002. *The Archaeology of Christianity in Africa.* Stroud: Gloucestershire: Tempus.

Finneran, Niall. 2007. *Archaeology of Ethiopia.* New York: Routledge.

Fisher, Daniel. 2018. "Memories of the Ark: Texts, Objects, and the Construction of the Past." PhD diss., University of California, Berkeley.

Fitzgerald, Mary Anne, with Philip Marsden. 2017. *Ethiopia: The Living Churches of an Ancient Kingdom.* Cairo: American University in Cairo Press.

Foley, Cyril. 1935. *Autumn Foliage.* London: Methuen.

Ford, J. Massyngberde. 1975. *Revelation: Introduction, Translation and Commentary.* The Anchor Bible 38. Garden City, NY: Doubleday.

Fraade, Steven D. 2019. "Facing the Holy Ark, in Words and in Images." *Near Eastern Archaeology* 82, no. 3: 156–163. https://www.jstor.org/stable/48571090.

Frend, William H. C. 1996. *The Archaeology of Early Christianity.* London: Geoffrey Chapman.

Freud, Sigmund. [1939] 1967. *Moses and Monotheism.* Translated by Katherine Jones. New York: Vintage Books.

Futterer, Antonia. 1950. *Palestine Speaks.* Los Angeles: Holyland Bible Knowledge Society.

Futterer, Antonia. 1982. "Adventures of the Golden Ark Explorer." Los Angeles: Holyland Bible Knowledge Society.

Futterer, Antonia. [1911] 1992. *Eye-Ographic Bible Course: A Layman's Training Course of Bible History and Geography.* Minneapolis: Holyland Bible Knowledge Society.

Gadamer, Hans-Georg. [1960] 1989. *Truth and Method.* 2nd rev. Edited by Joel Weinsheimer and translated by Donald G. Marshall. New York: Crossroad.

Gelb, Ignace J., Oppenheim, A. Leo, Erica Reiner, and Robert Biggs (eds.). 1956–2010a. "*karābu.*" In *The Assyrian Dictionary of the Oriental Institute of the University of Chicago, K,* Vol. 8, 192–198. Chicago: Oriental Institute of the University of Chicago.

Gelb, Ignace J., Oppenheim, A. Leo, Erica Reiner, and Robert Biggs (eds.). 1956–2010b. "*kāribu.*" In *The Assyrian Dictionary of the Oriental Institute of the University of Chicago, K,* Vol. 8, 216–217. Chicago: Oriental Institute of the University of Chicago.

George, Mark K., Frans van Liere, Christopher Rowland, Ori Z. Soltes, Günter Stemberger, Mark D. Stucky, Roberto Tottoli, and Kathryn Walls. 2009. "Ark of the Covenant." In *Encyclopedia of the Bible and Its Reception,* edited by Constance M. Furey, Peter Gemeinhardt, Joel LeMon, Thomas Römer, Jens Schröter, Barry Dov Walfish, and Eric Ziolkowski, Vol. 1, 744–767. Berlin: de Gruyter.

Geraghty, Lincoln. 2014. *Cult Collectors: Nostalgia, Fandom and Collecting Popular Culture.* London: Routledge.

Ginzberg, Louis. 1909. *The Legends of the Jews.* Philadelphia: Jewish Publication Society.

Goin, Jane. 2015. "Uhuru Given 'Ark of the Covenant' with Good Tidings for Kenya." *Capital News.* https://www.capitalfm.co.ke/news/2015/11/uhuru-given-ark-of-the-covenant-with-good-tidings-for-kenya/.

Gonen, Rivka. 2003. *Contested Holiness: Jewish, Muslim, and Christian Perspectives on the Temple Mount in Jerusalem.* Jersey City, NJ: KTAV.

Goodenough, Erwin R. 1953–1954. *Jewish Symbols in the Greco-Roman Period.* New York: Pantheon Books.

Gray, Jonathan. 2010. *Show Sold Separately: Promos, Spoilers, and Other Media Paratexts.* New York: New York University Press.

Green, Jack. 2017. "Museums as Intermediaries in Repatriation." *Journal of Eastern Mediterranean Archaeology & Heritage Studies* 5, no. 1: 6–18. doi:10.5325/jeasmedarcherstu.5.1.0006.

BIBLIOGRAPHY 231

Gressmann, Hugo. 1920. *Die Lade Jahves und das Allerheiligste des Salomonischen Tempels.* Berlin: Kohlhammer.

Griffith-Jones, Robin. 2004. *The Gospel According to Paul.* New York: Harper-Collins.

Grünschloß, Andreas. 2007. "'Ancient Astronaut' Narrations: A Popular Discourse on Our Religious Past." *Fabula* 48, Heft 3/4: 1–24. DOI: 10.1515/FAB.2007.016.

Gunkel, Hermann. 1906. "Die Lade Jahves ein Thronsitz." *Zeitschrift für Missionskunde und Religionswissenschaft* 21: 33–42.

Hachlili, Rachel. 1977. "The Zodiac in Ancient Jewish Art: Representation and Significance." *Bulletin of the American Schools of Oriental Research* 228: 61–77. https://doi.org/10.2307/1356500.

Hachlili, Rachel. 1997. "The Origin of the Synagogue: A Re-Assessment." *Journal for the Study of Judaism in the Persian, Hellenistic, and Roman Period* 28, no. 1: 34–47. http://www.jstor.org/stable/24669126.

Hachlili, Rachel. 2000. "Torah Shrine and Ark in Ancient Synagogues: A Re-Evaluation." *Zeitschrift Des Deutschen Palästina-Vereins* 116, no. 2: 146–183. http://www.jstor.org/stable/27931648.

Hachlili, Rachel. 2002. "The Zodiac in Ancient Jewish Synagogal Art: A Review." *Jewish Studies Quarterly* 9, no. 3: 219–258. http://www.jstor.org/stable/40753310.

Hachlili, Rachel. 2013. *Ancient Synagogues—Archaeology and Art: New Discoveries and Current Research.* Leiden: Brill.

Hancock, Graham. 1992. *The Sign and the Seal.* New York: Touchstone.

Hancock, Graham. 1995. *Fingerprints of the Gods.* New York: Doubleday.

Haran, Menahem. 1985. *Temples and Temple Service in Ancient Israel.* Winona Lake, IN: Eisenbrauns.

Harland, Philip. 2013. *Associations, Synagogues, and Congregations: Claiming a Place in Ancient Mediterranean Society.* 2nd rev. ed. with links to inscriptions. Self-published.

Harris, Jennifer. 2009. "Enduring Covenant in the Christian Middle Ages. *Journal of Ecumenical Studies* 44, no. 4 (Fall): 563–586.

Hartmann, Richard. 1918. "Zelt und Lade." *Zeitschrift für die Alttestamentliche Wissenschaft* 37: 209–244.

Harvey, John. 2013. *The Bible as Visual Culture: When Text Becomes Image.* The Bible in the Modern World, 57. Oxford: Sheffield Phoenix Press.

Hassinoff, Erin L. 2011. *Faith in Objects: American Missionary Exhibitions in the Early Twentieth Century.* New York: Palgrave Macmillan.

Hassner, Ron E. 2009. *War on Sacred Grounds.* Ithaca, NY: Cornell University Press.

Hausman, Gerald. 2020. *The Kebra Nagast: The Lost Bible of Rastafarian Wisdom and Faith.* New York: St. Martin's Essentials.

Henze, Paul B. 2000. *Layers of Time: A History of Ethiopia.* New York: Palgrave MacMillan.

Hess, Richard S. 2007. *Israelite Religions: An Archaeological and Biblical Survey.* Grand Rapids, MI: Baker Academic.

Hicks, Dan. 2020. *The Brutish Museums: The Benin Bronzes, Colonial Violence and Cultural Restitution.* London: Pluto Press.

Hillers, Delbert R. 1968. "Ritual Procession of the Ark and Psalm 132." *Catholic Biblical Quarterly* 30: 48–55.

Hitzlik, Michael A. 1992a. "Does Trail to Ark of the Covenant End Behind Axum Curtain?" *Los Angeles Times,* June 9, section H, p. 6.

Hitzlik, Michael A. 1992b. "A Passage to Ethiopia." *Los Angeles Times,* July 19, section SM, p. 16–19, 35.

Holder, Anthony, trans. 1994. *Bede: On the Tabernacle.* Liverpool: Liverpool University Press.

Holtorf, Cornelius. 2007. *Archaeology is a Brand!* Walnut Creek, CA: Left Coast Press.

Holtz, Barry, ed. 1984. *Back to the Sources: Reading the Classic Jewish Texts.* New York: Summit Books.

232 BIBLIOGRAPHY

Homan, Michael M. 2002. *To Your Tents, O Israel! The Terminology, Function, Form, and Symbolism of Tents in the Hebrew Bible and the Ancient Near East*. Culture and History of the Ancient Near East, vol. 12. Leiden: Brill.

Hornung, Erik. 2001. *The Secret Lore of Egypt: Its Impact on the West*. Translated by David Lorton. Ithaca, NY: Cornell University Press.

Hubbard, David Allan. 1957. "The Literary Sources of the Kebra Negast." PhD diss., University of St. Andrews.

Huckvale, David. 2012. *Ancient Egypt in the Popular Imagination: Building a Fantasy in Film Literature, Music, and Art*. Jefferson, NC: McFarland & Co.

Huizinga, Johan. 1938. *Homo Ludens: A Study of the Play-Element in Culture*. New York: Random House.

Hyatt, J. P. 1971. *Exodus*. The New Century Bible Commentary. Grand Rapids, MI: Eerdmans.

Japhet, Sara. 1993. *I & II Chronicles*. The Old Testament Library. Louisville, KY: Westminster/John Knox Press.

Jarus, Owen. 2018. "Sorry Indiana Jones, the Ark of the Covenant Is Not Inside This Ethiopian Church." *Live Science*, December 7. https://www.livescience.com/64256-ark-of-the-covenant-location.html.

Jones, Vendyl. 2005. *A Door of Hope: My Search for the Treasures of the Copper Scroll*. Springdale, AR: Lightcatcher Books.

Juvelius, Valter Henrik. 1916. *Valkoinen Kameeli Ja Muita Kertomuksia Itämailta*. Norderstedt, Germany: Kustanusosakeyhtiö Otava.

Kabbani, Rana. 1986. *Europe's Myths of Orient*. Bloomington: Indiana University Press.

Katz, David S. 2004. *God's Last Words: Reading the English Bible from the Reformation to Fundamentalism*. New Haven, CT: Yale University Press.

Keck, David. 1998. *Angels and Angelology in the Middle Ages*. Oxford: Oxford University Press.

Keel, Othmar, and Christoph Uehlinger. 1998. *Gods, Goddesses, and Images of God in Ancient Israel*. Translated by Thomas H. Trapp. Minneapolis, MN: Fortress Press.

Kenyon, Kathleen. 1974. *Digging Up Jerusalem*. London: Ernest Benn.

Kestner, Joseph A. 2010. *Masculinities in British Adventure Fiction, 1880–1915*. Surrey, UK: Ashgate.

Kletter, Raz. 2020. *Archaeology, Heritage and Ethics in the Western Wall Plaza, Jerusalem: Darkness at the End of the Tunnel*. New York: Routledge.

Kopytoff, Igor. 1986. "The Cultural Biography of Things: Commoditization as Process." In *The Social Life of Things: Commodities in Cultural Perspective*, edited by Arjun Appadurai, 64–91. Cambridge: Cambridge University Press.

Kugel, James L., and Rowan A. Greer. 1986. *Early Biblical Interpretation*. Library of Early Christianity. Edited by Wayne A. Meeks. Philadelphia: Westminster Press.

Kurlander, Eric. 2017. *Hitler's Monsters: A Supernatural History of the Third Reich*. New Haven, CT: Yale University Press.

Larsen, Mogens Trolle. 1995. "The "Babel/Bible" Controversy and Its Aftermath." In *Civilizations of the Ancient Near East*, edited by Jack Sasson, Vol. I., 95–106. Peabody, MA: Hendrickson.

Lawler, Andrew. 2021. *Under Jerusalem: The Buried History of the World's Most Contested City*. New York: Doubleday.

Layug, Benjie. 2019. "Ten Commandments Building (Baguio City, Benguet)." *B.L.A.S.T. Benjie Layug: Adventures of a Savvy Traveler*. http://benjielayug.com/2019/01/ten-commandments-building-baguio-city-benguet.html#google_vignette.

Levine, Lee I., ed. 1982. *Ancient Synagogues Revealed*. Jerusalem: Israel Exploration Society.

Levine, Lee I., ed. 1987. *The Synagogue in Late Antiquity*. Philadelphia: American Schools of Oriental Research.

Levine, Moshe. 1969. *The Tabernacle: Its Structure and Utensils*. Tel Aviv: Soncino Press.

Lieb, Michael, Emma Mason, Jonathan Roberts, and Christopher Rowland, eds. 2011. *The Oxford Handbook of the Reception History of the Bible*. Oxford: Oxford University Press. https://doi.org/10.1093/oxfordhb/9780199204540.001.0001.

BIBLIOGRAPHY   233

Linville, James. 2016. "The Bible and the Other Creation Museums." *The Bible and Interpretation.* https://bibleinterp.arizona.edu/articles/2016/08/lin408023.

Long, Burke O. 2003. *Imagining the Holy Land: Maps, Models, and Fantasy Travels.* Bloomington: Indiana University Press.

Luceno, James. 2008. *Indiana Jones: The Ultimate Guide.* New York: DK.

Luckhurst, Roger. 2012. *The Mummy's Curse: The True History of a Dark Fantasy.* Oxford: Oxford University Press.

MacDonald, Burton. 2010. *Pilgrimage in Early Christian Jordan: A Literary and Archaeological Guide.* Oxford: Oxbow Books.

Mander, Jerry. 1978. *Four Arguments for the Elimination of Television.* New York: Morrow Quill.

Maraval, Pierre. 2002. "The Earliest Phase of Christian Pilgrimage in the Near East (before the 7th Century)." *Dumbarton Oaks Papers* 56: 63–74. https://doi.org/10.2307/1291855.

Marcus, Harold. 2002. *A History of Ethiopia.* Updated ed. Berkeley: University of California Press.

Marcus, Ralph, trans. 1953. *Philo Supplement II: Questions and Answers on Exodus.* Loeb Classical Library. Cambridge, MA: Harvard University Press. https://ryanfb.github.io/loebolus-data/L401.pdf.

Master, Daniel, ed. 2013. *The Oxford Encyclopedia of the Bible and Archaeology.* Oxford: Oxford University Press.

May, Herbert G. 1936. "The Ark: A Miniature Temple." *American Journal of Semitic Languages and Literatures* 52, no. 4: 215–234.

Mazar, Eilat. 2002. *The Complete Guide to the Temple Mount Excavations.* Jerusalem: Shoham Academic Research and Publications.

McCarter, P. Kyle. 1980. *I Samuel.* Anchor Bible 8. New York: Doubleday.

McCarter, P. Kyle. 1984. *II Samuel.* Anchor Bible 9. New York: Doubleday.

McGeough, Kevin M. 2006. "Heroes, Mummies, and Treasure: Near Eastern Archaeology in the Movies." *Near Eastern Archaeology* 69: 174–185.

McGeough, Kevin M. 2015a. *The Ancient Near East in the Nineteenth Century: Appreciations and Appropriations. I. Claiming and Conquering.* Hebrew Bible Monographs 67. Sheffield, UK: Sheffield Phoenix Press.

McGeough, Kevin M. 2015b. *The Ancient Near East in the Nineteenth Century: Appreciations and Appropriations. II. Collecting, Constructing, and Curating.* Hebrew Bible Monographs 68. Sheffield, UK: Sheffield Phoenix Press.

McGeough, Kevin M. 2015c. *The Ancient Near East in the Nineteenth Century: Appreciations and Appropriations. III. Fantasy and Alternative Histories.* Hebrew Bible Monographs 68. Sheffield. UK: Sheffield Phoenix Press.

McGeough, Kevin M. 2018a. "The Problem with David: Masculinity and Morality in Biblical Cinema." *Journal of Religion and Film* 22, no. 1, Article 33: 1–52.

McGeough, Kevin M. 2018b. "Murderous Archaeologists, Doubting Priests, and Mesopotamian Demons: The Bible in Horror and Adventure Cinema." In *T & T Clark Companion to Bible and Film,* edited by Richard Walsh, 60–72. London: T & T Clark.

McGeough, Kevin M. 2020. "The "False Syllogism" of Archaeological Authenticity in Jesus Movies." In *T & T Clark Companion to Jesus and Film,* edited by Richard Walsh, 115–125. London: T & T Clark.

McGeough, Kevin M. 2022. *Representations of Antiquity in Film: From Griffith to Grindhouse.* Sheffield, UK: Equinox.

McClellan, Daniel. 2022. *YHWH's Divine Images: A Cognitive Approach.* Atlanta: SBL Press.

Melander, Henning. 1916. *Frimuurarnas Hemlighet Och Israels Förbundsark.* Stockholm: Wilhelmssons Boktrckeri.

Meskell, Lynn. 2004. *Object Worlds in Ancient Egypt: Material Biographies Past and Present.* Oxford: Berg.

Mettinger, T. N. D. 1999. "Cherubim." In *Dictionary of Deities and Demons in the Bible,* edited by Karel van der Toorn et al., 189–192. Leiden: Brill.

234 BIBLIOGRAPHY

Metzger, Martin. 1985. *Königsthron und Gottesthron: Thronformen und Throndarstellungen in Ägypten und im Vorderen Orient im dritten und zweiten Jahrtausend vor Christus und deren Bedeutung für das Verständnis von Aussagen über den Thron im Alten Testament.* 2 vols. Alter Orient und Altes Testament. Kevelaer, Germany: Butzon & Bercker.

Metzler, Maria J. 2016. "The Ark of the Covenant and Divine Rage in the Hebrew Bible." PhD diss., Harvard University.

Meyers, Carol. 1992. "Cherubim." In *The Anchor Yale Bible Dictionary*, Vol. 1 (A–C), edited by David Noel Freedman, 899–900. New Haven, CT: Yale University Press.

Meyers, Eric M., ed. 1997. *The Oxford Encyclopedia of Archaeology in the Near East.* 5 vols. Oxford: Oxford University Press.

Meyers, Eric M., and Carol Meyers. 1981. "Finders of a Real Lost Ark." *BAR* 7, no. 6 (November/December): 24–39. https://www.baslibrary.org/biblical-archaeology-review/7/6/1.

Milikowsky, Chaim. 2015. "Where Is the Lost Ark of the Covenant? The True History (of the Ancient Traditions)." In *Tradition, Transmission, and Transformation from Second Temple Literature through Judaism and Christianity in Late Antiquity*, edited by Menachem Kister, 208–229. Studies on the Texts of the Desert of Judah 113. Leiden, The Netherlands: Brill.

Miller, Daniel. 2010. *Stuff.* Malden, MA: Polity Press.

Miller, Patrick D., and J. J. M. Roberts. 1977. *The Hand of the Lord: A Reassessment of the "Ark Narrative" of I Samuel.* Baltimore: Johns Hopkins University Press.

Morgenstern, Julian. 1945. *The Ark the Ephod and the "Tent of Meeting."* Cincinnati, OH: Hebrew Union College.

Morrison, Tessa. 2008. "Villalpando's Sacred Architecture in the Light of Isaac Newton's Commentary." In *Nexus VII: Architecture and Mathematics*, edited by Kim Williams, 79–91. Turin: Kim Williams Books.

Munro-Hay, Stuart, Alexander Kaczmarczyk, and D. W. Phillipson. 1989. *Excavations at Aksum: An Account of Research at the Ancient Ethiopian Capital Directed in 1972–74 by the late Dr Neville Chittick.* London: British Institute in Eastern Africa.

N.A. 1929. "Japanese Author Traces Nippon Origin to Hebrew Race." *Jewish Daily Bulletin*, Thursday, August 15, 3–4.

N.A. 1956. "Ethiopia's Revised Constitution." *Middle East Journal* 10, no. 2: 194–199. http://www.jstor.org/stable/4322802.

N.A. 1983. "Tom Crotser Has Found the Ark of the Covenant or Has He?" *Biblical Archaeology Review* May–June: 66–67.

N.A. 2013. "Giant Ark of the Covenant Replica Donated to Israel." *Jewish Rhode Island*. https://www.jewishrhody.com/stories/giant-ark-of-the-covenant-replica-donated-to-israel,3137?.

N.A. 2017. "Large Model of Aron HaBris Destroyed in Downtown Jerusalem." *The Yeshiva World.* https://www.theyeshivaworld.com/news/featured/1288771/photos-large-model-aron-habris-destroyed-downtown-jerusalem.html.

Nakhai, Beth. 2001. *Archaeology and the Religions of Canaan and Israel.* Boston: American Schools of Oriental Research.

Neese, Shelley. 2019. *The Copper Scroll Project: An Ancient Secret Fuels the Battle for the Temple Mount.* New York: Morgan James.

Neusner, Jacob. 1970. *The Way of Torah: An Introduction to Judaism.* Belmont, CA: Dickenson Publishing Company.

Neusner, Jacob. 1987. *What Is Midrash?* Philadelphia: Fortress Press.

Neusner, Jacob. 1988a. *Judaism: The Evidence of the Mishnah.* Brown Judaic Studies 129. Atlanta: Scholars Press.

Neusner, Jacob. 1988b. *The Mishnah: A New Translation.* New Haven, CT: Yale University Press.

Neusner, Jacob. 1994. *Introduction to Rabbinic Literature.* New York: Doubleday.

Noegel, Scott B. 2015. "The Egyptian Origin of the Ark of the Covenant." In *Israel's Exodus in Transdisciplinary Perspective: Text, Archaeology, Culture and Geoscience*, edited by Thomas E. Levy, Thomas Schneider, and William H. C. Propp, 223–242. Cham, Switzerland: Springer.

BIBLIOGRAPHY   235

Noth, Martin. 1962. *Exodus*. Translated by J. S. Bowden. The Old Testament Library. Louisville, KY: Westminster Press.

Oftestad, Eivor Anderson. 2019. *The Lateran Church in Rome and the Ark of the Covenant: Housing the Holy Relics of Jerusalem*. Woodbridge, UK: Boydell & Brewer.

Olsson, Birger, and Magnus Zetterholm. 2003. *The Ancient Synagogue From Its Origins until 200 C.E.: Papers Presented at an International Conference at Lund University, October 14–17, 2001*. Coniectanea Biblica New Testament Series 39. Stockholm: Almqvist & Wiksell International.

Oyabe, Jenichiro. 1929. *The Origin of Japan and the Japanese (Nihon oyobi Nihon kokumin no kigen)*. Tokyo: Koseikaku Showa.

Pankhurst, Richard. 1986. ""Fear God, Honor the King": The Use of Biblical Allusion in Ethiopian Historical Literature. Part I" *Northeast African Studies* 8, no. 1: 11–30.

Pankhurst, Richard. 1987. ""Fear God, Honor the King": The Use of Biblical Allusion in Ethiopian Historical Literature. Part II." *Northeast African Studies* 9, no. 1: 25–88.

Park, Julie. 2010. *The Self and It: Novel Objects in Eighteenth-Century England*. Stanford, CA: Stanford University Press.

Pasulka, Diane W. 2016. "The Fairy Tale Is True: Social Technologies of the Religious Supernatural in Film and New Media." *Journal of the American Academy of Religion* 84, no. 2 (June): 530–547.

Pauwels, Louis, and Jacques Bergier. 1960. *The Morning of the Magicians: Introduction to Fantastic Realism*. Paris: Éditions Gallimard.

Pearce, Susan. 2013. *On Collecting: An Investigation into Collecting in the European Tradition*. New York: Routledge.

Porzig, Peter. 2014. "Postchronistic Traces in the Narratives about the Ark?" In *Rereading the Relecture? The Question of Postchronistic Influence in the Latest Redactions of the Books of Samuel*, edited by Uwe Becker and Hannes Bezzel, 93–105. Forschungen zum Alten Testament 2/66. Tübingen, Germany: Mohr Siebeck.

Price, Randall. 2005. *Searching for the Ark of the Covenant: Latest Discoveries and Research*. Eugene, OR: Harvest House.

Propp, William H. C. 2006. *Exodus 19–40: A New Translation with Introduction and Commentary*. Anchor Bible 2A. New York: Doubleday.

Le Queux, William. 1910. *Treasure of Israel*. London: Eveleigh Nash.

Quinn, Malcolm. 1994. *The Swastika*. London: Routledge.

Reinhartz, Adele. 2013. *Bible and Cinema: An Introduction*. New York: Routledge.

Reinl, Harald, dir. 1970. *Chariots of the Gods*. Anglo-EMI Film Distributors. West Germany: Terra-Filmkunst.

Renfrew, Colin, and Paul Bahn. 2019. *Archaeology: Theories, Methods, and Practice*. 8th ed. New York: Thames and Hudson.

Revel-Neher, Elisabeth. 1984. *L'arche d'alliance dans l'art juif et chrétien du second au dixième siècles*. Paris: Association des amis des etudes archéologiques byzanto-slaves et du christianisme oriental.

Rezetko, Robert. 2007. *Source and Revision in the Narratives of David's Transfer of the Ark: Text, Language, and Story in 2 Samuel 6 and 1 Chronicles 13, 15–16*. Library of Hebrew Bible/Old Testament Studies 470. London: T&T Clark.

Rinzler, J. W. 2008. *The Complete Making of Indiana Jones*. New York: Del Rey.

Ritmeyer, Leen. 2006. *The Quest: Revealing the Temple Mount in Jerusalem*. Jerusalem: Carta.

Ritmeyer, Leen, and Kathleen Ritmeyer. 1998. *Secrets of Jerusalem's Temple Mount*. Washington, DC: Biblical Archaeology Society.

Robinson, Edward. 1841. *Biblical Researches in Palestine, Mount Sinai and Arabia Petræa: A Journal of Travels in the Year 1838 by E. Robinson and E. Smith*. Boston: Crocker & Brewster.

Romano, Irene Bald. 2023. "Introduction. Antiquities in the Nazi Era: Contexts and Broader View." *RIHA Journal* 0282 (Sept. 15). https://doi.org/10.11588/riha.2022.2.92735.

236 BIBLIOGRAPHY

Rost, Leonhard. [1926] 1982. *The Succession to the Throne of David*. (*Die Überlieferung von der Thronnachfolge Davids*). Translated by Michael D. Rutter and David M. Gunn. Sheffield, UK: Almond Press.

Rowan, Yorke M. 2004. "Repackaging the Pilgrimage: Visiting the Holy Land in Orlando." In *Marketing Heritage: Archaeology and the Consumption of the Past*, edited by Yorke M. Rowan and Uzi Baram, 249–266. Lanham, MD: Altamira Press.

Ryan, Jordan J. 2023 "Jesus in the Synagogue." *Biblical Archaeology Review* 49, no. 1 (Spring): 34–41.

Sanders, E. P. 2015. *Paul: The Apostle's Life, Letters, and Thought*. Minneapolis, MN: Fortress Press.

Schmitt, Rainer. 1972. *Zelt und Lade als Thema alttestamentlicher Wissenschaft: Eine kritische forschungsgeschichtliche Darstellung*. Gütersloh, Germany: Mohr Siebeck.

Scholem, Gershom. 1965. *Kabbalah and Its Symbolism*. New York: Schocken Books.

Schrader, Paul. 2018. *Transcendental Style in Film: Ozu, Bresson, Dresser, with a New Introduction: Rethinking Transcendental Style*. Oakland: University of California Press.

Sconce, Jeremy. 2000. *Haunted Media: Electronic Presence from Telegraphy to Television*. Durham, NC: Duke University Press.

Seow, C. L. 1992. "Ark of the Covenant." In *The Anchor Yale Bible Dictionary*, Vol. 1 (A–C), edited by David Noel Freedman, 386–393. New Haven, CT: Yale University Press.

Sevensma, Tietse P. 1908. *De Ark Gods: Het Oud-Israëlitische Heiligdom*. Amsterdam: Clausen.

Shanks, Hershel. 1979. *Judaism in Stone: The Archaeology of Ancient Synagogues*. Washington, DC: Biblical Archaeology Society.

Shanks, Hershel, ed. 2004. *The City of David: Revisiting Early Excavations, English Translations of Reports by Raymond Weil and L.-H. Vincent*. Notes and comments by Ronny Reich. Washington, DC: Biblical Archaeology Society.

Shepherd, David J. 2013. *The Bible on Silent Film: Spectacle, Story and Scripture in the Early Cinema*. Cambridge: Cambridge University Press.

Shepherd, Naomi. 1987. *The Zealous Intruders: The Western Rediscovery of Palestine*. New York: Collins.

Shragai, Nadav. 2018. "A Rabbi, an Officer and a Mystic." *Israel HaYom*, December 7. https://www.israelhayom.com/2018/12/07/a-rabbi-an-officer-and-a-mystic/.

Silberman, Neil Asher. 1982. *Digging For God and Country: Exploration, Archeology, and the Secret Struggle for the Holy Land, 1799–1917*. New York: Alfred A. Knopf.

Solomon, Jon. 2001. *The Ancient World in the Cinema*. Rev. ed. New Haven, CT: Yale University Press.

Sommer, Benjamin D. 2009. *The Bodies of God and the World of Ancient Israel*. Cambridge: Cambridge University Press.

Staff, Toi. 2019. "Stone Slab Unearthed near Jerusalem Suggests Connection to Ark of the Covenant." *The Times of Israel*, December 19. https://www.timesofisrael.com/stone-slab-unearthed-near-jerusalem-suggests-connection-to-ark-of-the-covenant/.

Steinsaltz, Adin. 2013. *Koren Talmud Bavli: The Noe Edition*. Jerusalem: Koren.

Stern, David. 2004. "Midrash and Jewish Interpretation." In *The Jewish Study Bible*, edited by Adele Berlin and Marc Zvi Brettler, 1863–1875. Oxford: Oxford University Press.

Stewart, Susan. 1984. *On Longing: Narratives of the Miniature, the Gigantic, the Souvenir, the Collection*. Baltimore: Johns Hopkins University Press.

Strack, Hermann L. [1931] 1969. *Introduction to the Talmud and Midrash*. New York: Atheneum.

Tegegne, Habtamu, and Wendy Belcher. 2023. "The Solomonic Christian Kingdom of Ethiopia." In *Great Kingdoms of Africa*, edited by John Parker, 85–113. New York: Thames and Hudson.

Thomas, Elizabeth. 1956. "Solar Barks from Prow to Prow." *Journal of Egyptian Archaeology* 42: 56–79.

Tigay, Jeffrey H. 1996. *Deuteronomy*. The JPS Torah Commentary. Philadelphia: Jewish Publication Society.

BIBLIOGRAPHY   237

Tobolowsky, Andrew. 2022. *The Myth of the Twelve Tribes of Israel: New Identities Across Time and Space*. Cambridge: Cambridge University Press.

Tobolowsky, Andrew. 2023. "The Myth of the Twelve Tribes of Israel." *The Ancient Near East Today* 11, no. 4. https://www.asor.org/anetoday/2023/04/myth-twelve-tribes.

Touger, Eliyahu. 1987. *Mishneh Torah / Maimonides: A New Translation with Commentaries, Notes, Tables, Charts and Index*. New York: Moznaim.

Trigger, Bruce. 2006. *A History of Archaeological Thought*. 2nd ed. Cambridge: Cambridge University Press.

Truffaut, François, and Scott, Helen. 1984. *Hitchcock*. Rev. ed. New York: Simon and Schuster.

Ucko, Peter, and Timothy Champion, eds. 2003. *The Wisdom of Egypt: Changing Visions Through the Ages*. London: UCL Press.

Ullendorff, Edward. 1956. "Hebraic-Jewish Elements in Abyssinian (Monophysite) Christianity." *Journal of Semitic Studies* 1: 216–256.

Ullendorff, Edward. 1968. *Ethiopia and the Bible*. London: Oxford University Press.

Underhill, Evelyn. 1922. *A Book of Contemplation the Which Is Called the Cloud of Unknowing, In the Which a Soul Is Oned with God*. 2nd ed. London: John M. Watkins.

Van Seters, John. 2009. *The Biblical Saga of King David*. Winona Lake, IN: Eisenbrauns.

Vermes, Geza. 1995. *The Dead Sea Scrolls in English*. 4th ed. New York: Penguin.

Vincent, Louis-Hugues. 1911. *Jerusalem Sous Terre, Les Recette Fouilles d'Ophel*. London: Horace Cox.

Vincent, Louis-Hugues, and Charles Warren. 1912. "Recent Excavations on the Hill of Ophel." *Palestine Exploration Quarterly* 44, no. 3: 131–135.

Von Däniken, Erich. 1968. *Chariots of the Gods?* New York: Bantam.

Von Däniken, Erich. 1980. *Signs of the Gods*. New York: Corgi Books.

Von Rad, Gerhard. 1966. "The Tent and the Ark." In *The Problem of the Hexateuch and Other Essays*, translated by E. W. Trueman Dicken, 103–124. Edinburgh: Oliver & Boyd.

Walsh, Richard. 2003. *Reading the Gospels in the Dark: Portrayals of Jesus in Film*. New York: Trinity Press International.

Warren, Charles. 1912. "The Results of the Excavations on the Hill of Ophel (Jerusalem Sous Terre), 1909–1911." *Palestine Exploration Quarterly* 44, no. 2: 68–74.

Waxman, Sharon. 2010. *Loot: The Battle over the Stolen Treasures of the Ancient World*. New York: Macmillan.

Whiston, William, trans. [1737] 1981. *The Complete Works of Josephus*. Grand Rapids, MI: Kregel.

White, Chris. 2013. "Ancient Alien Evidence Examined." *Skeptic* 18, no. 4: 16–23.

Whitmer, Kelly. 2010. "The Model That Never Moved: The Case of a Virtual Memory Theater and Its Christian Philosophical Argument, 1700–1732." *Science in Context* 23, no. 3: 289–327. doi:10.1017/S0269889710000098.

Williams, Stephen. 1991. *Fantastic Archaeology: The Wild Side of North American Prehistory*. Philadelphia: University of Pennsylvania Press.

Wilson, Charles, and Charles Warren. 1871. *The Recovery of Jerusalem: A Narrative of Exploration and Discovery in the City and the Holy Land*. New York: D. Appleton & Co.

Wilson, Ian. 2005. "Merely a Container? The Ark in Deuteronomy." In *Temples and Worship in Biblical Israel*, edited by John Day, 212–249. Journal for the Study of the Old Testament Supplement Series 422. Edinburgh: T&T Clark.

Wilson, J. 1968. "British Israelism." *Sociological Review* 16: 41–57.

Woodman, Peter. 1995. "Who Possesses Tara? Politics in Archaeology in Ireland." In *Theory in Archaeology: A World Perspective*, edited by P. J. Ucko, 278–297. Routledge: London.

Wolters, Al. 2000. "Copper Scroll." In *Encyclopedia of the Dead Sea Scrolls*, Vol. 1, edited by Lawrence Schiffman and James VanderKam, 144–148. Oxford: Oxford University Press.

Zacks, Jeffrey. 2014. *Flicker: Your Brain on the Movies*. Oxford: Oxford University Press.

Zevit, Ziony. 2001. *The Religions of Ancient Israel: A Synthesis of Parallactic Approaches*. London: Continuum.

238 BIBLIOGRAPHY

Ziesler, J. A. 1990. *Pauline Christianity*. Rev. ed. Oxford Bible Series. Oxford: Oxford University Press.

Zinn, Grover A. 1979. *Richard of St Victor*. New York: Paulist Press.

Zwickel, W. 1999. *Der Salomonische Temple*. Kulturgeschichte der Antiken Welt, Vol. 83. Mainz am Rhein: Verlag Philipp von Zabern.

Scriptural References

For the benefit of digital users, indexed terms that span two pages (e.g., 52–53) may, on occasion, appear on only one of those pages.

Old Testament
Genesis 6:14, 16–17
Genesis 6:19–20, 21
Genesis 7:1–3, 21
Genesis 12, 21
Genesis 20, 21
Genesis 26, 21
Genesis 50:26, 16
Exodus 13:20–22, 156–57
Exodus 25:10, 73, 88
Exodus 25: 10–22, 13, 14, 15, 16–17,
    54–55, 63–64, 66–67, 83–85, 153,
    158, 173, 186
Exodus 25:18–20, 50–51
Exodus 25:22, 84–85
Exodus 28, 158
Exodus 35: 30–31, 14
Exodus 37: 1–9, 14, 22–23
Exodus 40, 14, 57
Leviticus 16, 14
Leviticus 25:10, 134–35
Numbers 3:16, 19
Numbers 4:4–8, 15
Numbers 4:5–6, 48–49
Numbers 10: 35–36, 15–16
Numbers 14:44, 19
Deuteronomy 10:1, 73
Deuteronomy 10:3, 22–23
Deuteronomy 31:26, 87–88
Joshua 3, 73
Joshua 3:11, 17–18
Joshua 6:3–5, 20
Joshua 8: 30–34, 20
Judges 2:1, 19–20
Judges 20:27, 19–20
I Samuel 4:1b–7:1, 23–27, 41
I Samuel 4:2, 41–42

I Samuel 4:3, 23–24
I Samuel 4:4, 17
I Samuel 4:21, 23–24
I Samuel 5, 42
I Samuel 6, 55
I Samuel 6:13, 25
I Samuel 6:13–15, 32
I Samuel 6:18, 25, 32
II Samuel 6:1–23, 23–27, 48
I Kings 8:6–9, 27–28
I Kings 8:9, 89
I Kings 8:21, 28
II Kings 12:10, 16–17
II Kings 19:14–19, 28–29
Psalm 114, 19
Psalm 132, 26
Isaiah 37:14–17, 28–29
Jeremiah 3:16–17, 29–30
I Chronicles 13:3–4, 26
II Chronicles 5:10, 89
II Chronicles 35:3, 28–29

New Testament
Matthew 1:20, 77
John 1:1, 80–81, 82–83
Hebrews, 8
Hebrews 9:1–12, 81–82, 158
Hebrews 9:4, 89
Hebrews 9:5, 83
Revelation 7:1, 112
Revelation 11:19, 70–71

Apocrypha
2 Baruch 6–7, 70, 71
2 Maccabees 2:4–5, 68–69, 98–99, 115–16
1 Esdras 1:54, 29
2 Esdras 10:20–22, 69–70, 71

Subject Index

For the benefit of digital users, indexed terms that span two pages (e.g., 52–53) may, on occasion, appear on only one of those pages.

Figures are indicated by an italic *f* following the page number.

2001: A Space Odyssey, 185–86

Aaron, 14, 48–49, 86, 90–91, 130–31
  staff of, 81–82, 89, 90, 122
Abinadab, 25, 26
Abraham, 11, 21
Abu Ghosh, 39–41, 76–81, 91–94. *See also*
  Kiryat Yearim
Abu Salih, 173
Acacia wood, 16
Adam and Eve, 85
adventure fiction genre, 123–24, 125–26, 148*f*,
  161, 180
advertising, 129–31
Adwa, Battle of, 170–71
Afeq Pass, 41
Afromet. *See* Association for the Return of the
  Maqdala Ethiopian Treasures
Agincourt, Battle of, 33–34
Akkadian terminology, 51
Aksum, 161–62, 166–69, 177–82
al-Aqsa Mosque, 96–97, 99, 102–3
aliens, 4, 5, 9–10, 124, 146–48, 175, 184–94, 208
Amaterasu, 114
Amda Seyon I, 165–66
Amsel, Richard, 147*f*
Amzey Bey Pasha, 102–3
anachronism, 33–34, 129
Ancient Aliens, 191–92
Ancient Apocalypse, 196
Anderson, Eivor, 90
angels, 50–51, 52, 84–86, 128, 164
Anglo–Saxons, 110–12
aniconism, 14–15, 59–60, 63–64, 87, 153,
  158, 200–1
anti–Semitism, 109–10, 197–98
Anubis, shrine of, 49–50, 50*f*
Aphek, 41–42
  Battle of, 23–24, 41–42

apocalypticism, 5, 69–71, 182–84, 203–4, 207
Apocrypha, definition of, 68
Aquinas, Thomas, 83, 85–86
Arabian trade routes, 163, 166–67
Aramaic, 122
arca, 16–17
archaeological methods, 9, 33, 34, 37–40,
  41–42, 43, 45, 47–48, 51–52, 117–18, 142–
  43, 205–6
Area 51, 193–94
Ark of the Covenant (rock group), 201–3
Ark Narrative, The, 23–27
Ashdod, 24, 32–42
Ashdoda, 41–42
Asherah, 29
Ashkelon, 41–42
Association for the Return of the Maqdala
  Ethiopian Treasures (Afromet), 172–73
Assyria (or maybe Neo–Assyrian Empire),
  28–29, 34–35
Atlantis, 4, 107–8, 175–76, 177, 180–81
atonement cover. *See* mercy seat

Baal, 39–40, 63
Baalah. *See* Kiryat Yearim
Babylonia, 29–30, 34–35, 69–70
Bar Kokhba Revolt (132–36 CE), 58–59, 62
Barfield, James, 204–7
Baruch, 70
Barrett, Wilson, 135–36
Baudrillard, Jean, 143–44, 159
Bede, Venerable, 83–85
Begin, Menachem, 108
Beit Alfa, 59–61
Beit She'arim, 61–62
Belloq, Rene, 2–3, 122, 127, 155, 184
Belzoni, Giovanni, 124
Ben–Dov, Meir, 106–7
Benedict XIV (Pope), 90–91

242 SUBJECT INDEX

Benjamin Major, 86–87
Benjamin, Tribe of, 40–41
Benjamin, Walter, 145–46
Beth Shean, synagogue at, 59
Beth Shemesh, 24–25, 31–33, 38–39, 76
Bethel, 19–20, 27
Bezalel, 14, 22–86, 190–91
BibleWalk Wax Museum, 157–58
biblical archaeology, 33–39, 42, 176–77
Bishop Joshua, 154–57, 202–3
Blake, William, 127
Boaz and Jachin, 57
Bochim, 19–20
Bond, James, 126
Borromini, Francesco, 90–91
von Bourg, Otto, 100
Branagh, Kenneth, 33–34
British–Israel Association of London , 110–12
British–Israel World Federation, 110–12
British–Israelists, 109–12, 207–8
British Museum, 171–73
Brody, Marcus, 121–22, 124–25
Brown, Dan, 180
Brynner, Yul, 130–31
Bubel, Shawn, 31–32, 53–54, 76–77, 95, 119, 140–42, 187–88
Buchan, John, 161
Buddhism, 112–15
Bunimovitz, Shlomo, 32
Burning Bush, 181–82
Burton, Richard , 102
Burtt, Ben, 127
Byzantine Empire, 93–94

camels, 33
canopic jars, 49–50
Capernaum, 53–57
    Synagogue at, 55
Capra, Frank, 194–95
Cargill, Robert, 207
Carter, Howard, 49–50
Cash, Johnny, 203
catacombs, 61–62
Cave, Nick, 203
Chariots of the Gods?, 185–88
Charisma (periodical), 203–4
Chartres Cathedral, 32
cherubim, 4, 13, 44, 48, 50–52, 55, 67, 78–79, 79*f*, 80*f*, 83, 84–86, 93, 127, 141–42, 155, 158, 160, 173, 186–87, 190, 191, 192
Chief Rabbinate of Israel, 106
Childress, David Hatcher, 191
Cho, Gene Jinsiong, 114–15

Church of the Holy Sepulchre, 93, 108–9
Church of the Nativity, 93
Church of Our Lady Ark of the Covenant, 39–40, 76–81, 80*f*, 91–94, 162
Church of Our Lady Mary of Zion (Aksum), 8–9, 161–62, 166–68, 173–74
    guardian of, 162, 173
Church of Saint John Lateran, 89–91, 92*f*, 167–68, 207–8
churches
    Byzantine construction of, 39–40
    as metaphor for the Ark, 83–85
civilizing heroes, 181–82
clairvoyants, 100
The Cloud of Unknowing, 86
codes, 99–100, 125–26, 180, 190–91, 193–94, 207
coins, 150–51
Cold War, 134–35
collectors, 143–51
commodification, 145–51, 159
conch shells, 60–62, 63, 64–65
Conder, Claude, 39–40
confirmation bias, 179–80
conspiracy theories , 5, 9–10, 182–84, 189, 193
Constantine, 89–90, 93
"contagious holiness," 14
contents of the Ark, 8, 81–82, 86–87, 89, 90, 122, 128, 143, 191
copia, rhetorical strategy, 191
Copper Scroll, 204–7
Copper Scroll Project, 204–7
correlation–causation fallacy, 179–80
cosplay. *See* playacting
Covenant Life Church, 158
cross (of crucifixion), 83
Crotser, Tom, 116–18
crusaders, 102
cultic statues, 45–52
Cupid, 85–86
cyphers. *See* codes

Dagon, Temple of, 24, 41–42, 64–65
Dale, Rodney, 188–89, 191–92
Dan, Tribe of, 110
Danger of the Ark , 2–3, 14, 120–22, 126–27, 136–37
Das Boot , 2
dating, archaeological, 37–38
David, 25–27, 34–38, 40–41, 48, 88–89, 99, 110, 136–39, 170, 189
David and Bathsheba (1951 movie), 136–39, 209–11

SUBJECT INDEX 243

Dayan, Moshe, General, 103–4
Dead Sea Scrolls, 204–7
Decalogue. *See* Ten Commandments
DeMille, Cecil B., 130–37
democracy, American, 134–35
Dennin, Michael, 192
Descriptio Lateranensis Ecclesiae, 90
description of the Ark, 6, 12–14, 47, 173,
  202, 208
  allegorical interpretation, 66–67, 83–
  84, 86–87
  cinematic interpretation, 119–20,
  127, 129–30
  rabbinic interpretation, 72–73
  replicas, 153
diabolus in musica interval, 128–29
Diodati, John, 203
Disneyland, 159
divine names, 17–19, 22
Dome of the Rock, 37–38, 74, 96–97, 102–3
dualism, 66–67
Dunne, Philip, 135–39
Dura Europas, 55, 63–65

Easter, 133–34, 197–98
"Easter Egg," 120
Eben–Ezer, Battle of, 23–27, 41, 64
École Biblique, 100–1
Egyptian funerary customs, 47–48, 49–50, 50*f*
Egyptian religion, 43–51
Eichler, Ranaan, 52
Ein Gedi, synagogue at, 59–60
Ekron, 24, 41–42
Eleazor son of Abinadab, 25
electric chair, 203
Electrical transmitter, 186–94, 208
Elephantine, Egypt, 178
Elgin Marbles. *See* Parthenon Sculptures
Eli, 23–24
Elijah, 90–91
Ephraim, Tribe of, 27
Ephrathah, 26
Epiphany, 169–70
epithets, 18–19
Epolemus, 69
Eros. *See* Cupid
escapism, 210
von Eschenbach, Wolfram, 180
Ethiopia
  and Christianity, 160, 161–63, 165–71
  early history, 166–68
  and Judaism, 168
  leadership, 162

Medieval, 161, 162, 167–68
  psuedoscholarship, 177–82, 191–92, 196–97
Eucharist, 87
Eudocia, 93–94
Eusebius, 69, 98–99
Exile, Babylonian, 34–35, 69–70
Exodus (from Egypt), 130–37
The Exorcist, 122
Ezekiel, 184–85
Ezra, 69–70

faith–healing, 154–57, 202–3
Falk, David, 47–49
fan culture, 5–6, 138–39, 143–51, 201
fedora, 138–39
Fenians, 110
Fingerprints of the Gods, 177, 181
Finkelstein, Israel, 40–41
First Spiritualist Church of Minneapolis, 100
formation processes, 47–48
Franciscans, 53–54, 77, 116–17
Freemasonry, 110, 180–81
Freud, Sigmund, 181
function of the Ark, 2–3, 6–7, 14–15, 19, 45–52,
  64–65, 73, 123–24, 126–27, 132–33, 157,
  163–64, 169, 170–71, 184–93, 196–97,
  208
Futterer, Antonio, 115–17

Gad, Tribe of, 114–15
Garden Tomb, 108–9
Garvey, Marcus, 166
Gath, 24
Ge'ez, 163, 168, 169–70
Gemara, 72
Geraghty, Lincoln, 149–50
Getz, Meir Yehuda, Rabbi, 103–8, 207–8
giant sculptures, 151–54
Gihon Spring, 97–98, 100–1
Gilgal, Sanctuary of, 19–20, 27
Giza, 191
Golden Calf, 12, 22–23, 51, 135–36, 181–82
Gonne, Maude, 111–12
Gorden, Charles, 108–9
Goren, Shlomo (Rabbi), 106–8
grace, 85–86
Graves, David, 201–2
Gray, Jonathan (author of *Ark of the Covenant*)
  182–84
Gray, Jonathan (author of *Show Sold
  Separately*), 146–48
Great Britain, 109–12
Gupana, Grace, 151–54

244   SUBJECT INDEX

Haggard, H. Rider, 161
Haile Selassie I (Emperor), 164–65, 166
Hammat Tiberias, 59–61
Han Solo, 1, 146–48
Hancock, Graham, 8–10, 162–63, 173–74, 177–83, 196–97
Haram as–Sharif, 96–108
Haran, Menahem, 13, 14, 29
Hausman, Gerald, 166
Hayes Code, 135–36
Head–Smashed–In Buffalo Jump, UNESCO World Heritage Site, 119
Heavy Metal, 128–29, 201–2
Helena, 93
Helios, 59–60
Henry V, 33–34
hermeneutics, definition, 13
Hermes, 180–81
Hermetic Traditions, 180–81
Herod the Great, 96
Heston, Charlton, 130–31
Hezekiah, 28–29, 99
historical geography, 39, 93
historicity of Ark, 38, 152–53, 197, 200–1, 202–3, 211–12
Hitchcock, Alfred, 126
Hitler, Adolph, 121–22, 193–94
Hollywood Production Code. *See* Hayes Code
Holmes, Richard, 171–73
Holy of Holies, 29, 56–57, 72–73, 74, 90, 99, 102, 105, 106–7, 154, 169
Holyland Bible Knowledge Society, 116
Holy Land Exhibition (Silver Lake) 116
Homer, 61–62
Hophni, 23–24
Hopkins, Clark, 63
horror genre, 122
Houston, Texas, 157
Howell, Leonard (Reverend), 166
hyperreality, 159

Ichabod, 23–24
imperialism, 123, 161, 166, 170–73
In Search Of (television show) 4
Indiana Jones, 1–3, 5–6, 29, 117–18, 119–31, 138–39, 143–44, 160, 161, 180, 193–94, 196, 201–2, 208, 210, 211–12
costume of, 138–39
Indiana Jones and the Dial of Destiny, 124, 150
Indiana Jones and the Kingdom of the Crystal Skull, 124, 130, 150, 193–94
Indiana Jones and the Last Crusade, 124
Indiana Jones and the Temple of Doom , 150

Infotainment, 4
Innocent X (Pope), 90–91
Institute for Restoring History International, 116–17
Ionic Columns, 54–56, 60
Ireland, 109–12
Isaac, 21, 60–61
Ise Shrine, 114
Ishtar, 197–98
Israel (Northern Kingdom), 34–35, 110
Israel Antiquities Authority, 31, 106–7, 108–9, 206
Israel in Egypt (1867 painting), 131–32

January 6 United States Capitol Attack, 9–10
Japan, 112–15
Jehoash, 29
Jeremiah, 29–30, 46–49, 98–99, 111, 115–16, 189, 203–4, 206, 207–8
Jericho, 20, 191, 192
Jerusalem, 23, 25–30, 34–36, 37–38, 95–109, 118, 140–42
City of David Excavations, 95–96, 97–98, 104–5
Old City, 95–96, 97–98, 108–9, 140–42, 159–60
public art, 151–54
water systems, 95–96, 97–98, 99, 100–1
Jerusalem Day, 153
Jerusalem Water Relief Society, 98
Jesus, 78–81, 79f, 80f
body of, 81–83
Second Coming, 70, 85
Supersessionism, 81–82, 90–91, 158, 162
Jewish Gladiator, 61–62
Jewish Revolt (66–73 CE), 58, 71
Jones, Vendyl, 206
Jordan River , 19–20
Joseph, 16
Joseph (husband of Mary), 77
Josephus, 67–68, 83, 105
Joshua , 17–20, 134
Josiah, 28–29, 203–4
Judah , 34–35, 36–37, 40
Judah, Tribe of, 40–41
Judea, 34–35, 36, 58
Juvelius, Valter Henrik, 99–100, 103

Kabbalah, 99, 105–6
Kagome, Kagome , 113
kami, 114
kapōret. See mercy seat
karābu, 51

SUBJECT INDEX   245

Kaufman, Philip, 127
Kebra Nagast, 163–67, 172, 173, 178, 189
Kenya, 153–54
Khalil, Sheikh, 102
kibōtós, 16–17
Kiryat Yearim, 25, 38–41, 76–81, 91–94
Kitchener, Herbert (Lord Kitchener) 39–40
Kitos War (115–17 CE), 58
Knights Templars, 178, 180–81, 191–92
Kohathites, 15
Kojiki, 112
Kol Israel (radio station), 107–8
kotodama, 112
Krieger, William, 140

Last Samurai, The, 113
Last Supper, 90–91, 157–58
Lederman, Tzvi, 32
Left Behind, 183–84
Lethbridge, AB, 1, 3
Levites, 14, 15, 25, 28–29, 142, 155, 156*f*, 158, 190–91, 200–1
Liber Axumae, 167–68
Liberty Bell, 134–35
literalism, biblical, 181–82, 192
location of the Ark , 5, 29–30, 69–70, 73–75, 95–118, 161–62, 168–69, 173–74, 178, 180
London Society for the Promotion of Christianity Amongst the Jews, 171
looting, 171–73
Lorenz Z1, 205–6
Lost Tribes of Israel, 109–15
Lot, 122
Lucas, George, 3, 120, 127, 146, 201–2
Luther, Martin, 13, 46–47

Maccabean Revolt, 68–69
MacGuffin, 124, 126–27
Magdala, Battle of, 171–73
Mahrem, 164
Maimonides, 87–88, 105–6
Makeda, Queen. *See* Sheba, Queen of
Manasseh, 29, 178
Mander, Jerry, 129–30
manna, 188
Manna Machine, The, 188–89, 191–92
Manor, Dale, 32
maps, 180, 204–7
Marian Apparitions, 77–78
Marion. *See* Ravenwood, Marion
Mary, Mother of Jesus, 77–81, 79*f*, 80*f*, 90–91, 92*f*, 162
Mazar, Benjamin, 104–5

Mazar, Eilat, 104–5
McCarthyism, 135–36
McLuhan, Marshall, 159
Medina, David, 190–91
Megiddo, 51
Melander, Henning, 99
Melchizedek, 90–91
Menelik, 163–66, 180
Menelik II, 170–71
Mennonite Life Visitors Center, 158
menorah, 60, 61–62, 90, 129
merchandising, 146–51
mercy seat , 13–15, 48, 55, 78–79, 83, 84–85, 127, 141–42, 173, 186, 192, 203
Mercy Seat, The (song), 203
Mesopotamian religion, 43–51
Messianic return, 5, 105–6, 110–12, 159–60, 203–4, 207
metasymbols, 6–7, 209–10
meteors, 181–82
Michal, 25–26
midrash, 71–75
Mikado, 114–15
mikoshi, 113
military, 123
millenarianism, 110
miniaturization, 144–45
minimalist–maximalist debate, 34–38, 200–1
Ministry of Religious Affairs, 104–5, 107–8
miracles
   cinematic, 130–31, 132–33, 136–37
   faith–healing, 154–57
   pseudoarchaeology, 181–82, 192
Mishnah, 55, 106–7
Mishneh Torah, 87–88
missionaries , 98, 115–16, 157, 171
Mithraism, 63, 114
Miyanaki, Yoshun, 113
Mona Lisa, 145–46
monasticism, 165–66
monotheism, 45, 164, 200–1
Mormonism, 3, 4
mosaics, 59–61, 91–93
Moses , 4, 11, 43–44, 67–68, 69, 73, 86, 90–91, 115, 127, 164–66, 181–82, 186, 187, 189, 191
   cinematic depictions, 130–37
   staff of, 83, 130, 132–33
   Tomb of, 78–79
Moses and Monotheism, 181
Mount Ebal, 20
Mount Gerizim, 67–68
Mount Nebo, 98–99, 115–17, 118, 134, 207–8

246 SUBJECT INDEX

Mount Pisgah, 116–17
Mount Sinai, 11–12
Mount Tsurugi, 112–13
Muhammad, 96–97, 102
mummy fiction, 122
Murphy, Maurice, 128
Museum of the Bible, 158
museums, 9–10, 116, 121–22, 154, 157–60, 171–73
music, 20, 113, 119, 128–29, 142, 201–2
The Mystical Ark, 86–87

Nabratein, Synagogue at, 62–63
Nachmanides, 88
Nadab and Abihu, 14
names of the Ark, 16–19
Napier, Robert, 171
Nathan, 131
National Parks Service (Israel), 53, 104–5
Nazis, 2–3, 6–7, 120–22, 123, 128, 193–94, 197–98, 209–10
Nebuchadnezzar, 29, 69–70, 189
Neese, Shelly, 206
Neo–Babylonian Empire. *See* Babylonia
Nero, 58
Noah's Ark, 16–17, 21, 83, 116–17, 168, 175–76, 208
Noble Stone. *See* Shettiyah)
North by Northwest, 126
nostalgia, 148–51
nuclear power, 123, 188, 190, 191–92, 208

Obed-edom, 25–26
object teaching, 158
Olivier, Laurence, 33–34
opening of the mouth ceremony, 45–46
Oral Torah, 72, 87–88
Our Lady of la Vang, 77–78
Oyabe, Jenichiru, 114–15

painting, Victorian, 131–32, 135–36
Pan-Africanism, 166
Pankhurst, Richard, 172
paratexts, 149–50
Parker Expedition, 99–103, 124, 127, 204, 207–8
Parker, Montague. *See* Parker Expedition
pārōchet, 14, 57, 60, 90, 157, 160, 169
Parthenon Sculptures, 172–73
Parzival, 180
Passover, 131
Paul, 81–82
Pazuzu, 122

Peck, Gregory, 136–39, 209–11
Pergamon Museum, 9–10
Persia, 34–35
Pharaoh (of Exodus), 130–31
Philippines, 151–54
Philistines, 23–27, 32–43
Philo of Alexandria, 65–67, 71, 83, 84–85, 86–87
Phineas, 23–24
Pi-Rameses, 13
pilgrimage, 77–81, 91–94, 143–44, 145
pirates, 125–26
Platonism, 7, 66, 84–85
playacting, 149–51
poles. *See* staves
Pontius Pilate, 67–68
popular culture, 7–8, 9
Post–Traumatic Stress Disorder, 136, 138–39
powers of the Ark. *See* function of the Ark
Poynter, Edward John, 131–32
prayer, 137–38
Prester John, 161
Price, Randall, 106–7
processions, 25–26, 27–28, 47–48, 113, 134, 142–43, 153, 157, 170–71
propaganda, 194–96
Pseudoarchaeology, 4, 5–6, 9–10, 52, 98–118, 121, 124, 125–26, 127, 159, 162–63, 173–74, 175–99, 201, 204–7, 210
    dangers of, 197–98, 207
    reasoning, 175–76, 178–80, 182, 186–88, 190, 191, 192–93, 194–96, 198–99, 206
Pseudo–Dionysius, 85–86
ptgyh, 41–42
putto, 13, 50–51, 78–79, 85–86

QAnon, 9–10
Quatermain, Alan, 161
Quinn, Malcolm, 6–7, 209–10
Qumran, 204–7

Rabbi Yehuda Ha-nasi, 61
Rabbinic Literature, 71–75
rabbis, 71–75
Rabin, Yitzhak, Prime Minister, 183
racism, 197–98
radiation, 181–82, 189, 191
radio, invention of, 185
Raiders of the Lost Ark, 1–3, 117–18, 119–31, 120f, 138–39, 143–51, 155, 160, 184, 193–94, 196, 201–2, 211–12. *See also* Indiana Jones
Rambam. *See* Maimonides

SUBJECT INDEX 247

Ramban. *See* Nachmanides
Rastafarians, 162–63, 166
Rav Getz Synagogue, 105–6, 108
Ravenwood, Marion, 2–3, 122, 128
Rebekah, 21
reception history, definition, 7–8
Red Sea, Parting of (check earlier), 130–31, 132–33
Rehoboam, 29
Reinhold, Leopold, 44
relics, 87, 90–91, 93, 157, 167–68, 173–74
remote sensing, 205–6
repatriation, 171–73
replicas, 157–60
Revelation, Book of, 8
Rhodesia, 161
Richard of Saint Victor, 86–87
Rinzler, J.W., 127
Ritmeyer, Leen, 96–97
ritual purity, 14, 46–47, 48–49, 81–82, 106–7
roadside attractions, 152–53
Robinson, Edward, 39–40
Rome, 89–91, 92*f*
Römer, Thomas, 40–41
Rost, Karl Leonhard, 23–27
Rothschild, David, 116–17
de Rothschild, Edmond, Baron, 101–2
Royal Engineers, 98

Sabbath day, origins of, 188
sacraments, 87
Sallah, 119, 201
Samaritans, 67–68
Samuel, 34–35
Sanhedrin, 36
Sarah, 21
Sassoon, George, 188–89, 191–92
Saul, 34–38
Schrader, Paul, 132
Scotia, Queen, 164–65
Scotland, 164–65
Semitic languages word formation, 51
Sennacherib, 28–29
Seow, C.L. 17
Sephora, 134
Serabit el-Khadem, 181–82
Seventh Day Adventists, 108–9
Shakespeare, William, 33–34
Sheba, Queen of, 162–65, 169
Shema, 153
Shettiyah, 74, 96–97, 102–3, 105
Shikoku, 112–13
Shiloah (Siloam) Pool, 97–98

Shiloh, 27
Shintoism, 112–15
Shishak, 3, 29, 119, 124–25
shofar, 128
Shugendo, 112–13
Sign and the Seal, The, 8–9, 173–74, 177–83
Sign of the Cross, The (1932 movie), 135–36
Silk Road, 114
Silwan, 104
Sister Joséphine Rumèbe, 77
Sisters of St. Joseph of the Apparition, 76–81
Six–Day War, 103–4, 153, 159–60
Snyder, Michael, 203–4
Society for American Archaeology, 196
Sodom and Gomorrah, 122
Solomon, 27–28, 34–38, 99, 105–6, 163–66, 169, 189
  sons of, 161, 162–66, 180, 189
Solomon and Sheba (1959 movie), 129
"Song of Myself, 51," 210–11
"Song of the Ark". *See* Numbers 10: 35–36
sound effects, 127–29
source criticism, 21–27
souvenirs, 93–94, 140–46, 142*f*
Spain, 111
Spencer, John, 44
sphinxes, 51–52
Spielberg, Steven, 3, 119, 120, 130, 201–2
spiritualism, 185
St. Crispin's Day Speech, 33–34
St. Michael's Church, Ethiopia, 170
Staff of Ra, 125, 193–94
Star of David, 113, 127, 155
Star Trek, 5–6, 132–33.
Star Wars, 1–2, 5–6, 120, 146–49
Status Quo Agreement, 103–5, 204
staves, 4, 12–13, 14, 15, 28, 48, 49–50, 55, 64, 67, 78–79, 84–85, 88–89, 113, 119–20, 141–43, 153, 155, 158, 159–60
Stewart, Susan, 144–46
supersessionism, Christian, 81–83
swastika, 6–7, 209–10
syllogism, 132, 152–54, 158–59, 210
synagogues
  activities in, 56
  architecture, 56–57, 60
  emergence of, 8, 58–59, 71
  Galilean, 55, 58–63

Tabernacle, 12, 14–15, 22–23, 28, 46–47, 48–49, 57, 68, 81–82, 83, 84
Tabot, 168–73
tahash, 48–49

248 SUBJECT INDEX

Takane, Masanori, 112–13
Talmud, 72
Tanis (ancient Egyptian city), 124–25, 193–94
Tara, Ireland, 109–12, 118
Targum, 72
Tea Tephi, 111
technocratic ideologies, 123, 181–82, 184–93, 210
telegraph, 185
teleology, 134–35
Television, 4, 122, 129–30, 133–34, 149–50, 191–92, 194–96
Temple, First, 8, 27–30, 34–35, 57, 69–70, 78, 83, 84, 86, 90–91, 95–109, 110, 189, 200–1
  cinematic depiction, 129
  destruction of, 29, 34–35, 68–70
  and Ethiopian Churches, 169
  treasures of, 69–70
Temple, Second, 8–9, 36, 95–109
  destruction of, 8, 52, 58, 62, 71, 90–91, 106
  location of Ark, 74
  replica, 159–60
  sacred vessels of, 67–68, 90–91, 94, 106–7, 108–9, 206
  symbols of, 60
Temple, Third, 101–2, 103–4, 106, 159–60, 203–4, 207–8
Temple Institute, 159–60, 203–4
Temple Mount, 37–38, 58, 73–74, 95–109, 118, 159–60, 203–4, 207
Temple of Solomon, São Paolo, 154, 157
Ten Commandments, 3, 4, 11–12, 20–21, 44, 45–46, 51, 55–56, 57, 62, 72, 80–81, 82–83, 87–88, 90, 106–7, 134–35, 150–51, 153–54, 168–69, 208
Ten Commandments, The (1923 movie), 135–36
Ten Commandments, The (1956 movie), 130–37
Tesla coils, 191
Tewodros II, Emperor, 171–72
Theme parks, 157–60
theophany, 11–12, 135–36
thing theory, 6–7, 126–27, 137–38, 143–51
Thoth, 180–81
Timqat, 169–70, 173, 174
Titus, 90–91
  Arch of, 90
Torah Arks (Shrines), 5–6, 55–65, 105–6, 122, 202–3
  terms for, 56–57
Toronto, 154–57, 202–3
tourism, 31, 53–55, 61, 76, 77–78, 80–81, 93, 95–96, 104, 105–6, 116, 140–46, 157–60
toys, 146–51, 148f, 210
Truffaut, François, 126

Tutankhamun, 49–50, 50f
Tyndale, William, 13
typological theology, 80–81, 84–85, 109–10, 131, 134–35

Ullendorff, Edward, 168–69, 173–74
UNESCO, 104
United Monarchy, 34–38
Universal Church of the Kingdom of God, 154–57, 156f
Uzzah son of Abinadab, 25–26, 88–89, 155–56, 186

Van de Graaf Generators, 191
Vatican, 89–90, 189
Via Maris, 41
Victoria and Albert Museum, 171–72
Victoria, Queen, 110, 171, 172
video games, 122, 125–26
Viet Nam, 77–78
Vincent, Louis–Hughes, 100–1
Von Däniken, Erich, 185–88

Wandering in the Wilderness, 15
Waqf, 103–4, 106, 107–8
Warren, Charles, 97–98, 99, 100–1, 105
Warren's Gate, 105–6, 108
weaponization, 3, 120–22, 126–27, 163–64, 181–82, 191, 193–94
Weill, Raymond, 101–2
Well of the Souls (Dome of the Rock), 102, 117–18
Well of the Souls (Raiders of the Lost Ark), 117–18, 119, 201
Western Wall, 37–38, 95–96, 103–4, 105–6
white supremacists, 109–10
Whitman, Walt, 210–11
Williams, John, 119, 128–29
Windsor, House of, 110
Wyatt, Ron, 108–9, 183–84

X-Files, The, 193

Yamamoto, Eisuke, 113
Yeats, William Butler, 111–12
Yehud, 34–35
Yohannes IV, Emperor, 172

Zara Yaqob, King, 167
Zedekiah, 111
ziggurat, 129
zodiac, 59–60
Zohar, The, 188